Famous Last Questions

'In this rollicking debut, Sanjana Ramachandran proves that hers is an exhilaratingly fresh voice: the sort that blitzes across the literary horizon once or twice in a generation and ends up defining it. The Millennials—who sprang forth into a rebellious India, locked in a tryst with liberalization and globalization—have long gone without a chronicler. Unlike the GenZs, they grew up without Instagram and TikTok, unable to capture and vlog their adventures, aspirations, and anxieties, and thus have only nostalgia to hold on to. But here at last is Ramachandran with *Famous Last Questions*, a sparkling collection of essays in which she explores the paradoxes of modern India through the prism of her generation, the 'nineties' kids', answering a question that haunts us today more than ever, when the very notion of Indianness that successive generations grew up taking for granted is being challenged: what does it *mean* to be Indian?

Interweaving a knack for storytelling with memoir, reportage, and rigorous research, Sanjana Ramachandran has composed a deeply introspective and hugely funny volume, rediscovering a generation in the process and reminding us that we, both as human beings and Indians, contain multitudes—and if we contradict ourselves, then, well (to rephrase Whitman), so what, we contradict ourselves.'

—Shashi Tharoor, politician and writer

'I can think of few people better than Sanjana Ramachandran, with her deft voice, keen observations and curiosity, to write about the millennial experience of coming of age in '90s India. These essays are humorous and insightful, and they elevate Sanjana's queries—"what is love?" "who am I?"—into something universal. These are no "last questions": once you read Sanjana's work, you'll keep looking to her to make sense of the world.'

—Sanam Maher, author, *A Woman Like Her*

'Sanjana's engaging voice—bombastic yet skeptical, pointed yet searching—makes her a lovely travelling companion through this book's territories, which range from the local to the fundamental. I am fond of this kind of company.'

—Sasha Chapin, author, *All the Wrong Moves*

'Who is Sanjana Ramachandran? Who does she think she is, to write a book about herself? What nonsense is this, and why is her VO2 Max above average? You have no choice but to read this book and find out.'

—Sidin Vadukut, author, *Dork: The Incredible Adventures of Robin 'Einstein' Varghese*

Famous Last Questions

A Confused Woman's Investigations into the
Country that Shaped Her

SANJANA RAMACHANDRAN

ALEPH

ALEPH

ALEPH BOOK COMPANY
An independent publishing firm
promoted by *Rupa Publications India*

First published in India in 2025
by Aleph Book Company
7/16 Ansari Road, Daryaganj
New Delhi 110 002

ISBN: 978-93-6523-186-1

1 3 5 7 9 10 8 6 4 2

Printed in India

For my family,
and everyone else who has hurt me,
and I them,
with loving-kindness.

FAMOUS LAST QUESTIONS

'Coming home from very lonely places, all of us go a little mad: whether from great personal success, or just an all-night drive, we are the sole survivors of a world no one else has ever seen.'

—John le Carré

'Fearlessly the idiot faced the crowd'

—'Fearless', Pink Floyd

CONTENTS

Introduction   *xi*

1. Who am I?: Or, What are The Norms?   1

2. Science, Arts, or Commerce?   46

3. Your Body or Mine?   78

4. Please Get Married Before I Die?   101

5. Work, Work, Work, Work, Work   137

6. What Is Love? Baby, Don't Hurt Me   172

7. God: Must I Believe in They/Them?   215

Epilogue: Famous Last Words   260

Acknowledgements   267

References   271

INTRODUCTION

I've always had a colourful and crazy life. Such a life seemed pointless to keep to myself. When I didn't constantly fantasize about storifying it, I would cease to want to live. I had to be arranged in service of storytelling, I realized, if I was expected to live at all. And there wasn't an option about the latter. Frugal, but quite real, investigations were made. When I grew wise, years after those innocent, half-serious, mostly helpless attempts at killing myself, I learnt that it is not a real escape. It merely prolongs suffering. It is immoral. It is wrong.

Never do it.

Instead, find meaning in suffering. Making stories is a fun and obvious way to do so. Behind every successful artist is a traumatized, lonely child. It could be something else for you, your purpose. Of course, I also defined 'fun' as trying to be the 'best' at everything. That is how I developed my deep and eviscerating insights into narcissism, which is the condition of being attached to and loving a certain self-image, rather than loving and being an actual, messy self.

I know about narcissism from my own personal and generational experience of it.

I wouldn't claim to not be a narcissist now, however, because you might not believe me. Even attempting to influence your opinion of me makes me lose some ground. Nobody can objectively claim anything about themselves. Somebody calls you crazy; you insist you're not. You've already lost.

So, think what you will about me. I can only speak to

my intentions and aims. When I started writing this book, it was because:

- I wanted to irrevocably settle the matter of my genius, and never have it be questioned again, especially by myself. I also didn't want to be a commonplace genius, merely literary, merely scientific, merely anything. I wanted to show you my multitudes, partly because cultivating them had entertained and occupied me, partly because I was wedded to this self-image of being-the-best-at-everything-no-matter-what-especially-if-somebody-else-thinks-otherwise, and partly because these somebody-elses seemed to live at close quarters—at home. This is how I earned safety and respect in an achievement-driven society. There is no use not being honest about this.

- Since I started to heal—or even through the early wounds—I recognized the above as overcompensations. Sufficiently loved individuals are perhaps not motivated to do much, much less invent complicated truths and set out to prove them as true. Such is magical thinking. It got me through it all, but now that I have made true some of the magic, my hope and endeavour is that my stories are useful to more than just me.

- Now, that too sounds grandiose. What a hope! That one's sordid coping mechanisms could be convoluted and justified as some kind of public entertainment. Yet I believe it is this kind of megalomania that drives every artist. Do not shy away from it. Many present modest, sane fronts—and the worst believe in them—lest they be ridiculed for unwarranted self-confidence, for 'hubris'. But a basic need for greatness, for death-denial, for imprinting your individuality upon the world, underlines the artist's moves, camouflaged or not.

- In following this call to express the truths I saw, as I saw them, hubris and megalomania gradually devolved. I suffered many absurd defeats. But when reality didn't keep up with my desired self-image, I somehow also found the strength to keep going. Perhaps the inflations were only ever embryonic indicators of the 'daimon', which creative people 'live in the grip of'. The word comes from the Greek 'daiw', which means 'to divide or distribute destinies'. The 'daimon' is thus an energy or godly force that gives us our fate, allots human destiny, and is 'as real as hunger and the fear of death'. (It is the root word for both 'demon' and 'daemon', the background process that automatically executes certain maintenance tasks on computers.) The daimon makes demands of us; we are not as in control of our lives as we think we are.

- So, as I stopped resisting and attended to my daimon, I stopped getting as many headaches, I stopped falling sick as much, and I was able to get over the blows to my ego and persist from some sense of duty towards something more—something unknown.

- Perhaps this work *is* socially useful. The collective consciousness is shaped by individual consciousness and vice versa. Feverishly investigating mine through various modes and questions led to natural sub-questions about my life, the environment(s) I grew up in, my personal, familial, and social histories, the nature of consciousness and the self, morality, truth, god, gender, sexuality, religion, technology, capitalism, mental health, identity, all of it. Even if I do say so myself, this is intriguing and wide-ranging ground to cover while moving concentrically outward from the self.

- Specifically, we are examining the conditions of being born in '90s India, into rather traditional Indian families, mostly upper-caste and upper-class Hindus, who found themselves assaulted by the forces of 'modernity', or values that were both aspirational and contradictory to their own. Whatever was forbidden in our culture—intoxicants and sex and materialism and less rigid ideas of gender and sexuality—were suddenly not forbidden in the economy and culture we aspired to be part of, having been colonized and plundered by another version of it before. This gave birth to interesting and gripping conflicts in the individual and cultural psyche, complexes planted by colonialism colliding with Indian history. India's '90s kids were only the second or third generation to ever have freedom, and they enacted these complexes differently than their parents. Investigating this clash of values within families, and their effects, is one way to state the theme of this book.

- The answers are long—as long as a book—because the search for a moral, healthy way of life in a complicated country and world is long-form. This is the format best suited for subjective truth, for ambiguity, and good answers; neither this nor that but a secret third thing (this *and* that; paradox).

- These are my famous last questions, for now. I hope it is interesting, gripping, accessible, and novelistic.

So, you see, I wrote this out of desperation, not just for glory. I wrote it because I couldn't not. I remain convinced that nobody could've had so much to absorb and reconcile if it weren't to construct meaning from it and share it with the world.

Hoping, of course, to be loved for it.

Ultimately, then, I am looking for love. I wrote this out of love, and for love.

From myself, from you, from my parents, from everybody.
Forgiveness and acceptance too, of your worst and mine.
And through it all: some kind of enlightenment.

1

WHO AM I?: OR, WHAT ARE THE NORMS?

'There's an old saying. The place you're born in is the place that half-buries you. That's why "birthplace" is also called "blood land".'

—Jia Zhang-ke

'Don't think you can drink and go out and do things like that. Understand?'

My father was on the phone with me, and it was right after we'd said goodbye. It had barely been a minute since I'd entered my hostel room again.

'You are not a modern woman,' he said. In a few minutes, he would drive off from the engineering college I'd joined in Goa, India's 'party state', back to Mumbai, where my family lived.

I knew how far I'd come, and how easy it could be soon. Over the last few days, I'd explored the college campus at night with a girlfriend. We had made some friends and acquaintances. I knew about Bogmalo.

This beach, the nearest at 7 kilometres away, was home to John's, where the cheapest drink, a peg of Romanov vodka, cost ₹40.

So, I responded quietly: a sound from the small of my throat versus my father's assertion about the kind of woman

I should be. We said goodbye—again—and I left my room determined to find people and make plans.

I suppose my father had good reasons then for warning me. Two years before, when I was sixteen, I had been carried back home by Raman, who said Appa was 'aghast' at receiving my unconscious body at about 4 a.m. This was after Shivam's birthday party, where they had served flaming shots. Shivam had just turned seventeen, and there were over ten people at the bar in Andheri West he'd called us to, including somebody called Jalat or Jalaj, who later that night became the first boy I ever kissed.

Amma woke me up with Kellogg's and milk the next morning. I slept again for a few hours. As I sat across from my parents later, a cloud of suspicion, scrutiny, and shame was born. It followed us afterwards for more than a decade, its stench growing as badly as my hangovers.

Appa suspected that my subsequent deference was obviously affected and that I had no real remorse. I would go on to confirm his worst fears—and expand them beyond his wildest visions—by getting expelled from the first engineering college I joined.

In a remote part of Chennai, at the age of seventeen, I was...caught with a boy.

The priests who ran the college were upset—they hadn't even seen us making out—but Appa was too. He slapped me before helping me pack my bags and leave.

That was the first and only time I've been slapped.

As I looked over my father's shoulders on the bike ride back to my paati's home, it dawned on me that my life must be a movie. But of course: the mission was to correct these wrongs and earn my parents' love. But my character also believed in and wanted to protect her own moral integrity.

So, I would achieve everything they wanted for me, but not in the ways they may have wanted.

An Achievement Complex is Born.

As Tamil Brahmins born in South India in the 1960s, Amma and Appa staunchly believed that drinking, smoking, non-vegetarian food, sleeping and waking up late, sex, members of the opposite sex—because only they could fathomably be had sex with—were all dangerous elements. They did their best to keep me away from them. Before I left for college—the second time—at the age of eighteen, my mother told me, in Tamil, that she'd 'slice me up' if I ever ate non-vegetarian food. She told me I could marry whoever I wanted, except a Muslim. She did understand the idea of love, and always wanted me to find it. When I was thirteen, she suggested in the kitchen that there was nothing wrong with 'love marriages'.

'Be careful what you say in front of your daughter,' my father told her.

Such aggressive aversion to 'sinful' pursuits attracted my teenage subconscious to them more than casual indifference or open deliberation might ever have. And without seeing their abstinence correlate with virtue, which seemed to be religion's central promise, I wondered about religion itself. Why should anything 'fun'—done for oneself, without hurting anyone else—be so morally reprehensible? Although Appa was proud of never drinking or smoking, he was sinful in what I thought were more gross ways. He never left the house, cursed everyone, and was especially cruel towards Amma, who did all the work and complained about him whenever I entered the kitchen.

She herself never wanted to do anything else about it. Suffering and sacrifice had become her virtues.

Carl Jung said that every form of addiction is bad, 'whether the narcotic is alcohol or idealism'. He also said that the greatest burden a child must bear is the 'unlived life of its parents', of their unconscious desires and whatever they've repressed from 'fear, or an excess of conformity'. I sensed that Appa's disgust for vices came not only from religious idealism, but also from repression, if not of desire, then at least of some basic curiosity. When Amma and I were travelling once—I must have been seven or eight or nine years old—I heard him say on the phone, 'I will go to a pub today.'

'Are you going to drink?' she immediately asked.

He denied the idea, as far as I remember.

Both seemed to me amoral for being so distant to their unhappiness—surely the most virtuous way to live was happily—but instead, they invested in codified morality. They worried about keeping fights down instead of not having them, living for neighbours and strangers more than themselves. I wondered about their ideas of 'good' and 'bad', and perhaps lived by everything 'bad' to verify that I would not only be okay, as I suspected, but also not be 'bad', actually. And if, while doing so, I could give them everything they thought was 'good', I could show, surely, that the 'bad' things were not, in fact, strictly so. Perhaps neither were the 'good'.

And they would have to still love me.

Because parents, by definition, love their children unconditionally—do they not?

In hindsight, I'm divided on the mathematics of my adolescent moral scheming. Logically sound, but lacking major adult learnings: life's frequent failure of logic. But I perhaps remain a literal asshole.

As with other Tamil Brahmin or 'TamBrahm' families in newly liberalized '90s India, Amma and Appa wanted with fervour the following 'good' stuff: for their child to speak good English, to get into IIT, India's foremost engineering institution, and then IIM, India's foremost management institution, and then to marry somebody similar, before the age of thirty or any pre-marital sex. If you weren't aware of this primal Indian aspiration, you've probably escaped the following: *Two States, Five Point Someone, The Three Mistakes of My Life,* and other English novels with numbers in their titles converted into blockbuster Hindi films, authored by IIT–IIM graduate Chetan Bhagat. His literary career is often exalted as the benchmark for creative success, especially for the 'non-Arts' types in India—as everyone, including my parents, reminded me when I told them I was writing this book.

So, these 'good' things I achieved in full, I guess. Almost.

I spent the six months after I got expelled studying religiously. We kept our secret from the rest of the family and the world; like scores of Indians who couldn't 'crack' the engineering exams on the first go, I too 'dropped' a year to sit them again. My sadness at picking up books I thought I'd dusted off, my anger at the priests' righteousness, it could all only last a week. I had time for nothing but concentration.

As a Dropper, I could not fail again.

And I didn't.

So, all I wanted to do afterwards was party.

Thus, I broke even more rules of what it means to be a 'good' Indian, or a good woman, or perhaps a good Hindu, or maybe a good Brahmin, or just a good Indian Hindu Brahmin woman. I didn't know that's what I was doing then. I thought I was just exercising my moral prerogative—by having fun.

I was in the company of the rest of my generation, India's millennials, the first in the nation's history to grow up with the internet, full-fledged neoliberal capitalism, and a stronger-than-ever 'Western' influence that elders have always resented for corroding 'traditional' Indian values. Others from this group, stifled by the values of an earlier generation, unaware of their origins, may also have a touch of this 'TamBrahm Rebel Syndrome': a tendency to secretly, perhaps extremely, indulge in whatever is forbidden to them without due explanation or reason. They may still not know why anything was forbidden in the first place, because they've faced no real loss from their 'heresy'. Indeed, now that it is no longer cool to be regressive about things like drinking and marrying for love, Brahmins behave as they want and continue to be Brahmins.

At a recent, highly contemporary TamBrahm wedding, the morning's Vedic rites and rituals were followed by an evening cocktail party. The marriage was arranged by the parents, but the children, both TamBrahms plucked from freshly graduated IIT–IIM stock, wanted to change the story because 'arranged marriages are lame now'. This is a twist to the quintessential Indian tendency of too-much-parental-involvement-over-course-of-child's-entire-life, because the children have now internalized methods that follow tradition but look modern. So, marriages may be caste-bound and arranged, but on Instagram should look like 'love'.

This tension between wanting to look 'modern', 'global', 'Western', and 'advanced', while also remaining 'traditional' and 'Indian' 'at heart', has been a defining theme of life in contemporary India. After it liberalized its economy in 1991, entering a world evermore awash with identities and their abstractions across the internet, we are careful about all our appearances, working like full-time brand managers of the self, and, directly or otherwise, the country.

At the wedding, Appa laughed off an invitation to drink stating that he had a hard time 'controlling himself', sounding more like a spent socialite than a camouflaged conservative. Amma then remarked that she had 'always liked' the inviter, a thirty-five-year-old unmarried man who was moving around with his drink in one hand and his girlfriend in another. Meanwhile, their daughter, now twenty-eight years old and also unmarried, had spent the evening fearfully, doing what she had always done: living hypocritically.

I had tried to hide everything. My secrets spanned not

only social evils like my clothing and drinking and other 'bad habits'—Appa's umbrella term for my moral health—but also my deepest problems, the times I needed help the most, my likes and dislikes, my friendships and relationships, my aspirations, my whole self. Unlike characters in these Western movies and TV shows I watched—where parents knocked on their children's doors, openly discussed sex and relationships, and seemed to understand their children emotionally, offering friendship, respect, and autonomy; where children and women were equals to adults and men—I gave up on the idea, growing up, that I could ever 'be myself' at home.

Like my family and everyone else I knew, I was wearing multiple masks all the time, alienated from myself and largely unaware of it. If 'all the world's a stage and each man in his time plays many a part', as Shakespeare believed, Indians are prolific actors performing constantly for their families and loved ones.[1] This may seem to be free work, but there is a cognitive payment for these double and triple lives. Hiding your sexuality, partner(s), true desires, careers, and lifestyle at home or work is not easy. There is a 'constant feeling of having to choose between distinct versions...each feeling like a betrayal'; 'As we seek acceptance from our families and society by trying to meet their standards, we move away from our true selves...and develop a kind of duality within us'; 'Constant conflict within one's mind...suppression of oneself can lead to identity crisis and depression in many'.[2]

It can lead to madness if my life is true.

The ground between who we'd like to be, and who we choose to be, is sown with the seeds of our deepest conflicts—psychic, interpersonal, and societal—so much so that India's best films and stories are about ordinary characters fighting to be themselves with those closest to them.[3]

The results are mixed. In the 2016 Marathi film *Sairat*, an inter-caste couple is hunted down and murdered by their families for falling in love, getting married, having a child, and even trying to live away from the crime scene. In the 2015 Hindi film *Masaan*, cops in Varanasi 'catch' two lovers in a hotel room, driving the man to kill himself in the toilet. Stigma and shame follow the Brahmin woman he slept with, who contends with a hostile father and gossiping town afterwards. In *The Newlyweds*, Mansi Choksi writes about the couples who overcome inter-caste and inter-faith norms for their love, and whether it remains worth it after all.[4]

Serious drama isn't the only genre to tackle these obstacles to self-actualization, of course. In an Instagram reel on the 'Three Signs of Childhood Trauma', @vineeth_sri stops at 'Sign #1: Having Indian parents'. Ankur Warikoo, a doyen of the Indian creator economy, wrote about the '11 things that Indian parents get wrong', from 'comparison' and 'looking at the world only through their own experiences' and 'emotional blackmail' and 'dismissing mental health' to 'unreasonable expectations'.[5] One reel thus suggests that 'healing from generational trauma together' is one of the 'Five Signs of a Loving Relationship'.[6]

Controlling Indian parents are a favourite of 'desi' social media, which includes not only resident Indians but also the sizable diaspora the country has exported across the world. 'Trauma' became the word of the decade.[7] Google searches for it peaked in 2022, and related terms like 'cultural trauma', 'collective trauma', 'historical trauma', and 'intergenerational trauma' have been on the rise since the 1990s—tongue-in-cheek references in pop culture and online are concomitant with its more serious usage.[8] The term is at the altar of modern life's assault on language. Most political crises today are debates over terms we've come to associate with structures we'd rather not live by anymore. But language is both our tool of communication and our tool of thought, so battles about language are battles within our minds.

The upper-caste, 'privileged' woman who cries 'trauma!' may well be left alone by the rest, especially if they're her family, or if they're on Twitter (currently X), or if they belong to more marginalized identities. After all, the virtuous and extremely online of the human race have invented the scientifically tested sliding scale for suffering, wherein your trauma can be calculated in neat proportion to your identity. Caste, class, religion, age, disability, sexuality—all these axes of identity are but variables for the polynomial equation that outputs How Much You Have Suffered, or How Legitimate Your Victimhood Is. It's easy-to-use and available at a rotting online discourse near you.

According to this scale, your suffering is obviously the least if you're a man—you could never have had hardships, of course—and it's least-most if you're a straight man, but not-so-least if you're a queer man, unless you're a queer man and of a marginalized caste or religion, but all of these are still inferior sufferings to women at large, unless, of course, you're upper-caste women, because then you still have class privilege, but, if not, god save you, because you have it the worst-most.

This is proven.

But don't go down that road with me. If you construe my suffering some way and then filter it through your borrowed hivemind formulae, I will call the cops. Don't tell me your compassion is so conditional and your empathy so rarefied that you can only extend it to those you've been told deserve it. This kind of comparison and ranking could only be perversions of a hivemind, worrying in its lack of empathy. Individual suffering is a function of such complex factors that identity, or any such single cause, can hardly explain it.

I sometimes think it's only people who haven't really

suffered who would try to classify its magnitudes and make some kind of status game out of it.

If you've really suffered, you would never wish it on your worst enemy.

The rightful evolution is towards redemption, however hard that is. The Buddha did not perceive the universal nature of discontent and suffering to only help those who suffered the most by his calculations, which would certainly have been more accurate than yours and @cowboyintellectual on Twitter, by the way. He didn't bemsirch his insight and wisdom that way; he wanted to help whoever might need it—everyone.[9]

Listen properly now.

But even then I may not trust you.

The fault is mine. The joke is on me. There are people talking about their worst traumas while applying make-up in sixty-second reels, as #childhoodtrauma (and related) hashtags on social media indicate. But instead of commodifying mine into such snackable formats, I've saved it for formats as quaint and unprofitable as books and films. It's almost like I want to construct a self through this storytelling—not pander to an audience with no stake in my life.

Such purity of effort hardly bodes well. You see why these are my *Famous Last Questions*?

But now that I have this space, I am going to make proper use of it. Several Indian stories address the same problem—the pain caused by The Norms, their easy internalization by the social human brain, and our difficulty with breaking out of them—but only few talk about how they came about and why.

All stories are equal, but some stories are more equal than others.

This, as I would find out too late, is one secret to how The Norms endure.

In July 2009, soon after I was brought back home drunk, I could quantify the costs of having to hide myself at home, and before the world. *Sach ka Saamna*, the Indian version of American reality show *The Moment of Truth*, was premiering on Star Plus. If contestants could answer personal and compromising questions before their loved ones, without being caught by a lie detector, they would win ₹1 crore.

I knew I could never go on the show.

Soon people demanded that it be stopped anyway. Such public admission of misconduct, especially by celebrities, would make everyone break the rules and cause a 'weakening of society's morals'. An MP took up the issue, stating that the show's questions were 'against Indian culture'. Unbeknownst to myself then, but with an intuitive grasp of what constituted this culture, I began to conform to it soon after the internet and my puberty hit India.

Things were complicated by how drawn I was to technology, which I associated with cool, both a thing and a means to learn, its emancipatory vibe exalted early in my life. As Appa likes to say, 'I love tech.' He bought his first cell phone, one that had an antenna on it, in 1999. He bought us our first computer three years later, when I was nine years old and in the fourth standard. I used this Pentium 4 with its protruding monitor to play games like Sky Roads, Road Rash, Midtown Madness, and Solitaire, and to look things up for the odd school project with a crackling dial-up connection. I also wrote my first story, about a tiger, on it. Appa had taught me how to use a QWERTY keyboard the year before, after we got one free with a video game, but beyond knowing these mechanics of writing, I don't know where I got the sense that I should.

Amma introduced me to books at the age of five, starting with Enid Blyton and Agatha Christie and Ruskin Bond, but I only got hooked after I read *Harry Potter*. She gave me everything she had read as a child, even letting me touch Sidney Sheldon and Jeffrey Archer a few years before she had, shaping my reading life until my teens, when, through school friends and bookstores, I discovered Wodehouse and Ayn Rand too. The stories I consumed weren't limited to books, however. I sat in front of the television a lot, a real couch potato with routines around *Tom and Jerry, Popeye, Scooby-Doo*, and Cartoon Network. After we shifted to Bombay/Mumbai from my birthplace, Madras/Chennai, I told a prospective new friend, who asked me why I would rather watch TV than step out to play, that it was better company and also improved my English.

By the time I was thirteen, I was—understandably—fat, and I'd taken part in a few essay competitions and also started writing for myself. One early treatise was about how my parents would be happier if my father got a job and my mother stood up for herself instead of 'wallowing in self-pity' and complaining whenever I entered the kitchen. I was, by now, also using the landline (not yet cordless) and Orkut and MSN Messenger to communicate with school friends. We'd have long conversations and make jokes on comment threads, and I could chat with boys—and others, about whatever—without being overheard. The girls worried that their display pictures could be right-clicked-upon and saved—a quirky concern now. I still use the email ID that Appa made for me then—sanjana7ramachandran@gmail.com—which he said would be more long-lasting than the one I'd made myself on Hotmail, and, like many of us, would rather not admit now.[10]

Everyone in school made a Facebook account in 2007. There was a feature called 'Compare People', which let you rank your social network on personality things and showed you where you stood too. I was always voted second-funniest amongst the friends and friends of friends I was friends with on Facebook. The feature seems like an obvious hint about what we now understand as the fundamental driver of all social media, the concept of 'mimetic desire'. A theory of desire as a social process, mimesis was studied by the French social scientist René Girard, who is revered by all techbros who know he taught Peter Theil, Facebook's first outside investor. Girard posited that human beings want what others want, and compete with each other to get it. 'Man is a creature who does not know what to desire, and he turns to others to make up his mind. We desire what others desire because we imitate their desires,' he wrote.[11] All human behaviour could be thought to rest on imitation; simplistically, AI systems too are programmed with impressionistic paintings or Sylvia Plath poems until they learn to spot patterns and replicate what they have been fed, and get better with feedback. We learn everything through this imitative reinforcement, this pattern-matching mechanism, from language and skills to morals and values. We are the only species to transmit them to each other through stories and culture.

The principle was in action in my offline life, too. Studying science felt like a natural choice for me—I loved math especially, which was always chalked up to Appa, who then should also be held responsible for my talent in migraines and impatience—but it was also what my friend Garima did then, and what 'South Indians' were supposed to be good at. As I went through school and tuitions to junior college, however, I was picking up behaviours from my friends and the people around me in 2000s Mumbai.

The first time I tried a hookah, in tenth standard, I untagged myself from all pictures of the outing, and subsequently spent hours on such clean-up acts, removing photos with boys and anything 'personal' or 'compromising'. When I suspected that my parents had created accounts, I looked them up proactively and blocked them. Although I was mostly sharing things I'd read or watched, back when

Facebook still had a 'wall', delinking these incompatible parts of myself felt like the smartest thing to do.

Then, Facebook also became how I kept in touch with my cousin Lata, who lived in another city. Appa had forbidden me from speaking to her and her family, his list of vices growing proportionate to his fading sense of control. An account manager in advertising, he worked at Rediff.com, one of India's first internet companies. When I was seven, I heard him say in the living room of our rented 2-BHK, 'And you tell him I've quit, okay? Tell him I've quit!' It turned out that Appa had left his job after a quarrel with his boss, and upon a promise from his brother-in-law, Lata's father, that he would get a new one at British Physical Laboratories, or BPL Limited. This didn't materialize, so Appa stopped talking to Lata's family. Amma became the only working adult at home.

The only breaks she took over the next thirty-five years were to birth and parent two more children, my brothers. Appa distanced himself from them early on, having wanted exactly one more child, not two. I spent much time with my brothers, sometimes caring for them and otherwise terrorizing them, as I'd imbibed the old could treat the young. I grew up quickly in those years, though; quite literally, I was so fat by the time I was fifteen that the other kids in the building sometimes mistook me to be the twins' mother.[12]

We now recognize the trauma of the 'Eldest Daughter', particularly in South Asian households, from the expectations from an early age that they should get everything right, from taking care of themselves to not having a reaction to the dysfunction around them, so that being unaware of their own needs and bodies in order to keep everyone happy and meet external goals is how they relate to the world by default. This unpaid third parent pays the price for perfectionism and rigidity in adulthood, when anxiety and guilt become associated with being yourself. I tend to scoff at how quickly we spin theories and 'syndromes' for every facet of human experience, but looking back at my childhood provides plenty of evidence that I was hyper-attuned to the emotional states of people around me, and always moulding myself to meet their needs for my own survival, in ways that now expose me to trauma and remain somewhat maladaptive in adulthood. Even before the age of eight, I became conscious of how we spent money. Although Amma and Appa never made me feel an overt lack of it, they did check the price of everything and calculated costs and disliked the loss of an umbrella or tiffin box. When they once offered to buy me a whiteboard, I asked how much it cost; a third person near the family expressed mild surprise that someone so young bothered to ask this question. All of us lived in a small one-bedroom apartment in Andheri East, and we moved from one rented apartment to another frequently. Appa did not believe this recurring 'one-time' activity could take a toll on us, and home ownership came much later than it did for my friends, who never moved homes.

Still, they also tried to provide us with whatever might make us happy and smart. I was given everything I needed and more. I got my first cell phone—a Nokia 3300—quite early, and I remember downloading and saving some Linkin Park songs to it for a school trip, painstakingly renaming them all in l33t speak, only to be judged by the actual 'cool' kids, who just listened to the music. Unlike children today, for whom the smartphone is necessary, I didn't use mine for assignments or classes yet. I once put it aside for an entire day to see if anyone would message or call me—two friends did—as if with an early idea of how obsessive our need to constantly know and measure what other people think of us would get.

It was also because I needed my phone for legitimate reasons, though, that I was even allowed to keep one after The

Expulsion. I have always been very grateful that, in 2010 India, I didn't have to manage a digital footprint across LinkedIn and Twitter about that career move: 'Thrilled to announce rustication from conservative college for briefly? allegedly? being in the same washroom as a boy!'

I continued my relationship with the boy I got caught with through SMS, short, whispered Skype calls late at night, and WhatsApp starting in 2011, when the app didn't yet have blue ticks or even two of them. When I went back home from college, I would save certain contacts with a different name. For a while, Lata was 'Vinny', à la the 1992 film *My Cousin Vinny*, which I'd watched on Zee Studio, one of the five or six 'English channels' in pre-2010 India. Vinny was a lawyer who defended himself and his cousin at a murder trial, and Lata was often the one to aid me in life's emotional trials. We laughed together—'who gets expelled; that *is* a movie'—and could talk about most things. We picked up influences and tastes from each other, and discussed humour and music and Tina Fey and *The Simpsons* and early YouTubers like Jon Lajoie.

Our families liked to engage in subtle forms of one-upmanship. Everything mundane and otherwise could be a source of status-anxiety, clues into what was important and desirable: our respective English- and Hindi-speaking skills, educational qualifications, lifestyles and expenditures, the kind of vacations we took, how the men and women in both families behaved, what Lata and I weighed, how much we ate. Because Appa didn't like us talking, we hid our pictures and albums together on Facebook. One time, after I lied at home to take a trip to meet her in Bengaluru, I was caught when my parents called me and the IVR spat out Kannada instead of the usual Hindi.

It is dizzying to recall now how these trackable extensions of ourselves multiplied innocently over time, and how suddenly they changed the scope of our lives. It was only my second, better attempt at engineering in Goa that provided an era of relative freedom. I had overcome the worst thing a South Indian could do (study badly), and had started living with an ease that befit my age—until I went home, of course. When my parents once glimpsed an SMS, seemingly about alcohol and seemingly from a boy, I urgently requested a girlfriend to act like she'd sent it instead, speaking to her hurriedly from the bathroom. The lavatory remains one of the last real sources of privacy in modern society.

In hindsight, having to wear masks all the time made me acutely aware of myself. Especially after I started 'making mistakes', I would keep track of all my actions, where I might leave traces of them, who could see those, and whether they would add up with what people were supposed to know of me. I know I'm still not alone in this: another Sanjana, a friend, a model, and a businesswoman, explained how she uses different profiles for work and for family. One of the first questions desi content creators are always asked is: 'What do your parents think about you doing this?'

But, ironically, this period of 'feeling like myself' is also when I adopted the masks I did want to wear. I joined the college drama and literary clubs, continuing from schooling in extracurriculars like writing and acting and 'elocution' and 'public speaking'. I met my second boyfriend too, who had a taste for the 'non-mainstream', and told me about Reddit and Woody Allen and Beat literature and world cinema. Unaware of our place on the spectrum of Indian identities, we judged people with 'lesser' tastes, once making an Excel sheet called *Ghati_Trendz* to laugh at the English mistakes that other people made. Mimesis, that deeply unconscious process, had nonetheless led us to imbibe certain tastes that would cement our belonging to 'our' social strata. Despite our troubles with them, we were carrying forward the previous generation's cultural complexes: their conscious admiration and unconscious resentment for all that India's erstwhile colonizers held superior, such as the English language and Western, 'cultured' sensibilities.

To spend nights out with this second bf, I would write fake emails as my mother from another account, giving myself permission to leave campus. We'd rent scooters and cars and drive to Baga and Candolim, staying in hotel rooms that cost ₹1,000 a night then. When he told me he wanted to be a film-maker, I knew my life and ideas were meant to be, and I latched on to that desire too.

My writing from that time is telling now: an evident struggle with naming characters as my worlds trying to blend some real-world observation or experience, therefore 'Indian', with the kind of art I aspired to make, 'in English'. Although I watched Hindi and Tamil 'content' aplenty, English was the language I read the most, thought in, and believed I could create in. The output at the time, however, was awkwardly constructed stories with characters who didn't fit in in places that were not real. That was perhaps my relationship with my country then.

India has not known and encouraged creative careers as stable, even possible, professions until recently. But as my artistic exposure and inclinations grew in college—I acted in and directed plays; I was the editor-in-chief of the college magazine; a friend and I wrote each other letters after we learnt that Ernest Hemingway and Scott Fitzgerald did too—I slowly started to fathom a future for myself where life would be no different. Through the classical engineering-and-MBA-or-medicine-and-other-national-competitive-exam-topping-aspirations that plagued what we thought of as middle-class India, I kept the dream alive, once buying a DSLR camera with money saved up from a software internship. I wanted to make a 'mockumentary film' about zealous religious mobs and the news-hungry media in Zuarinagar, Goa. My friends in the film club and I stopped midway, oblivious to the content gravy train on YouTube and such that today's most successful creators must have hopped onto around then. We were already defined by and enmeshed in the safety and prestige of the traditional '90s Indian kid career.

Think about it, though: there is the coming-of-age Hindi drama *Udaan*, released in the same year I was expelled—2010— about a boy who was also expelled from school, for watching a porno with his friends. The rest of the film is about him fighting his abusive, oppressive father to fulfil his lifelong dream of becoming a writer. The Viral Fever (TVF), one of India's first 'homegrown' digital content companies, was founded by a group of IITians-turned-writers; they produce relatable shows for 'progressive young Indians' often centred around the stress of taking India's various competitive exams, such as the JEE for engineering, the CAT for business, and the UPSC for civil services. There are, again, the likes of Chetan Bhagat and Sidin Vadukut, both engineers-turned-MBAs-turned-writers.[13] Their earliest works are fictionalized accounts of what seemed to be their 'hero's journey': born into a life and career that stifled them creatively, they overcome society's expectations and stable but boring jobs to find a girl and/or write, mostly about their lives. They wrote about writing about their lives.

Before I could attempt fame with my stories, though, the world as I knew it started to collapse. The year 2016 is when I registered that things surely didn't make sense anymore. This is the year that 'post-truth' was declared *Oxford Dictionary's* Word of the Year.[14] But it wasn't that Trump became the American president then or that the Indian currency was redefined overnight or that Modi was elected two years before and again in three years.

Instead, definitions of 'good' and 'bad' felt dubious again. Life presented what could be considered both 'good' and 'bad' simultaneously. Reality felt surreal. Consider for yourself my time.

August 2013: I withdraw from directing a college adaptation of *Skeleton Woman* by Kalki Koechlin after Amma calls to tell me that Appa is going through her phone. They are fighting more. The insults about her intelligence, family, and appearance are getting more creative. Amma also appears to be talking to a colleague. The second bf, who is next to me, jokes that I should gift her a divorce for her birthday. I laugh, quite seriously. To be able to laugh at anything meant detachment and strength.

April 2014: I'm in the hospital for the twentieth time in four years—this time for malaria. I have now started dating Bf #4, a most special character overall. He lies down next to me in the hospital, and I am immediately comforted. Our chats are teeming with ideas and jokes and endearment. I have finally understood what people mean by 'love'.

August 2015: I tell him before we start drinking, so he knows this isn't some intoxicated admission of hurt, that my parents are getting a divorce.

3 October 2015, 4 a.m.: A phone call about Amma's bleeding ear. Appa has run away from home. I make a call to the nearest police station.

5 October 2015, 6 a.m.: A weekend break from my first job and a flight to Mumbai to be with my mother as she gets her eardrum stitched back together. Appa sobs as he apologizes. He later tells me I'm going to be a periyaal—a 'big person'—for having the guts to call the cops on my father. Amma's ear is never the same again. Eight years later, even after years of meditation, when she is getting another surgery for the same ear, the man who's responsible for it but blasé about the damage he's caused—I break down. I can't take this.

November 2015: I now own a Bajaj Pulsar (150cc), having told my parents to accept my decision because I was going to drive a motorbike anyway. I'm averse to scooters after an accident from three years ago with Bf #1—I'd broken my jaw and lost an incisor. As I looked up from the blood soaking my slippers, I told him, 'I'm never going to smile again.' I spent the next year getting my mouth replaced. Pictures of those toothless days can still be found in internet backwaters.

December 2015: I'm not intelligent if I can just code—perhaps anyone can get a job at Oracle after studying for ten days—so I have to get a 'Top 4' job in software. That's Facebook, Amazon, Apple, or Google—now FAANG, with Netflix.

January 2016: I blank out during the interviews.

August 2016: I've studied more—properly this time, scouring Geeks4Geeks and YouTube channels and Coursera—and gotten the job. Amma's resolve, too, is solid now.

October 2016: The fourth bf and I have started fighting. Folks at the new job—mostly men, but one woman too—are discussing things I've said and done, questioning whether I really know what I claim to. I want to let myself accept that that I don't belong there, but I also can't. I can't stick to 1,300 calories a day anymore. I can hardly keep counting them.

November 2016: A dentist at Fortis leaves behind a piece of equipment in my jaw while operating on my wisdom teeth. He tries to take it out without telling me, without anaesthesia. The fourth bf faints.

4 December 2016, 1.30 p.m.: I'm getting a photograph clicked before the CAT exam. The previous night was spent drinking and smoking up, the usual weekend in Bengaluru for most 'techies'. Friends insist I shouldn't 'enjoy the arrogance of missing an exam in India', and that I could just give it and see what happens. Nothing to lose. But my most paranoid

trip happens later that evening, after the exam. I run into a Nilgiris outlet, screaming about the light coming towards us, and the inevitable apocalypse. People around us are alarmed.

23 December 2016: The divorce is final. I'm twenty-three years old and my brothers are thirteen. I've been prescribed something called Nexito Forte by a psychiatrist I found in BTM. Nobody knows but Bf #4, who finally believes I'm unhappy. So what if some colleagues thought I was stupid, he would say, perhaps because he knew exactly what being intelligent meant to me. Perhaps I understood what it meant to him too. I was about to ace an exam that he'd studied for and I'd rolled out of bed for. But that never got in the way of him trying to care for me, sincerely.

9 January 2017: I'm in the top 0.67 per cent in a competitive exam sat by more than 200,000 people. Rare for someone with no preparation. 'Disgusting,' in Lata's words. 'A golden opportunity Sanju,' Amma squeals, 'that cannot—should not—be missed.' I finally feel like the genius I've always wanted to be.

March 2017: Interview after interview amidst a demanding job and panic attacks and long fights and unstable relationships (and several supremely kind ones) and Bengaluru's execrable roads and traffic. I am stared at by every man on the road when I ride my bike. I buy a jacket that billows in the wind and obfuscates me, even as I am expressing, supposedly, my strongest self. Joints at night, along with *Gossip Girl*, are my salvation.

April 2017: I cheat on Bf #4, by hugging someone I have a crush on—after he cancels on me one more time, seemingly only to upset me. After a sleepless night, I finally give way and cry in one of the lesser rounds of the lesser colleges—where they love asking you stupid questions because they believe in 'stress interviews'. In all the others, I give 'normal' ambitious answers ('I want to combine my love for storytelling and tech and business to create a media company!'). I wished I could speak instead about adversity and gender and forced perseverance.

There is a second semi-real suicide attempt. Bf #4 is the only one to know, again. You can imagine the kind of stress he was in. There was no need for interviews to attempt to recreate that.

May 2017: I've quit that stupid job and Bf #4 to attend one of the country's most prestigious B-schools, according to PagalGuy.com. I've gotten in thanks to my sudden excellent score, but perhaps also the points for gender diversity given to women. It is another leg of doing what everybody does, but Amma is happy. It *is* a new beginning.

June 2017: I am reading *One Flew Over the Cuckoo's Nest*. I don't yet know what the book is about—the subtle ways in which institutions and authorities 'process' and manipulate individuals, so that they do not even recognize they are being controlled—but I have, in the same week, gone through a job factory disguised as 'preparation for life', hazing rituals disguised as college ice-breakers, drug-fuelled parties with doses of sexism, ableism, and homophobia, all under the guise of 'bringing seniors and juniors together' and 'building the brand'. I am, of course, one of them. I want to fit in, so I am either anxious or high. I'm mostly high. As confident and dramatic as I always am.

August 2017: The achievement complex does its job. No substance or man gets in the way of success. I'm the first one to get the coveted summer internship; the first one to get the job out of the internship; the only one to unironically get an award called 'Universal Crush of the Batch'. I joke about having to pay less dowry while collecting it. Some of the girls don't look me in the eye later. I don't say anything when a professor asks us if girls really should get extra points for 'diversity' in the entrance process, because I am sick of being seen as a 'feminist' or 'campaigner' or 'lesbian', as some guys had already called me. I am the hot cool girl, always one of the guys, and, also, I'm high. I run rounds to lose the kilos I've put on. I'm bringin' sexy back! I am diplomatic and spaced with male superiors and their sometimes excessive attention. I have to work with them, I cannot displease them. Appa threatens to tell my office I was expelled. He wants to get me fired. A male superior will later fire me. Is it the men, or is it me? I fret that I cannot be as outspoken, confident, unapologetic, only sometimes ironic as I want to be, because only I know my intentions are not one-upmanship, but 'how I really am'. Perhaps I really was 'arrogant' as Appa had called me. I am called, in addition to these adjectives, 'emotional' on a day my face betrays some emotion. On the days it does not, I am called 'dead inside'. What *am* I, then, why don't you decide and tell me? My email ID is still sanjana7ramachandran@gmail.com. My new love interest is a TamBrahm with a JEE Rank befitting my ancestry. I want to get married by the time I'm twenty-eight—twenty-nine, latest—so I can 'have my shit together', which includes ensuring intelligent children so as to not suffer like Amma did. No matter how hard I try, though, I cannot enjoy what we have. I do not have the courage to end things either. I read *Tender Is the Night*, which explains what's happened: 'Diver's profession of sorting the broken shells of another sort of egg had given him a dread of breakage.'[15] I'm broken. I careen from one boy to the next, either collecting sexual escapades or trying to anoint 'The One'. This is my checklist: does he want to get married? Is he the kind of funny that would guarantee we're never bored—how else do two ordinary human beings survive forty years of only each other—and is he intelligent, so that we don't have stupid children? I know I don't want children, but what if we have them? Is he attractive? A is funny, smart, attractive, but three years younger than me and unsure of his sexuality—risky;

J likes me too much; M's dick is too small, and he thinks I've never watched porn; S ghosts me; the dating apps are stultifying, commodifying connection and people more than even I can. The only thing worse than giving this mad chase up is becoming 'one of those single old women'. I share this anxiety with every other woman I know, so it feels utterly sane. It is also sane to work twelve hours a day, or more; in fact, the more the better, so you can talk about busy you are in back-handed ways and give 'gyaan' online. So what if I get six migraines a month? I read *Migraine* by Oliver Sacks. Everyone is reading a lot these days. We talk about the news, self-improvement, diets, and first principles. One has to make an effort to concentrate. Why did I open my phone again? Pot helps. Amma does not understand that. During one particularly notorious migraine, for which I am admitted to the hospital, she insists that I should 'relax'. I didn't get it; wasn't it an abnormal desire to appear 'normal' and 'relaxed' that caused all this?

Can't she tell that I have PTSD?

What about our lives, or anyone else's, was relaxing or 'normal'? Sacks writes that migraines can be circumstantial—triggered by light and sound; or situational—'a sign of the body rebelling against what is repressed'; 'not being in its natural environment'.[16] I'm crying in bathrooms—sometimes outside them—so a mentor and friend at work recommends his therapist. Everybody needs help, he knows, and Shreya tells him I'm 'brilliant'. As much as I doubt my sanity, I doubt others' more, so I ask her how she knows this. She tells me I can 'join the dots'. I continue working in sickness and in health. I am 'doing a fantastic job'. I have had a 'wonderful start' and 'could be CEO someday'. I'm obviously doing what I was always meant to. Michael Dearing has a study on the 'Five Cognitive Distortions of People Who *Get Stuff Done*'; it turns out to be a comparison between founders and the mentally ill. Both use 'overgeneralization', 'black-and-white thinking', 'personal exceptionalism', 'blank canvas thinking', and 'Schumpeterianism' ('I am a creative destruction machine').[17] I want to get promoted quickly. Before everyone else. How horrible, though, to wait thirty minutes for a cab twice a day, carpool a few hours to and fro, and still only get any real work done at home *after* office hours. I have no time to myself, between my job and living at home so I can save rent-money to pay off student loans I undertook to get this job that pays for things I never really needed, like student loans. One time, I injure my knee during a morning run and work from home for a few days. I'm thinking about the ongoing atrocities in India, living in times comparable to fascist Germany, and how I'd have liked to answer the question of 'What would you do if you were alive during the Holocaust?' with 'Be part of some kind of resistance, obviously,' instead of 'Just try to get promoted before everyone else at my job!'

Most people want to think favourably of themselves. Are the evil banal by choice? Offended by my impotence, disgusted by religious divides, desirous of another by-line, I write something about the Kafkaesque lives of Assamese citizens and minorities after the CAA–NRC issue, drawing comfort from how Kafka also wrote on the side while being sickly and well-regarded in his bureaucratic job. It gets six likes on Twitter.[18] That is okay, though.

Wouldn't it be great if everyone could just work from home?

March 2020: Wait. What just happened?
Was this manifestation?

As the pandemic and lockdowns sank in, during what felt like the eve of mankind's end, like so many people around the world, I risked being buried by my usual way of life. I didn't enjoy thinking about how I'd gotten here, but at least I finally could.

I could participate in my life again.

Around me were my mother and my brothers, colleagues on a screen, and, on the internet, everything everywhere all at once. I started picking up desire, guilt, and regret in real time.

A girl from school was now a model with 400,000 followers on Instagram and her fashion brand. *She* hadn't organized her life around her parents' desires, I thought, having the courage to follow her path instead of doing what society upheld. Another, an actor, posted brave stories about his mother's 'narcissistic breakdown'. He was an activist too, with highlights about India's farmer's protests and the issue of misandry. Yet another friend of a friend had been cancelled on social media for appearing gleeful about his job, which involved charging at protesting Indian farmers.

People were making sketches, but TikTok got banned. I couldn't be as weird on Instagram. I took part in online open-mics and screenwriting competitions, desperate to create in my hours off of work. What if I could never self-actualize later? I saw funny tweets and tried to think of some consistently. I was shocked that the recommended amount to 'grow' was some five per day and that even Appa was on it and had blocked me.[19] I decided to call myself @ramachandranesk; meaning 'in the style of, or resembling'. Everyone had a newsletter suddenly. Everyone was starting up. I got some cool job offers, but I also wanted to act on my own ideas. The term 'side-hustle' peaked in Google searches and grew seven-fold in this time.[20] What side-hustle should *I* invest in? The mind was racing.

The Platforms suggested being 'consistent', being

'authentic', being yourself—but I didn't get it. Wearing one mask too many over time had confused my idea of who 'I' was.

Which self? What is the self, even? Slicing and dicing myself variously led to abstractions that all seemed to contradict each other. I wished I could easily 'brand' myself—didn't I work in marketing?—but mapping my traits onto the brand pyramids and positioning gizas I'd learnt through my management career didn't teach me who I was. I thought I was 'tech-forward'; couldn't I somehow be favourably mutated by these technological advancements that had upturned our lives? As an aspiring writer and artist, I wanted foremost to be true to myself—but what was true about me?

Weren't all my actions over my lifetime derived from looking at other people anyway? Hadn't I also enjoyed my life—or at least I thought I did.... So what were these new pains and itches?

Why couldn't I monetize my existential angst properly? I'd then be rich enough to sponsor a reality show featuring other Indians trying to monetize their existential angst.

So: how could I know that what I wanted *now* was what I actually wanted? What *were* my thoughts and ideas, or even 'me'?

Who *am* 'I'?

Behind all these tensions and versions of myself was a grand incongruity with the only ostensible 'me'—my physical self, my body, an irrefutable presence, surely—which occupied one room at home but presented itself differently in the next, at work, online. But only through it did I begin to find what I was looking for.

The answers turned out to be in my knees, my lungs, my liver, in the splits of my pulsating headaches, between the lips of my vagina; as the bodymind revealed me to myself, I traversed scenes from my life, the land I grew up in, and the world I'd grown into.

I encountered, like every other being, the composites of matter and energy that made me, producing this feeling of sentience, some sense of self. Perhaps it had been here before.

Above this layer, though, like a refurbished computer in the hands of a new owner, various programs had been installed. Since '6.19 a.m.' on '8 April 1993', a 'Thursday', I have been, apparently, an 'Indian', a 'woman', a 'Brahmin', born in 'Isabella Hospital, Madras', qualified and overladen with abstractions I don't quite recall choosing.

I am trying to square these installations off with what I think are my own now. *Famous Last Questions* is the story of this dangerous endeavour, how I peeked into dynamic cultural source code, and what it says about all of us.

Things I've written since April 2020 have gotten more than six likes on Twitter. Not that that should matter, but people don't respect you until they see other people respecting you. Such is the herd. But in my drive to live my many unlived lives, I found I did have the energy to enjoy tweeting multiple times a day, and to produce 'proper' writing outside of it, and to work other jobs and sustain this writing and the soul, while also excelling at them, I might add—even if I do say so myself.

And I have to say so myself.

If a tree falls in a forest and no one is around to hear it, does it make a sound?

If a person exists in the crowd, but no one ever sees them, do they even exist?

'Pics or it didn't happen', basically, but about your whole life.

The 'personal brand' is a natural by-product of the rise of social media and the gig economy, and in repeating a few times a day that I am a writer, that I am a marketer, that I am conventionally successful, that I exist, I have adopted the beliefs that I sell—successfully, I might add again (that's what the algorithm wants). 'ramachandranesk' is now also known as 'sanjubobbygeorge', the trickster version of me on X who's had comedic writerly hits and is occasionally recognized on dating apps, and other circles where just about everyone has had their taste of internet microfame, most way more than me: the city of Bengaluru.

Just in time—I'd become a writer—before the very relationship between humans and writing was to be changed forever by that pattern-matching artificial intelligence.

Still, fame today lies in the eyes of the beholder. My family were somewhat supportive of my deviation from the corporate-CEO-married-and-settled-by-thirty path, but they were trained to look for success in older ways. They might not understand or find internet fame useful, or even cute, even though the network and visibility allowed me to get paid while being myself.

'Oh. It takes only one book to become big,' some merciful relative might understand, when I tell them I'm writing one. There is no question about the work itself, although we are capable of having that conversation. 'You should reach great heights,' someone else will say, unaware of the weight of the expectations that were always foisted on me, oblivious to how I may be happy doing what I want, whether or not that's 'successful', which also it is—I repeat.

'How many followers do you have?' a former-day corporate colleague might ask. 'You want to be the next Chetan Bhagat, huh?' asks another who knows we share an engineering-and-

MBA background. I flinch at these questions. Effin plebs. Only people without an artistic bone would imagine that outward wins can endlessly compensate for the sheer nervous system benefits of being yourself.

Meena Kandaswamy, an author who won awards previously gifted to Gunter Grass and Harold Pinter, tweeted about her #indianparents reaction that she get a 'permanent job with a regular salary'.[21] One meme after Kamala Harris was elected as the American vice president showed #indianparents asking, 'Why only Vice President? Why not an actual President?' These ideas of success, marked by the highest knowable, comforting externalities, have been passed down through generations.

But all I wanted to do was write books like the ones I'd read and loved, to talk about the things in my head, and to be funny. One way to do that was through personal essays about Appa and my family, insights into a more real-world Homer Simpson, someone so oblivious to his misogyny and entitlement that the idea of by screaming at people for things like being slightly late would never strike him as counter-productive.

But in trying to become a professional, published writer in India, while also selling products to its people, I ended up being able to write about myself *and* the world outside—my country. And in the process, I learnt that it is not so different from me.

The paradoxical aspirations that defined independent India were always superimposed on my life, starting with my very name. You may know about the 'Sanjana Effect', from an essay I wrote about how Indians name their children, told through the story of my name, and all my namesakes from the '90s.[22] Our families were all smitten by Aishwarya Rai, or 'Sanju', from a 1993 Pepsi ad, in which she symbolized the ideal new Indian woman—modern and internationally successful, yet definitively traditional and Indian—as India itself aspired to be after it opened up its economy in 1991. I found those same pressures applied to the fields of science and technology, when I learnt that some Indian researchers were still trying to make AI systems through the use of Sanskrit, because it is 'Indian' and traditional, even though the world was racing forward with deep-learning-based AI.

These are the complexes that explain the older generations' paranoia about Western culture and vices contaminating the morality of young Indian generations. In our collective desire for branded accomplishment no matter what the—scientific, managerial, or artistic—endeavour; in our hunger to leave a mark on the world—there are now over 100,000 start-ups in India, up from 500 just nine years ago; a 'demographic dividend' and 'burgeoning middle-class' and billion-people consumer base that investors are betting on—we now have a promising 'India story' that the world is invested in.

It is about a nation finally poised to realize its own potential. Born through violence and to widespread scepticism about the prospects of its very existence, the Indian nation-state has always had its own achievement complex: to be as successful, advanced, and modern as the Western forces that colonized and birthed it, but through its own traditional, 'Indian' means. This need for public, national self-actualization in turn feeds constant internal paranoia about who, or what, is truly Indian, with various groups and identities constantly evaluating each other's claims to Indianness, in all the country's 'richness', 'diversity', and 'contradictions'.

Your stance on Kashmir and whether it should be part of the Indian nation-state is a litmus test of patrioritsm. What you say about beef-eating and vegetarianism will get you labelled as casteist or anti-caste. 'Hindi' becoming the national language is a matter of erasure for the Dravidian identity. NRIs are 'out of touch' with their homeland, but also touted as global proof of 'how far India has come'. Your opinions on these hot issues are how people slot you as 'in' or 'out', or 'like us' and 'not like us'—god forbid you don't subscribe to binaries, or believe in the value of ambivalence, because then people won't know what to do with you or how to react. You see these battles playing out on the media and internet daily—from questions about how we should look and speak to what we should eat and know—and in #desicontent that did not exist a decade ago.

Those descended from the groups that helped create the Indian nation-state—upper-caste and upper-class Hindus, who still control most of India's mainstream business and media—have been in the position to define these in-groups and out-groups most broadly. While celebrating every instance of 'Indian' success on the international stage, they sometimes let slip their particular brand of Indianness by pointing out, for example, the religion and castes of the CEOs of Twitter, Google, Microsoft, and the American vice president—they're all upper-caste Hindus.

But quick to point out the flaw in such claims are the voices of India's several minorities and sections of the majority. When PEN America's released it's 'India at 75' edition, it was criticized for featuring majorly only upper-caste writers.[23] Now, for the first time in history—thanks to the internet, capitalism, and this 'Western' influence that has corroded 'traditional Indian values'—Dalits, Bahujans, Adivasis, and other communities disadvantaged by India's caste system have been able to communicate at scale, no longer mediated by groups that have a vested interest in suppressing their stories. For them, Indian nationalism was always a caste-Hindu variety, upheld only by an elite minority of the country's population. Even its purportedly secular strand, represented by the Congress today and derived from its leaders, Nehru and Gandhi, is 'problematic' for having a history of exclusion as serious, perhaps more insidious, than the more nakedly militant and conservative BJP and RSS. Both are marked by a leadership of mostly upper-caste Hindus, who represent about 30 per cent of the Indian population.[24]

The manufactured homogeneity of the Indian identity could only sustain itself until the internet, and the access it provided non-dominant groups, shattered it. Some proportion of India's upper-caste, or savarna, population was edified by this shattering, confronted by a history of exclusion and oppression they'd been complicit in, inadvertently or otherwise.[25]

A moment of reckoning.

If you ever felt proud of your religiosity or intellectualism or 'simple' lifestyle as a Brahmin, it would follow that those lower in the caste-order should also be defined by their caste-norms. Banias proud of being 'dhandho'-minded should wonder if they agree that Dalits are really untouchables, and whether they deserve to inherently run businesses more than other Indians. Do you believe that meals must be segregated, that vegetarianism is 'pure', that period-blood is 'impure'—or, fundamentally, that the concepts of 'purity' and 'pollution' that define 'caste' are valid?

After more than two decades of socialization that valorized a monolithic 'secular' 'idea of India', which treated caste as some banal system from the past, simply brushing past how it is responsible for the Indian view of gender—it took weeks and months to internalize what this really meant in my life. It was caste-Hindu ideas of who people should be that had shaped our lives, which are the underlying reasons for most female trauma in India—including the controls on my sexuality, the shame and inferiority of girlhood, the domestic violence, the love conditional to materialistic overachievement, clothed as spiritual purpose—while all the time, I was seen as and called 'privileged' by the outside world.

'We are all from somewhere. And it's the artist's job to question the values that went into the making of that somewhere,' wrote Hilton Als.[26]

What made my 'somewhere'?

Until very recently, most stories from India's mainstream media—from TVF to Bollywood to its big news channels—singularly centred those in power, causing material and psychic harm to anyone who didn't conform to those images. The 'woke movement' world over demanded our screens be more 'diverse and inclusive', and the new generation of Indian content has finally caught up with the complexity of being Indian. The average Indian OTT programme will now feature a bouquet of the 'right' characters, identities, and situations, reflecting a 'changing modern India': upper-caste Hindus, lower-caste Hindus, Muslims, LGBTQIAs, their intersections too, with narratives of new Indians self-actualizing, pursuing their creativity or unconventional career paths, becoming influencers or start-up founders, or living in with their partner(s), or choosing to stay single, contending with the consequences of their choices for older generations and in a fast-changing world.

Growing up, however, I received stories and ideas of who to be devoid of such subjectivity. I had little awareness of conditioning as a process of man-made labels and constructs, much less their national and political associations, and all their contradictions too.

They were more simply encountered as the expectations and 'best practices' of elders, relatives, teachers, friends, colleagues, people you rely on and trust.

That their genuine expressions of love and care were intertwined with unconscious, externally-programmed status-seeking goals and definitions is an adult realization—and a complicated one.

If you do not choose your history and life, neither did those who lived by theirs and hurt you as a result. And if you, while living your history out, which you always are, inadvertently hurt someone, shouldn't you forgive yourself too? Because you have to?

Shouldn't everyone be forgiven then?

What of justice, then? What of love?

Much has been written about these ideas of India, religion, morality, philosophy, psychology, and human nature, more than I ever thought I'd read with the imperative of understanding my own life. The norms we're handed down travel through stories from screens and institutions to families and children into our very psyches, varying by religion, caste, gender, age, the times we're born in, the places we live in, their laws, the people we encounter, and the languages we speak—which is why all their different definitions combined mean no single definition of 'Indian'. The country's and our own many sub-minds have each got different values and ideas of who belongs: in Mumbai, I may be told I don't look 'South Indian' but also that my Hindi isn't good enough. In Chennai, I look 'North Indian' and my Hindi is too good. In both Delhi and Bengaluru, I have been stared at and groped by men nonetheless. In Kolkata, I was once laughed at for not knowing the date of the Babri Masjid demolition. My Class X scores in Hindi and History were ninety-six and ninety-two, if you must know, but what I really want is to not have to prove my Indianness in any way.

It's not *that* important.

Your identity *is* perhaps the most important determinant of your experience on the planet. But you still probably only control some single-digit-percentage of your experience in life overall—if at all.

Yes, it was shocking to find out that Amma's and Appa's control over my interactions with the opposite sex came less from pragmatic concerns about my safety—that I may get pregnant, for instance, and that might keep me from other selfish activities—but more from internalized notions of the 'purity' of the Hindu upper-caste female, so central to maintaining an endogamous religious caste order. All the customs that I associated, as a child, with illogical ritualistic ideas of happiness, were, in fact, the creations of a culture they had inherited and did not question, because they did not—and do not, and perhaps will not—believe it to be harmful. We operate under no usual patriarchy in India; to attribute sexism here to simply gender is to believe we feel hot because of the concept of temperature, not the presence of heat.

Even though Amma has been denied housing for being a divorced woman, and although she struggled to get divorced despite being denied basic freedoms at home, and although Appa denied her those freedoms because of his ideas of man, woman, and success—the norms strike back!—both ascribe their life outcomes to less systemic and more intractable reasons, such as fate, being born on the day eight, and, in Appa's case, having a terrible, 'interfering' daughter.

And I'd certainly interfered, by suggesting for over a decade that nobody should live an unhappy—immoral—life. I don't think I did it very well, though, because my brother now believes that I am the cause of our dysfunction, a blame my father does not take upon himself, and that my apologizing for has little effect on. And I could not help Appa, although I could have perhaps tried harder to; the need for it was palpable when, even as words like 'mental health' and 'gaslighting' were entering popular vocabulary, he told me I was crazy for trying to both help and get help.

I have now recovered enough to recognize, and he may agree, that his worst moments—like mine—were of a person who was, at times, not in sufficient control of their mind.

In Jung's theory, a complex can be conscious, partly

conscious, or unconscious. An emotionally charged pattern of beliefs and memories, organized around themes like power or status or belonging, complexes 'can have us'. They can 'usurp power from the ego and cause psychological disturbances and symptoms from the development of a neurosis'. Without resolution, they exert an 'unconscious, maladaptive influence on our thoughts', and 'an active complex puts us momentarily in a state of duress, of compulsive thinking and acting....'

The psychological knots and habits that caused Appa to seemingly intentionally hurt his own wife and children— insisting that Amma reach home by 7 p. m., or else penalizing her by keeping my brothers at a mall; implying her use of kajal and perfume was a desire to be raped; belittling her intelligence and education by trumpeting his own in 'maths', even though my mother was a state topper in her chosen subject, law; trying to get me fired for opposing him in all this; calling me 'arrogant' and 'egoistic' at any protest or display of independent thought—originated from deep-rooted complexes about men, women, intelligence, age, and power. They manifested across multiple axes of a full human life, revealing this Brahmin male's idea of his place in society relative to others. And Amma too, for the longest time, would rather have remained miserable and 'sacrificing' than question the norms that defined her self-image and life, even if they compromised her freedom and happiness.

Though we believe men to be privileged, they sometimes don't see themselves as such, suffering from their ideas of who they should be; just as women sometimes don't perceive themselves as subjugated, even as they suffer from their ideas of who they should be; just as we believe ourselves to be free, the makers of our own choices and identities, when in fact they are handed down to us, directly or otherwise, and even if we decide to redefine them, we need and would like others to agree.

We are hardly independent of each other, or totally free. It is for this reason that The Norms have a powerful grip on us. It is only by questioning my own unthinking adherence to them, and the complexes and strange behaviours they'd engendered in me, that I was exposed to the universal humanity of living by them.

I already told you that my achievement complex had nearly killed me, pushing me willy-nilly, in opposite directions but with equal force, splitting me up until I did everything my parents—and India—wanted me to do, but in ways that my parents—and India—would hate, because I unconsciously hated following anybody else's ideas of how to live, but I also wanted to follow them just to show that I could.

How could I not? And how could I not do it better than anyone else?

And for what? Just to prove a point? Draw the boundaries of unconditional love with my own hands? Cement myself as the 'best'?

'The goals we pursue are always veiled,' wrote Milan Kundera. 'A girl who longs for marriage longs for something she knows nothing about. The boy who hankers after fame has no idea what fame is. The thing that gives our every move its meaning is always totally unknown to us.'[27]

This invites the obvious question now: why am I writing this?

If Kundera is to be believed, I am speaking about that which cannot be known. But, as Joan Didion wrote—and if quoting her doesn't cement me as a Writer-Writer: 'I fail to see how [objectivity] can be achieved if the reader does not understand the writer's particular bias.'[28]

Here I try to reveal mine: my biases, my agenda.

The idea of being honest and telling stories about life became, at some point, my only salve through the imagined 'bad' and 'good' of it. Art saved me, entertained me, and made me think. It was there for me whenever I needed it. So, I felt compelled to create some in the same vein.

And I do it now happily, but also with compunction and confusion. It isn't the life of dignity I imagined. My extended family thinks I 'sit at home'—they don't respect me. Like many artists and creators today, my internet 'fame' is an outcome of being embarrassingly online, 'putting myself out there' several times a day, a kind of long-term grovelling for my work to be read and shared, to be made a career out of, while also working several less precarious jobs that provide the actual capital, enabling me to question the methods of that capital.

I know I have more friends than ever now, but I like them less than I pretend to, especially the snivelly kind who only want my attention so they can advance their career or interests. They're not cool. They're like any other boss or colleague who I have to appease lest they stop 'supporting' me.

And support me they must—otherwise how am I going to achieve my aim?

Look here, I've hardly been secretive about it. The title of the book is a dead giveaway. I am telling you I'm looking for 'fame'.

It's not just in the title—look at when I was born.

'Me, me, me'! My generation was called the 'me, me, me' generation by TIME—woohoo, now that's a brand you can trust—who reported a 58 per cent rise in narcissism between 1982 and 2009, three times higher in people in their twenties than those four times their age, who aren't as 'obsessed with fame' and 'getting promoted every two years'.[29] It also states that everyone has narcissistic traits, since it is a spectrum. The healthy kind is self-aware about their narcissism and channels into something larger than oneself, which is how great things get done. Think Gandhi, Nelson Mandela, Elon Musk, etc—those people wouldn't have been able to defy everyone around them without some narcissism.

(Look at me! I'm aware of it! Channelling it into high ends!)

Speaking of 'high', I told you once that I was 'high' all the time. But I'm definitely not now. I just want to tell you about all the pressure I am under, all the expectations I have to live up to—which you do too, by the way. Liah Greenfeld wrote in *Mind, Madness and Modernity* that the rise of nationalism expanded the human emotional repertoire, adding to it new feelings like ambition, aspiration, and, remarkably, even happiness and romantic love.[30]

Capitalism and nationalism both function on the premise of the individual endlessly constructing his own identity. But 'the more choices one has, the less secure one becomes in the choices already made (by one or for one) and making up one's mind—literally, in the sense of constructing one's identity—grows increasingly difficult.'

It grows maddening.

And we've only gotten more ways and more ways to construct ourselves. There isn't a platform you're not on. Of course we've gone mad.

And in questioning all the values that brought me here, I risk growing madder, because I might blow up the ones that cushion me, without even becoming the 'periyaal'—the big person—that Amma and Appa want me to be. I might do it just to become the writer and jester whose stories are now within me.

What stories!

Imagine if I stick my neck out and tell you everything and get arrested or something. And AI just solves it in two months anyway. It already sounds more coherent about the problem than me:

Smashing Brahminical patriarchy requires dismantling the interlinked systems of caste and gender oppression embedded in Indian society. This means questioning not only the visible caste hierarchies but also the seemingly benign customs and rituals that uphold them. For example, we need to critically examine everyday norms around arranged marriages, religious ceremonies, and the glorification of "traditional" family structures that privilege Brahmin men. Education, awareness, and increased representation of marginalized voices (particularly Dalit, Bahujan, and Adivasi women) in media, politics, and literature are key strategies.

At the same time, there's a need to redefine masculinity and deconstruct the association of power, purity, and control with Brahmin male identity. Men who benefit from these systems must confront their own conditioning and choose to relinquish the privileges conferred upon them by caste and gender. Allyship should go beyond performative acts to actively support anti-caste feminist movements and implement policies that disrupt caste-based entitlements in education, employment, and cultural capital. Real change will come from a fundamental shift in how we understand equality—breaking free from hierarchical thinking altogether.

Now, before you judge me for thinking I can get killed, let me tell you: India's best writers and artists are always at risk. I'm not some stand-up comedian talking about how hard it is to get rickshaws in Bombay and comparing it with Delhi to be relatable and get some stupid laughs. And if you think it's hubris that makes me believe I am that good, I know better than to admit that. I'd prefer you attribute my caution and fear to legitimate worry—to my sanity instead.

Because what sane person would even slightly risk their safety? See this line from *Catch-22*: 'There was only one catch and that was Catch-22, which specified that a concern for one's own safety in the face of dangers that were real and immediate was the process of a rational mind.'[31]

So, I'm being rational, unless you disagree that the dangers are not real or immediate. But if you agree that they the dangers are real and immediate, then you agree that it is sane to be worried.

What is so worrisome, though? What am I going to say here?

Nobody's insane.

Perhaps the question is answered more easily by addressing an opposite.

A sane mind is one that is not crazy.
And I'll be the first to tell you I am not crazy.
But a crazy person wouldn't know that they are crazy.
And if they were crazy, they definitely wouldn't know it.
They definitely wouldn't tell anyone.
So, I'm telling you: I'm crazy.
But now I'm crazy.
And if I tell you I'm crazy, I'm definitely not.
You see the problem?
I can't be an authority on this subject.
We have to turn to a third person.

Post-Traumatic Stress Disorder is a psychiatric disorder that may occur in people who have experienced or witnessed a traumatic event, causing them to have intense disturbing thoughts and feelings long after the event has ended. They may relive it through flashbacks; nightmares; have sadness, anger, and fear' and hypervigilance to sensations, noise, and touch. It may be caused by war, natural disasters, accidents, rape, historical trauma, domestic violence, bullying. Women are twice as likely to contract it as men.[32] Even while reliving it, patients can find it hard to remember aspects of the offending event.

They may struggle with feelings of detachment or estrangement from oneself and others, leading to ongoing thoughts like, 'No one can be trusted.'

I never said that, though.

I just said that I may not trust you. Even if you listen well.

I said it a few pages ago. Look how perfect my memory is.

How can I be crazy?

Even the average third person doesn't think I am. She just thinks I've been through a lot. That I should be careful. That I shouldn't jeopardize my life or my lifestyle, however middle-class it is, just because I've discovered some normal truths about the establishment. It's a part of adulthood. Be anti-establishment, but just the right amount.

Now you'll tell me my lifestyle is hardly 'middle-class'. Yes, you fall in India's top 10 per cent if you earn more than ₹25,000 per month. And for this luxury, I have to thank my parents for everything they have given me, from my education and this privilege to their initially begrudging but eventually quite full acceptance of my chosen ways of being. And I love them not just because they birthed me, or named me Sanjana, and made me the writer I am today. My desire to tell the truth about the places I come from doesn't mean I don't want to lose the people or relationships that came with them. I don't feel better than anyone I share this culture with.

So, you must understand why it is necessary that I say one thing and do another. 'Hypocrisy is the grease that keeps society functioning,' wrote Janet Malcolm, the journalist who exposed the questionable methods of her own profession: ingratiating sources, making them feel safe while speaking to them but twisting their words later.[33]

And my brushes with authority, especially older and male, have also taught me this: honesty is not the best policy, especially for women. Of course, it makes me terribly uncomfortable. It is an important Buddhist precept, not to lie. Now, I'm not saying I'm Buddhist—I'm still Hindu—but I just don't like to lie. I told you I want to be honest. That this is my moment of truth. That is what I want.

But also I have to lie. Not only to protect myself and the people I love, but also to tell the truth. I'm just exercising that peculiar ingenuity we all have today, in cultivating multiple images and selves and not adhering to any one of them to still maintain all relationships.

It's best that I too speak in metaphors and riddles. You understand, right? That is how Hindus talk, anyway. What better way to critique its 'plural culture' than by using its own language? I hate to have to explain my own jokes like this. But I do want to be read by as many people as possible, so that everyone will know that I am the successful author of this successful book.

And yet I am also not writing e-books or posting #hustleporn on LinkedIn or dancing in front of a camera—I'm not saying I won't; I just haven't yet—all of which are more effective routes to fame.

I told you, honestly, that writing honestly requires immaculate dishonesty.

So, what is happening?

Am I playing some cheap trick to drive home the fallibility of the idea of truth, or the chaos of being alive under the weight of a hundred thousand contradictions daily, from trying to have a coherent sense of self from all the parallel realities we occupy in a given moment, in front of our screen(s), before our families and friends, and our own reflection in the mirror? What *Black Mirror*-ass shit is this?

Anyway, the following essays are attempts to understand my behaviour over the last three decades, and they have sadly become larger questions about my generation and my country. This is difficult. I am sifting through everything I've been fed about religion and gender and science and education and people and love and marriage and drugs and achievement and the body and the mind and the self and reality itself, with the intent of making one or more lives better. But it is hard to pretend to know what 'better' is—ignorance was bliss—and that this isn't an exercise that does more than honour my own life and suffering. Because the myths and norms and selves I'm writing about may never appear again. But still, let the questions be asked, and let them be answered, but let them be the last—it would be funny to now work on a *Famous Last Questions 2.0*—because the answers are as much modes of healing as they are warnings about the folly of the human condition, windows into some version of truth, and, 'non-fiction' or not, hopefully definitely literary.

2

SCIENCE, ARTS, OR COMMERCE?

'When logic and proportion have fallen sloppy dead,
feed your head...feed your head.'

—Jefferson Airplane

You remember that bit about how my father slapped me after I got expelled from an engineering college on the outskirts of Chennai?

Well, here is the never-before-told-at-parties story of how it happened. The boy and I had just started seeing each other. It was a time when love and freedom were worth it—and we never imagined they could have such dire consequences anyway—so we decided to make out in one of the under-construction toilets on the fourth or fifth floor of this under-construction college building. We were soon interrupted by a bunch of construction workers who thought it was necessary to gather at our erotic enclosure and, I don't know, resume constructing it or something. It was the lunch hour, so we hurriedly covered our torsos back up and rushed out to resume our day.

A few classes later, we made another attempt. Having been caught once, we really didn't think we'd get caught again—big-time.

This time it was a fully constructed toilet, on the first floor. We occupied the first of six cubicles. Before we could kiss, however, we heard footsteps. Somebody had entered the restroom and was checking to see if it was occupied. Ours was the only door that didn't open up, so I spoke up, in Tamil. 'I'm inside. I'll be out in some time.'

We had two minutes to figure out how to escape. It didn't strike us then that it was impossible. We couldn't speak; the guard would hear us. Even the bottom of our cubicle would have given us away, because there were four feet—not two. I screamed with my eyes at my cohabitant that he should put his feet on the toilet seat, but he didn't get it.

There was nothing left to do.

I non-verbally indicated that I'd give the boy some sort of signal if it was safe for him to leave after I did, but I don't think that transmitted either. The restroom was empty when I stepped out, but the guard was right outside. As I retreated towards the sink, as if to wash my hands but really to find some way to tell my boyfriend that he should remain inside the cubicle—the man stepped out. Just then, the guard stepped in.

Guard, Boyfriend, and I—face to face—a blank second or two.

'Run,' I said, and m'amour sprinted towards the nearest stairwell, the guard at his heels. I fled in the opposite direction, but in a few metres, the under-construction building came to a literal end, and I had to decide.

I could jump off this floor, I thought, assessing the protruding beams of iron and mortar beneath me for potential damage.

A broken arm? Hurt legs? So much for my weight loss journey. But at least I'd avoid a worse disaster: whatever lay after this misadventure.

But I didn't choose death then either. I turned around and started running again. Seeing that I was the easier catch, the guard also turned toward me, and soon grabbed a hold of my bag.

In the two weeks that followed, I lost a lot of innocence. I have only been losing it since. I couldn't believe what was happening, but that it was happening made me feel like an observer in my own life. A story was beginning to form, seemingly due to my own actions—so I *had* to change the ending.

We were part of an interrogation by one Professor Reddy that very evening. Before I entered the staff room, I told Reddy I had to go to the bathroom. 'Why?' he asked angrily.

'I have my period,' I said, and watched the blood leave his face instead. It was 2010, an era when fifty-five-year-old conversative men weren't used to the idea of a woman—nay, a girl—openly mentioning her bodily processes. Truthfully, though, this wasn't a white lie. I had to get rid of a bottle of vodka in my bag, lest the bag was searched later. On my way to the bathroom, I ran into Shiva, who knew what had happened and quickly took it away from me.

The boyfriend is now in the staff room too. His hands are behind his back, his face is lowered; he is the picture of abashed. Good.

'Where are you from?' Reddy asked. 'Sir, I'm from Rajasthan,' he said. Not good.

My mother is on the phone with me later, aghast but also threatening the institute. If 'anything happened to me', she, a lawyer, wouldn't let it go.

It was decided by the college authorities that we would give our term-end exams first, which were due to begin the next day—bold of us teenagers to still act upon our every hormonal whim, I know—after which our parents were summoned and schooled by the white-haired, dark-skinned Tamil Brahmin man who was the dean of the institution.

'A good girl doesn't do these things,' he said to my father

and I, as we sat opposite him in his cabin. 'A good girl wakes up at 5 a.m. She says her prayers. Studies dutifully. Attends all her classes. She is back in her hostel room by 5.30 p.m. in the evening.'

I nodded along, playing to the crowd, desperate to avoid a more unpleasant fate, slapped and willed into cautious obedience even if it meant becoming a morning person. 'But you know, even if you change now...we can't have people like you around.'

We were sent off with a warning that the verdict on 'our case' would soon arrive. When it did, I was back in Bombay, being woken up by my father swinging into my bedroom with a letter in his hand.

'They've expelled you,' he said, quietly and very seriously. He seemed to care less about my mistakes now, and more about my future.

Below is a list of more recent events, presented in increasing order of absurdity:

On 11 July 2022, twenty-nine-year-old M. Athira was suspended by Swathi Thirunal College of Music in Kerala for one year, a punishment equivalent to debarment, because she was found having lunch with a few people, some of whom were men, in a room in the vocal department. The boys were advised to leave because they were apparently in a girls-only space. But Athira was punished for their presence there. True to the location of the crime, though, she was speaking up and fighting a case against the college.[1]

On 21 July 2017, sixteen-year-old Gayatri and her friend Rahul were expelled from their school, also in Kerala, for an 'act of indiscipline'. They were seen hugging—'that lasted about two seconds'—after Gayatri's performance at a Western singing competition.[2] To build their case against the students, the school obtained some of their pictures from their private Instagram accounts. Their families were sent for; the girl was slut-shamed. She was also offered a way out: 'The Secretary asked me to write a letter against Rahul—that it was a forced hug—and that if I did so, I could avoid expulsion,' Gayatri said. 'I wish my teachers were more considerate towards me…. I don't think I deserved to be expelled, for my education to be hampered for five months already. I don't want to lose a year because of this.'[3]

On 2 June 2023, twenty-year-old Sradha Satheesh, a student of food technology at another college in—guess where? Kerala, was caught using her mobile phone in a lab. A few hours later, she killed herself. In the meantime she had been mentally harassed by her professors, who called her a 'red-street girl' and told her she would never succeed in life. Her parents were summoned too. The girl came out crying, and told her friends she wanted to die.[4]

See how I supplement incidents from my life with other people's so that I can paint an anti-establishment picture? See how I avoid admitting, 'Well! We shouldn't have done that!'

Of course we shouldn't have risked ourselves like that. But you know what? Instead of just Dropping a year the vanilla way, both of us went to some godforsaken collage, met a soulmate, got a heck of a story to tell for the rest of our lives, and made everything that happened after objectively better for ourselves. We are so risk-taking and resilient—hire us!

Sigh.

I did not want to kill myself—not then.

There was definitely a how-could-you-do-this or four at home, but Amma and Appa were also taken aback by the extremity of the situation. To be sure, they were appalled, ashamed of me, but they knew I had to rescue myself, and they wanted me to. 'At the end of the day, she's only seventeen,' I heard my mother tell my father one morning after the incident, when they thought I was asleep. 'This has been the hardest on her.'

Even people who haven't been expelled from an engineering college may want to kill themselves, merely by undertaking the journey to one. Tens of thousands of Indian students die by suicide annually, with 'failure in examination' listed as one of their reasons, so much so that there are calls to regulate the coaching industry in cities like Kota, where students arrive in hundreds of thousands every year to live in hostels and study for India's competitive exams.[5]

But they are a bit too competitive: around 65,000 seats are available to the 2.7 million people who sit for the STEM (engineering and medical) entrances, lured into betting against their own odds by 'those in the business of selling dreams'.[6] Indeed, the Indian coaching industry is reliant on millions more believing in their shot at a higher education, with its promise of social prestige, upward mobility, and material safety, than the number of people who can actually attain it. After a certain age—depending on how much of a hard-on your family has for the big names, but you may start as early as ten or eleven—coaching for higher education is more important than the state-mandated exams you must pass to attend them. In an industry estimated to be worth $4 billion, coaching centres thus collaborate with state-level institutions so that students can skip the latter, allowing attendance only for lab assignments and the final board exams. This allows students to focus exclusively on competitive exam prep, which is usually more challenging than state-level syllabi anyway.

I too had begun to attend a reputed coaching class in Andheri West when I turned fourteen. It was called IITian's PACE, where my best friend from school was also going.[7] We were on the phone sometime after our tenth-standard board exams, talking about how everyone had already decided what to do next. But I had no idea what 'engineering' was, this thing that supposedly happened once you took 'science' (but not 'medicine', because if you 'took medicine', you'd be a doctor, whose meaning I was aware of)? Did you build a car? My friend assured me that I would enjoy PACE, so I followed her there.

This level of complex original thought is rare, however, for a fourteen-year-old Indian deciding what to do about their career. Typically, if you've displayed any proficiency in the science subjects by the end of school, you are not supposed to think further. Counter-intertuitive though it may be, it does not matter; you will find yourself in engineering or in medicine depending on your particular scientific temper.[8]

This is around the age when people first become acquainted with the concept of depression. One friend told me it's when she discovered Buddhism. My brother, ten years younger than me, perhaps still does not get why I went through the grind and still goaded him towards it. He took the JEE in 2020, in the middle of a pandemic that roused a historic protest from Indian students in the form of 800,000 dislikes on a YouTube video of the prime minister announcing that their exams would take place that year anyway, despite the disruption and impossibility of studying online.[9]

Eleven years later, even after much learned wisdom and 'work-ex', I had no better advice for him.

We are talking about a gendered achievement complex that haunts the nation. I first encountered it in my parents, my family, my friends' parents and their families, until it became indistinguishable from what was always propelling me. Its roots can be traced to the first time I seriously wanted to die...by suicide. It wasn't, like I said, after the expulsion, nor even during JEE prep.

I was fifteen. My tenth-standard board exam results had just been announced.

I lay on the bed with a knife next to me, telling myself that I could act whenever I felt ready. Amma had stopped talking to me over the past few days. She was upset that despite my 'decent' score overall—91 per cent—I had underperformed in mathematics. 'It's not bad, but you can't get these marks in that subject,' she said, without looking at me. 'If it was some other subject, I'd have been okay.'

I had gotten 88 per cent in Maths.[10]

I agreed that it was less than I could have gotten, but I didn't intuitively hate myself for it. There may have been a sum or two that flustered me—whatever.

She didn't notice me then, nor does she recall her punitive reaction now, but after years of being belittled by my father over this, with the rest of the culture she grew up in also glorifying mathematical and scientific prowess as the highest form of intelligence, or the only conclusive one, Amma felt betrayed, perhaps, or hurt that I had missed my shot, because in her eyes, I could have had it.

I enjoyed science deeply, so much that I loved pouring myself into it with the hopes of being among the few thousand people in the country who would get to exercise that effortfully sculpted competence. When I first started studying for the JEE, I felt like I'd found the meaning of life. Really. I would study through the day and through PACE, until evenings sometimes demanded I rush from classes to lab assignments in a bus only to return home and, if the day still permitted, study more. Through coaching, I became part of the 'special batch' that is formed at the start of every year, based on performance in an internal test that emulated the JEE. Sometime later, I got a zero—exactly zero; not a quarter, not half—in a class optics quiz. There was a stunned silence within me, as if my heart had been swallowed by my stomach and dispensed out of my body, sent away for a few days. I didn't check anybody else's score, lest I was the only one who got a full-on fucking zero. Later I was able to articulate this deadness as a resolution: if there was one thing I couldn't be, it was stupid.

I couldn't be stupid.

I especially couldn't be a stupid girl.

This is the natural response to the fetishization of intelligence within the average Indian household—obvious when you examine its methods. I can speak to the Brahmin procedure, but the principle is psychological and so fairly universal.[11] The process involves a rejection of the self that does not produce the narrowly defined idea of intelligence respected by the culture. Instead, it induces the making of the ideal Pavlovian-self for familial, social, and cultural rewards like acceptance, appreciation, love, and, hopefully, eventually, *prestige*. This spectrum of status is best captured by one Hindi word: aukaat.

Ghar pe bhi aukaat honi chahiye. Even at home you have to have status.

In *Being Brahmin, Being Modern*, a book about contemporary Brahmin selfhood, academic Ramesh Bairy notes the aukaat of different children in one household depending on their professional choices.[12] A respectable offshoot of the great Indian dream is to move abroad and realize the great American Dream. Thereafter, not only will outsiders be judged for not appreciating new markers of status such as the latest foreign tourisms and consumptions, but even members of the same family. 'My two elder sons are employed in the US— one works for Infosys and the other General Electric,' Bairy quotes one father. 'But my youngest son is a journalist here in Bengaluru. He has a research degree in sociology.'

'*What—journalism, is it?*' he is pained to hear from friends and relatives. 'It is a way of saying, "Oh, a calamity has struck!"'

To prevent such calamities, you may attempt the following procedure at home. Observe the results for yourself. As a child, I was told that Tamil Brahmins have to be good at studies. And I have flaunted the results enough. *Simple living, high thinking:* that was the oft-repeated motto. Some others—North Indian—may be pushed towards their destined life of the mind with variants like 'स्वदेशे पूज्यते राजाए विद्वान् सर्वत्र पूज्यते (A king is praised in his kingdom, but a wise man is praised everywhere)'. There are also many oft-cited examples used to prove the Brahmin's claims to God-given talent. Consider Srinivas Ramanujan, a 'conventionally pious' Sri Vaishnava Brahmin and 'marginal member' of the middle class in 1920s Chennai, who failed to get a degree and ended up as an underpaid clerk.[13] He was removed from the social issues that occupied his community at the time, but interested in astrology and numerology, and claimed that his theorems and formulas were revealed to him on his tongue and in his dreams by Lord Narasimha (aka Lord Vishnu) and his consort Namagiri, to whom his mother was devoted. Like Aryabhatta, Bhaskara, Charaka, J. C. Bose, C. V. Raman, and other Brahmins, Ramanujan is upheld as evidence of the special 'Indian knack' for science and mathematics.[14] (We have the token but formidable female representation here in Shakuntala Devi.)

My 'IIT–IIM' Telugu-Brahmin friend, P. K., confirmed how social and moral values are also transferred through this attitude to education and intelligence. 'A lot of people in the family used to keep saying that, you know, we've got nothing else. There are no family riches. All we've got to give you is an education.'

And as for math?

'You don't come home with anything short of a hundred.'

Like me, like so many other kids, P. K.'s 'failures' stung him badly enough for the soreness to have colour even in adulthood. 'I had cases where I came home with, like, ninety-five or ninety-six and [his parents] were like, "Oh, that guy got ninety-eight. Oh man, what a smart kid." And you're like, "I got ninety-six! I didn't get fucking zero. I got ninety-six."'

When I asked him how these comparisons affected him, he instead told me about a friend who, 'if he [had] deep-seated psychological issues, [P. K. didn't] know about it'.

'He went to Hyderabad Public School and got second rank—not in his class, but in the entire section. Obviously very smart. But his parents asked who got first rank, and it was a girl. The modern parents of today might say, "Oh, you came second. That's great, let's celebrate." But this guy's dad,'—P. K. is considerate enough to disclaim him as a product of his times— 'this guy's dad says, "Oh. A girl came first? *Should we get you bangles?*"'

Here we are, then, plumbing the psychological nerve-endings of these socio-politico-cultural forces. Girls were frequently the 'teacher's pets' in school, per P. K.'s observation, cherished for their meticulous note-taking and handwriting, which he resented because 'I got dogged marks because of my handwriting, but, like, who gives a shit? What does it say about *learning?* What does it have to do with the real world?'[15] P. K. would go on to work in fields like management and politics, which are utmost proof that presentation is at least as important as subject matter, if not more. But he can be excused for being a sore loser—because who from our generation isn't?—so we can focus on his observation instead, which is petty but telling.

The gendered need to achieve, as a means of self-redemption in a competitive, status-obsessed, rigidly hierarchal universe, isn't limited to female suffering. As you've seen, both men and women are hurt by what is expected of their own genders, and their ideas of the other's role. The girl is naturally assumed less than; her burden is to disprove it. The boy is assumed more than; his burden is to live up to it. Should she succeed, her burden is to prove that it wasn't just for her hard work or good handwriting, but her own genius. Should he succeed, his burden is to prove that it wasn't just because of his genitals and the resources that are always afforded it by default. Whether or not these are justified burdens are for each to understand later—but suffering is universal.

Fundamentally, neither receives unconditional love.

Neither is free.

Produced as a result of these coagulating forces of status are not only unaddressed 'deep-seated psychological issues', but also their manifestation in the collective consciousness as resentment between genders, between historically disadvantaged castes and advantaged ones, between the arts and sciences, and self-doubt so toxic that these are mostly enacted as a culturally sanctioned drive to achieve, no matter what.

In July 2023, these man-made dualities manifested in the box-office sales of *Barbie* and *Oppenheimer*, two blockbuster films that released on the same weekend. While Western markets saw Greta Gerwig's capitalistic-anti-capitalistic femme film outperform Nolan's typically opulent science history film, it was the opposite case in India. The widespread prognosis behind this was the sexism embedded in Indian culture, which was expected to favour the traditionally masculine themes of Oppenheimer (despite the outrage it provoked by featuring the Bhagavad Gita in a sex scene). Here is the editor-in-chief in a local Brahmin organization's monthly magazine: 'What stood out as far as I am concerned is Oppenheimer's admission to his girlfriend that he is learning Sanskrit. It made me feel good that the best of the scientific world have learnt Sanskrit or studied our scriptures to understand the marvels and secrets of creation.'[16]

A bit about the tryst between masculinity and scientific

chauvinism in India, which is also just religious chauvinism. Far from science and religion being in conflict with each other, for upper-caste Hindus, they have long tried to ally with each other. When British colonial rule insisted on the superiority of the English language and Western scientific methods, they were pit against India's 'native' ways and 'effete savagery', so Indian elites, largely upper-caste Hindu men, sought parallels for scientific thought in their own past. The Brahmins and Bhadralok, the educated high-caste Bengali, used their proximity to the British to fashion a kind of 'scientific' status for their own culture. They positioned the Vedas and other canonical Hindu texts as containers of modern truths, synonymizing their culture, and its exclusions, with the modern Indian nation.

Now even educated Indian elites today believe that their talents are a direct function of their births, and not the conditioning that arises from those births, which elevated certain social groups over others. Sudarshan, a Tamil-Brahmin scientist, believes that Brahmins are the only ones to inherently value 'learning', whereas others only care about 'money-making'.[17] From here, the most mentally flexible also jump to the conclusion that their successes have nothing to do with caste (!)—only all that their caste position provides, of course. The internet is strewn with Brahmins answering other Brahmins' questions about how they all came to be so intelligent, citing their own #BrahminGrindset, which involves piety, worship, studiousness, rigorous habits that involve waking up at 4 a.m., chanting the right shlokas, eating only sattvic foods, which keep the body 'clean' and 'cool' and the mind 'sharp'. There is no suspicion in their answers about the early access to resources or, material privileges aside, the Pygmalion effect of being spoon-fed caste-ordained self-belief in their own divine talent, which is the psychological equivalent of crores of generational wealth.

Some Brahmins may at least acknowledge the incestuous mechanisms of this accumulation. 'Imagine, dude,' a batchmate once said, 'for 3,000 years they have been marrying each other and all of them have been studying all the time, so the kids will also be smart and keep on getting smarter, no?' Or, eugenics aside, they might cite the 'hard work' spawned by not being privileged by the system that privileges them. Listen to this: 'The main secret behind [Brahmins' intelligence] is the caste reservation system. Brahmins belong to general merit category, and they do not have any advantage. They know that the only way of thriving in this society is by working their socks off. That is why most of the Brahmins achieve things in life which other caste people can't. The SC, ST, and other castes get maximum advantage in many government institutions, and they don't even have to pay anything. Even in government exams, they don't have to score much to clear it. So, I feel most of them take things for granted. They can enjoy the benefits without having to work hard but Brahmins, on the other hand, don't get any advantage. The only way they can make their presence felt is by working hard.'

Deviously thus, a caste that was most distanced from hard work insinuates itself as the one that is most prone to it. Not only are tasks like manual scavenging and human cremation, typically relegated to Dalits, the outcastes, noticeably harder, if only by dint of being more physically demanding and widely stigmatized, even India's engineers were once produced by another varna in the hierarchy, the Shudras, whose caste-ordained professions included architects, stonemasons, sculptors, and builders. But as the British realized their need for trained Indian professionals, their education in fields like engineering and medicine was undertaken differently from how it happened in medieval India, or in Britain itself. Instead of engineers learning their trade in factories and in workshops, the modern apprentice would be taught mathematics and the applied sciences in a university setup. Such an approach historically favoured the literate peoples, upper-class and upper-caste Indians who were attracted by 'social status and well-paying careers', even if they 'avoided anything that smacked of manual labour'.[18] By 1947, engineering had become 'a coveted, high-status profession', seen as integral to nation-building by Jawaharlal Nehru, who envisioned India's growth and development through state-led industrialisation. The engineer was thus the new 'nation-builder', a vehicle, according to Nehru, for 'the Brahminic spirit of service'.

And then this early sense of entitlement, corelating caste and profession, creates resentment towards anyone who encroaches upon it. In an essay for *Himal Southasian*, Aparna Gopalan, a Tamil Brahmin, writes of her mother's warning against 'friendship', especially with 'them'—said in Tamil as avaal.[19] 'Think about it', her mother urged. 'If you become occupied with emotions, phone calls, and sharing experiences, you lose focus, you lose direction and they take advantage. They get you out of their way in class. They win. I didn't ask who "they" were and she didn't tell me. She was a Brahmin woman in post-Mandal India. We both knew who haunted her dreams.' Gopalan's mother believed that a jealous classmate had cursed her son when he fell two flights of stairs and lost a kidney, to stop him from getting first rank.

Indian schools supplement this kind of homeschooling, i.e. upper-caste conditioning, both directly and by proxy. Directly: teachers impart that certain castes are 'naturally' able to do certain things. Kshatriyas can fight, Brahmins can read and preach—all of that.[20] Brahminism is the predominant aspirational culture in this type of school; you have holidays on Diwali and other Hindu festivals, there will be idols of Saraswati, the Hindu goddess of learning, who is worshipped every year on the Sarawasti puja. In my family, we would write 'Sri Rama Jayam' multiple times on the first page of a few choice textbooks, which would be placed in front of Saraswati's idol at home over the period of the festival. This would ensure good academic performance. I grew up to learn that Saraswati is the same goddess who could bring death to Dalit and Bahujan children if they tried to get educated.[21]

This is the basic social reality for the average upper-caste Indian; for millennials, it framed their early lives; for their parents, their entire lives. An exposure to the right parts of the internet and further reading may change the millennial. In his book *Caste Matters*, Suraj Yengde writes that some Brahmins are pushed by their personal history to investigate themselves and their pasts. There is often a 'spiritual transformation'.[22]

You will learn of mine soon.

But for many upper-caste Indians, adulthood brings no such self-reckoning or transformation. People can become even more defiant and defensive about their privileges: having grown up feeling that the system was rigged against them, they struggle to reconcile a new story that challenges their reality on every level.

Instead, the achievement complex intensifies.

The lament of the General Engineering Male (GEM) overflows.[23]

[Enter Stage Left: A GEM in tight black leggings and a tight black netted crop top, armpits shaved, eyes made dark with kohl, a stream running down his cheeks as he begins swaying gently, then vigorously, until the lyric overpowers him and he, metaphorically speaking, implodes (does a full split).]

What is rightfully and innately mine is being taken away from me—by people who don't deserve it.

Why is the system biased against the GEM? Why are benefits being doled out to other sections of society while we get reverse discrimination? How is this different from nepotism? Isn't this caste-based discrimination?

[Muddy-brown women and various Others from

marginalized communities emerge from behind our GEM, dressed in Evil, grabbing his arms and legs, restricting his mobility as he tries to climb up a golden ladder with the weight of all the world's gold on his delicate dainty back.]

I have to score so high in CAT just to be considered for a shortlist. But our friends from 'Reserved Category' just need to appear for the exam. *[Women and Marginalized (WAM) race ahead, trampling all over him as they too climb the ladder.]*

Without even solving a question, they stand a chance to get into the best B-schools! Students with as low as the fortieth percentile can get into old IIMs just because of their category. But me?

I'm a GEM. I'm a hard worker. I take the rigours, burn the midnight oil, and score 99.xx percentile in CAT.

But that is not enough.

[He is a puddle at the bottom of the ladder. The Others are devouring his black blood.]

Because I am a 'male'. I won't get free the 'Gender Diversity' points that my female friends will.

They're so lazy, these children of labourers. She must be stupid if she got in with just 96 percentile and a few extra points. Maybe they did well in their board exams. Must have got in thanks to English or History or something dumb like that.

I got a 100 percentile in Quant.

They don't deserve it like I do.

There he lies, the GEM, glowing, seething, drowning, but static, left behind by humanity.

This is the person who does not believe that caste or gender inequality still exist. Instead, their view is that large malevolent groups of Others exist in immediate society to leech from them.

Years later, in the hallowed halls of 'one of the best B-schools', a professor would ask his students, as a matter of intellectual engagement, whether girls and backward castes indeed deserved reservations. Ignorant of our social and political histories, and what a policy like this was meant to achieve, one girl was stumped by the question, as if coming to terms with her wildcard entry into the institution. Another thought that reservations should be based on economic status only, since that was the chief determinant of outcome in the modern secular nation. These may have been valid arguments if they were at all informed and considered, but given the brainwashing that passes for an Indian education, we were mostly ignorant and defensive.

It had been a masculine definition of intelligence that I had been dancing to unconsciously, studying left, right, and centre to excel at engineering, then B-school, not even considering once, after an event that already threatened to ostracize me from civilization, that I might want something else. How could I? My femininity and intelligence were put in opposition to each other, both entwined around my ego, but in trying to prove that they weren't exclusive, as assumed externally, I didn't realize I would marr the very feminine principle I thought I was empowering.

No—its true form receded further into my psyche, so that a contortion would emerge, one that could succeed in patriarchal neoliberal modern India.

Please find below a description of three scenes at one of the best B-schools! It may be hard to believe, but I, a girl (!), a fully-loaded vagina-bearing autonomous self-driver of aspiration, had scored well, with hardly any preparation, which is important to restate because it came to me *naturally,* a girl(!)—not because of my handwriting—in Quantitative

Ability, Verbal Ability, *and* Data Interpretation and Logical Reasoning.

What gives?

Am I some kind of genius jerk? No, I'm not a man.

It was the steroids (drugs). But to hoodwink any authorities reading this, names and identifiers have been modified, as usual.

It also helps that I don't remember what I'm talking about.

I

Upon your entry into the country's pre-eminent B-school, reputed for their curriculums and rigorous culture that produces the captains of industry and leaders of tomorrow, you are initiated into a ritual that seeks to impress upon you that you have, in fact, entered the country's pre-eminent B-school, reputed for their curriculums and rigorous culture.

The initiation ceremony is an 'orientation', with seminars usually held by faculty. But there can also be a panel of seniors who invite you to the auditorium, where the entire batch gathers to be introduced to their new way of life. Before you're allowed to enter, you're studied from top to bottom by some members of the committee.

'Stand straight.'

'Your dress has a crease.'

'You think this is business casual?'

'Your lace is undone.'

'Wait here.'

Sometimes for hours. This continues for about five days, with long lines of students waiting for the start of every session, where every session is about How to Behave. Mind: the sessions are conducted by individuals who are a few years older than you. There is no option to not attend these sessions lest you are banned from placements, or worse, ostracized by the people who are necessary for your success in campus life.

Some of the ways in which you must behave include getting your CV reviewed by seniors, getting placed by following the placement process, realizing these are both being done 'for you', never being late to them, not checking your phone during, always sitting straight, not yawning, not looking sideways or chit-chatting, always being a worthy reflection of the Pre-eminent Institute, never assuming that the rigorous culture is anything less than rigorous because it is not, you have a brand to uphold.

I am forgetting some important details about how to behave for which I am sorry because as an observer in my own life the least I could do is observe well. But some of it was difficult to observe because my foot was bleeding from a shoe-bite since we had to wear formal shoes and I didn't have any that didn't bite me and that was my bad but the man shouting made me think of my father and I couldn't explain to the shouting man or the rest of them about either the shoe or my father because they wouldn't let me get a job and the very idea of explaining their problems to the people enacting them with complete self-assurance felt dystopian so instead I forgot some of it.

Sometime, though, I broke down, and one of the seniors took me aside and told me it was all a lie. He was sympathetic and said that I didn't have to attend the sessions any further now that I knew, and now that he knew what I was going through and that I had decided to leave the college the night before and that several legitimate joyous activities such as homosexuality were illegal in the country but did that make them wrong to which he said that was an intelligent question but that I shouldn't worry anymore because it was all a lie.

It's not an orientation ceremony.

It was called—and this I registered—'The Con'.

On the last day of The Con, all 450 students are shifted from the auditorium to a lecture room, one where the actual

Placement Crashers are held. It's a big room, but too small for so many people, so people occupy the benches and also the space between the benches, seating themselves shoulder-to-shoulder on stairs. The same rules of How to Behave apply in this room, but not today.

Today, after The Con, all the seniors—not from the Placement Committee, but The Con Committee, as we now know—come in plainclothes, not business casuals, like, in shorts and in T-shirts, and amidst fanfare and rabble-rousing they draw sticks out of their pockets and light them up and the thumping on the desks grows louder and louder until the night is spent getting drunk and lighting more sticks and celebrating the fact that the school is, in fact, the country's pre-eminent B-school, reputed for its curriculum and rigorous culture that produces the captains of industry and the leaders of tomorrow.

<h1 style="text-align:center">II</h1>

Hundreds of students shuffle in single files into the lecture room, where they will be coached on How to Get a Job by the Placement Committee. Dressed in formals, students seat themselves on benches and on the stairs, shoulder-to-shoulder. Shuffling or rustling or whispering or yawning of any sort through the four hours, however accidental, will draw ire. You might be stood up and asked to explain why you shuffled or rustled or whispered or yawned when you should be finding out How to Get a Job, and what if you did this during a job interview so if you keep racking up such penalties, you will be fined until you are debarred from placements. This is supposed to be terrifying (it is) because placements are ostensibly the only reason you are here (it is).

Your CV is key. It is what companies will first see of you, along with hundreds of other yous. Only if you are shortlisted do you stand a chance. You must therefore Stand

Out, even though every resume looks the same to company officials who spend a mere eight seconds, tops, glancing at each. It's good to have 'CV Spikes', therefore, especially if you're hoping to get into Finance or Consulting.

Your CV should be stacked from left to right and top to bottom with words, all of which must be in service to your singular accomplishments. A '998' or '999' is ideal— basically, a ninety-plus in tenth standard, ninety-plus in twelfth standard, and eight-plus GPA in engineering.[24] Even better if you have participated in five to six extracurricular activities like debating, squash, tennis, or music, at a non-trivial level. To create such a CV is not a simple matter, of course, but the committee can guide you. You start by creating a Master CV, which may run up to as many as six pages, wherein you list down, in point format, every potentially noteworthy activity you've engaged in since you turned six. It may happen that your big 'spike' was winning a national-level swimming competition that you didn't remember or think was useful, or a high-school classical singing competition, or college theatre, or wins of whatever kind, so long as wins are there. The placement committee verifies each of these 'CV points' by asking you to submit proof, like the certificates you must have won for these things, or emails from former managers and teachers that confirm you really did increase revenue by 30 per cent, or if you really were your school's head boy or whatever else you might claim to make your candidacy.

After weeks of such dedicated Master CV activity, you select—in consultation with other students, those people you may have befriended by way of getting ragged by them—you select the CV Points that make it to the final CVs that will be used while applying to companies. You submit them on the Placement portal before a certain date, until which time you can refine things over and over, after which they're sent en masse to companies that students have chosen.

SCIENCE, ARTS, OR COMMERCE? 67

By this time, you have learnt a lot about the English language. You know that sentences like 'worked in a team of six to create a customer dashboard' don't sound nearly as good as 'Single-handedly improved team productivity by 25 per cent and revenue by 30 per cent by launching first-ever customer retention dashboard.'

Started a film club in junior college? This is position of responsibility (PoR) that is only done justice by 'Spearheaded and launched Film Club with 40+ members leading it to first-ever national competition;'—and, to hit the right margin— 'securing first runner-up twice.' (Never say 'second place'. Which words to bolden is a subtle art form that can sway the attention of the harried but impressionable CV reviewer.)

This transformative new and improved grammar is brought to you by the 'Power Verb', which helps you communicate your message more strongly and confidently than ever before. They are also called Action Verbs, but how this differs from other verbs I am not sure yet. The Power Verb confers a sense of authority and leadership and strips you of the sense of inter-relatedness that is behind every human endeavour. Power verbs empower you to stand out as a heroic achiever in a sea of heroic achievers. A PDF list of Power Verbs is easily found on campus groups.

By the time the CV shortlists are done and the in-person dinners and interviews roll around, you are sufficiently preened to sell yourself and your work as the best thing to have happened to the Indian workforce—that is if you have truly 'cracked the system'.

Just as the upper-caste and middle-to-upper-class student has the wherewithal to 'crack the system', those from poorer socioeconomic backgrounds are acutely aware of their distance from it. S. K., a student at one of the IIMs, thought himself to come from a small town—even Goa may count as one—compared to those from Mumbai and Delhi and the more cosmopolitan Indian cities. 'Hamein kya pata,' he'd expressly say with a self-deprecating smile in 'mixed' groups, where someone with a 'more polished' background might confidently speak in English or refer to the latest global pop culture, without knowing they were wielding, at least partially, the results of inequities that S. K. held responsible for his life. The story a '998'-type has about their own success would centre their own hard work, intelligence, decision-making and tastes, differentiating them from similar peers.[25] But for those from disadvantaged positions, self-concept is centred around personal inadequacy, even when there is an understanding of systemic inequities.

Students from underprivileged backgrounds hide their CAT scores or surnames because these are seen as proxies for 'quota students', easy idientifiers of who got through via reservations or 'quotas'. This information then becomes further grounds for exclusion on campus.

And the present-day need to 'put yourself out there' and build a 'personal brand' presents another conflict for reserved categories. 'While the upper-caste worker can maintain a "strictly professional" online presence full of "thought leadership" content, [caste/reservations] is supposed to be a hush-hush thing,' said Vineet Kumar, a male student from a reserved category. 'The students of [India's top B-schools] are smart enough to understand that they aren't supposed to talk about discrimination openly. But when it comes to social media, it directly comes on your wall and the things you share. If I share a certain kind of news, about the lynching of a Dalit, then people might think that this person could be from reserved category.' Kumar worried that people would treat him differently if his online presence included this.

Perhaps the biggest tragedy of this job factory is not the

deliberate, 'single-handed' cultivation of narcissism at scale, nor the loss of soul that follows, but that the people this cultivated self is designed to please have little capacity to appreciate what has been undergone. What I mean is: after all this contortion to fit into the market, Indian parents may not even recognize the names of the companies their children have clawed their way into. McKinsey, BCG, Bain, Blackstone, Gaja—these are the names from newly liberalized '90s India, and although no parent might be able describe what it is exactly their child does, it matters least in comparison to what they can tell their friends: 'This is big, this is prestigious, this is safe.'

And although there are now more ecosystems to encourage people to take risks, build, create, and deviate from the norms—they still come with a need to show success, to reassure normalcy, in ways that the family understands.

III

I am tired now of talking about everything that's wrong with a young country's pre-eminent schools, so it is time to move onto something more positive, and, as a byproduct, also explain this memory loss I keep talking about.

One of the first images to surface when you Google certain keywords is a picture of a bed in a student hostel, whose cover is strewn with what can only be 4,000 marijuana joints.[26] These have been made in preparation for something called the 'GGP'—let's call it the 'Great Green Pastime'.

On the left-most side of this picture is the 'Big Fat Lady', pastime the size of a newborn baby, which, legend has it, inaugurates the festival. A ten-member committee is in charge of planning and hosting the GGP. Some versions of the legend hold that the sixty-five-year-old professor of introductory statistics goes up on stage with the Big Fat Lady with the kids he once taught.

Over the next three days, the remaining approximately 3,999 pastimes are lit and shared amongst the students and the pass-outs, who grow in number even though no more academic years are completed. The committee has probably rolled a little over and above the public count of pastimes, a quota reserved for them for the time spent on this service.

I'm going to confirm: it was a blast.

It is common enough for a college-goer's entire personality to be about weed that I think we can skip to the highlights here. Depending on who is listening, and what they are likely to think of me, I might include that I have been part of such committees. (I could've been elected head of the committee, you know. But hopefully my professional successes through and since then reassures everyone of my extremely high calibre and competence.)

At the time, I wasn't aware that this effortless-high-achieving-party-girl-persona was borne of a desperate need to collapse the 'bad' and the 'good' onto each other, to prove that nothing is as it's made to seem through my very way of life.

Intense, I know.

But what I thought was a benign tranquilizer that helped me study and bear social anxiety was also easy to abuse; it numbed my feelings entirely, so that I could ignore my nervous system and continue running on the hamster wheel I needed to run to survive.

Think about the word too. *Stoned.*[27] You can do anything to a stone. You can use them to create fires. You can lay roads, build things. You can throw it somewhere and nothing will happen to it. It won't feel a thing. On its own, it's inert, immobile, incapable of action.

You get stoned.

Like so much of my personality that I thought was irrevocably unique and edgy of me, I was sad to discover that a mid-to-late-twenties dependence on pot was not only unhealthy but also unoriginal as fuck. And it was characteristic of my generation for the same reasons as mine! In her essay about India's competitive exams, Gopalan describes a friend who went to study at Kota.[28] 'She was surrounded by people involved in self destruction. The drug scene on campus was vibrant and diverse. She would talk about thirteen-year-olds snorting cocaine at a joint on campus because what else were they going to do? They were people who had been stopped from happening, trapped in the abyss of a twisted version of "real life".'

'Stopped from happening.'

It really does not behoove a writer to plug so many of her own pieces in her own book, but such are the evermore self-involved times we live in. In a *VICE* piece on how technology is shaping the drugs market in India, I mention that the number of drug users has gone up 70 per cent in the last decade, a rise that the law enforcement attributes to increasing westernization and declining traditional social control, and a need for instant gratification brought about by technology and social media.[29] All this is true.

But a book called *Stoned, Shamed, and Depressed,* 'an explosive account of the secret lives of India's teens,' confirms my theories: in the book, Jyotsna Bhargava writes about 'Rock N Roll Generation 2.0', and how India's urban teenagers resort to drugs to make studies bearable, to fill a parental or emotional void, or, to remain socially connected for the 'cursed overachiever', or to 'rebel against an extremely strict upbringing'.[30] Embarrassingly me. But these kids started in school, much before I did, because of how available things are today. The latest is mephedrone or 'meow meow', especially popular with twelve-year-olds; it is ingested by sniffing and leaves no smell, lasting about forty-five minutes to a couple of hours, which means it suitable for undetected use at school, in tuitions, or at friend's places.

New-age Indian television that captures such Delhi youth life induces FOMO in me because the kind of adolescent I was would have thrived there. The 2023 web series *Class*, in particular, depicts the vagaries of interwoven distractions that children are mired in today, from drugs and casual relationships to increasing westernization and declining traditional social control, the pressures of performing your best self on social media, while grappling with mental health and dysfunctional families and intergenerational trauma, whether by collecting achievements or posing as generally aware or 'woke', which holds that the issues that divide our society have a right answer.

To wit: for the privileged, awareness, followed by shame, guilt, and online performances of morality are a chase to what they have inherited. But according to the identity politics framework, the final judge and gatekeeper of morality is the province of oppressed identities. Once a 'Privileged' has become alert to how their identities have helped them at the cost of others, rightful redressal should take the form of whatever an 'Oppressed' defines, whether it is changing the language you use, or being in favour of meat-eating, or excusing their own narcissism, or their hatefulness towards those who deviate from these right behaviours. Those we do are 'problematic', 'hypocritical', 'morally bankrupt', and so on.

But you don't need me to spell this out for you. You're extremely online, surely.

This is all too simple.

It is complicated by love.

An early memory I have is that of my parents standing outside the school I attended from the time I was six till the age of fourteen. We had just moved to Bombay. Cars and autos whizzed past us on this road in Vile Parle East, on the other side of which stood the new school, the impasse between us a metaphor for how far my parents would go for my education.

Looking from one to the other, I heard them discuss me.

'What do you think?'

'ICSE is definitely the best board.'

'Better she goes there. English isn't taught so well in the other boards.'

'Narsee Monjee is a good brand of schools also. NM and Jamnabai are part of the same family.'

'Yes, and those are very old schools.'

'And because this is a new school from the same family, it'll have good infrastructure also.'

Soon, they had me enrolled in every imaginable activity. My life as a seven-year-old was more vibrant than most high-functioning adults. I attended skating classes. Drawing classes. Tennis classes, which I quit after three days when the warm-up run around the court gave me fits of asthma. Carnatic music classes, which I was continuing from Chennai, but which I quit after I saw Amma sleeping through my singing, drool on her chin. I also went to *the* theatre classes by Alyque Padamsee, where even Alia Bhatt went. There may be a picture of us somewhere together, in a mimed production of the Ramayana (??), in which I played Sita (???).

Their vision for me persists, as you know. On the day before those fated tenth board exams, Amma bought me a new Reynolds pen with roller gel ink—black colour, that too—which cost ₹60 and made me feel older than I'd ever felt before. I hoped to sit my exams with the dignity that pen commanded. Before one of the exams, when my usual mode of transport was disrupted by some local event, Amma and I walked set out forty-five minutes in advance to hail an auto in time, which also abandoned us half way to school. We walked and walked, hurried and tense about making it.

One last illustrative memory before I tie it all up, please: in sixth standard, in a unit test of twenty or thirty marks, there was a question I missed that irked my father so much he carried himself to the school. The subject was *that* one, mathematics, and the question went like: some outbreak caused many people in a town to die, so how many were left? But the answer was a fraction. Now, whatever I wrote on that sheet was probably wrong, but my father entered the cabin of Mr Venugopalan, the supervisor of our class, to argue that no number of humans, dead or alive, could ever be a fraction. The question was wrongfully phrased, my father argued, hoping for a settlement.

I don't think this got me more marks, but Venugopalan acknowledged my father's point and offered that the teachers would try not to confuse students with the wrong units and dimensions in questions.

No more fractions of humans. Later, my math-teacher aunt, my father's sister, took Venugopalan's side: 'It's just a question paper,' she said. 'You write what the answer is.' They argued with each other.

This was my father, the same man who sat with his daughter in another cabin six years later as she was about to get expelled.

What a man. What a family.

But, once again, I am driven to say that even if we are unique, we are not special. A friend remembers—against his will—this one time he scored poorly on a school test. When he informed his mother about it as she drove them back home, the car swerved suddenly under her barely contained emotional upset. Aarohi Ramesh, a Tamil-Brahmin millennial, spoke to me about how earnestly she believed that chanting the shlokas were essential to her performance in school. 'I used to sing the shlokas and prayers as soon as I showered in the morning and before going to school. I anyway had a double life, one at home, one at school and outside it, so I only stopped doing it in my late teens.'

Usually, we are quite far into our lives before we realize we haven't been ourselves. 'This wasn't so much a case for me—I mean, a little bit, maybe—but a lot for my sister,' said P. K. 'She's a doctor, but if you ask me, she should have never been a doctor. All she likes doing is arguing. She's also good at language, she could have studied the law.' But P. K.'s sister was constantly compared to Namrata, a classmate who 'basically topped everything all the time'—All India Rank 3 in her CBSE board exams, eighth in the country in AIMS, fifth in the state in that exam—to the extent that 'she not only knew the subjects, but if you asked her something, she'd tell you what page of the textbook it was on. *Who does that?*'

'My sister took biology because of her. Colossal mistake, if you ask me,' said P. K., 'but I suppose if your parents keep saying some Namroo is so good, what is she doing, how did she do it, you're like, let me also walk in those footsteps.'

Like Namroo, I too had a usual set of comparators whose well-being (academic performance) Amma would regularly inquire into. The last time she did that, I was twenty-seven, I think. These things are hard to get over. Despite always making it to great colleges in extreme circumstances, I harboured a complex about being better at math than anyone—espeicaslly men who assumed women couldn't be good at it—because that sentiment is emasculating.[31] Not getting into an IIT or IIM can remain a wound, one that I've known has caused people to start entire businesses or develop other addictions to get over it.

Any complex—in this case, the achievement complex—is like a tree with deep roots in the human psyche. Some branches may grow old and wither, but so long as the roots are in place, supplied with nourishment, as any contact with the outside world tends to—in a culture that still unceasingly valorizes achievement as the chief end of a good life—the branches sprout and grow. Branded recognizable 'wins', no matter what your endeavour is. Narrow, chauvinistic definitions of intelligence, which privilege the conventionally masculine disciplines and denigrate the conventionally feminine.

Even if it's not the JEE or the CAT or the USPC—even if it's just writing a book, or taking care of your body, or finding a mate—the last battle to be fought is the conditioning that tells you you're only making it if you're at the glorious centre of it all.

3

YOUR BODY OR MINE?

'It is no measure of health to be well-adjusted to a profoundly sick society.'

—Jiddu Krishnamurti

Next to the laptop in front of Karen was an array of biscuits and cakes and snacks she would never actually eat. Some packets were open; some were waiting to be opened. On the other side was a white plastic bag.

Over the next couple of hours, it turned brown.

Karen barely took her eyes off the screen as she spat out all that she chewed: gooey, viscous regurgitations of items too inexpensive to worry about buying, but too expensive to actually swallow.

A moment on the lips, forever on the hips.

Really, a stuffing of Parle G Milanos and Bauli Moonfils (choco flavour) would have cost her 1,000 calories, at least. And she could only eat that much the entire day. But now that she spat it all out, after getting just the taste, this would amount to much less. Meanwhile, she could enjoy an episode of *It's Always Sunny in Philadelphia*—or maybe it was *Quite Interesting*, when the quiz show was still hosted by Stephen Fry—as she did with every 'normal' meal.

Nobody else knew. Not even her boyfriend, whom she told everything. Not even her flatmate, Arya, who was in the next bedroom. And definitely not her parents; no, she couldn't imagine.

But she also didn't think too much about it. She just disposed of the bags in garbage cans outside the house, where Arya's suspicions would never be aroused by what looked like half a kilogram or more of wrapped up shit. Karen felt that this was her biggest secret. Arya and she still worked out together sometimes; in college, they'd shared an obsession for Shaun T's sixty-minute *Insanity* workouts. It was around then that Karen was at her thinnest-ever, at 51 kilograms. One time, when they were drunk and entertaining Dubey and Parth at their apartment, Arya told them, 'This chick is the most disciplined person I know.'

So even if Karen knew she was up to something extreme, it was only a tad more so than what she and other women her age were already up to. It wasn't until a decade later that she understood that avatar of what was actually a longer, more sinister compulsion.

This much we know, though: there are 52 calories per 100 grams of apple. Sixty calories per 100 grams of mangoes. Eighty-one calories per 100 grams of banana. And only 10 grams of protein per 100 grams of lentils, or dal, contrary to what most Indians believed and espoused circa 2010.

In 2023, we will tell whoever listens that dal actually has a great deal of carbs, like roti or rice. I knew this before it entered popular internet discourse, though, because I was Karen.[1] I didn't suspect, however, when I was her in that bedroom, that I had a *disorder* of any sort.

Other, less extreme labels described my generation's pursuit of the extreme.

What I indulged in for a few weeks—Chewing and Spitting (CHSP or CS)—is a compensatory behaviour associated with eating disorders (EDs). EDs are 'severe and persistent disturbances in eating behaviours, accompanied by distressing thoughts and emotions about food, body weight or shape, and eating and its consequences'. They affect up to 5 per cent of the population internationally, across gender and age, developing mostly in women between twelve and thirty-five years old.[2] Individuals who partake in CS have a heightened desire for thinness, increased lack of control, and high body dissatisfaction. CS is hardly talked about, not yet recognized in diagnostic schemes, and is often an accompaniment or replacement to vomiting or binging. More well-known are anorexia nervosa, characterized by extreme food restriction, and bulimia nervosa, which is binge-eating followed by purging or fasting.

The visible symptoms of these disorders—that heightened desire for thinness; food restriction; sometimes purging; acute body dissatisfaction—I shared with several female friends. I was fifteen when I first understood that being fat would affect my chances in life. A male classmate, who I think I had a crush on, asked me in all seriousness, 'How are you going to get guys to go out with you?'

'Can I just rape them?' I'd said, to what I thought were guffaws from those around me. The question stayed with me, though, and as I later stood in front of the microwave, I resolved to lose weight after giving the JEE and other engineering entrance exams. Until then, I would drink as many green teas as I could.

I continue to bristle at the idea of 'getting fat', even in my advanced (thirty) years, full of awareness. It makes me uncomfortable that I weigh more than 65 kilograms, even though elevators recommend that range as the average weight per human being.

As I thought about the origins of my obsessive need to look a certain way to feel attractive, I remembered a specific moment from 2008, that had coincided with the vulnerable teenage years of millions of young Indian girls.

'I remember this point in my life so vividly, omgggg,' concurred Nina, a school friend, in my Instagram DMs. Monal too. 'I was triggered by that image,' she said, at the beginning of our two-hour-long conversation about it.

Both Nina and Monal were referring to the picture I'd shared online of the Indian actress Kareena Kapoor. In a still from her film *Tashan* (2008), Kareena is stepping out of the ocean, a lime green bikini glinting off her pale skin. Her taut abdomen and toned thighs and arms—and, at close glance, a few ribs—were testament to what had already been immortalized by the national news: Kareena's new 'size zero' figure.

'It was exactly at that time,' continued Monal, 'that I was looking at myself and thinking, "Oh my god, I look very ugly."' Monal was born in 1995, two years after me. Like Nina and I and the other young Indian women in this story, she was 'maturing' at the time—realizing how crucial her body was to how she was perceived in the world.

I was fifteen and weighed 79 kilograms when *Tashan* came out. A year and a half later, I weighed 54 kilograms. That male friend tried to kiss me soon after. For this triumph, I had run, counted calories, cut out all sugar, and eaten no carbs but fruit; when I stopped getting thinner after all of this, I ran even more and replaced a lunch of one roti, salad, and veggies with raw tomatoes.

Monal too decided to 'do something' about the tummy on her otherwise slim body after a friend told her it was 'coming out of her saree'. 'I didn't do anything specific,' she said. 'It's just that I started starving myself.'

Zara, who lives in Hyderabad, told me that her obsession with 'fitness' began around that age, age sixteen, and went on for ten more years. 'I gymmed, went on multiple diets, became thin, became fat again, cried, hated myself no matter what size or shape I was, [and I] had a close brush with bulimia.' What is sadder, according to her, is that she was always a thin girl. 'I weighed some 38–40 kilograms,' she said. 'But I became fat in my head.' Most girls from her Bengaluru law school suffered the same condition, 'always dieting, exercising, taking walks of the campus at night, obsessed with how their tummies should be flat, their arms should be thin and toned, they should have bikini bodies…. A lot of these pretty girls used to not eat a lot'.

'There was this senior in college who was anorexic,' recalls Zara. 'She was thinner than the thinnest models I've seen on-screen. And she would faint, and we never saw her in the mess, and we would hear stories. She was a very pretty girl. And she'd done that to herself. Her arms were noodle-thin. It was a sad story.'

Despite this widespread sadness, almost no news report linked *Tashan* to the '90s girl's quest to *become size zero,* and the lengths to which she went to achieve it. Most research papers on EDs in India begin with a comment on the lack of literature on the subject, attributed to how the condition is believed to only be prevalent in Western countries. One 2019 paper suggested that the recent upsurge in eating disorders was caused by the glorification of the 'size zero' body type, and the culturally sanctioned drive for thinness.[3]

EDs and related psychopathologies are especially hard to detect in India, where eating is communal, an expression of interfamilial relations, and a function of religion, caste, and class. Vegetarianism is a powerful social norm too, deviating from which can result in costly discrimination. And for a woman, marital and economic prospects are so imperative that families often prescribe how she should look and what she should eat in order to conform to a certain social standing. Such norms complicate EDs and their workings in India; in one study, it was found that Indians tended to explain disordered behaviours in medical or physical terms, rather than psychological, leading to a different, and limited, understanding of what they were facing.[4]

'It was only around 2018 that I started following these #bodypositivity pages on Instagram and realized that I was sick,' said Zara. 'I was cured after that, but I wish I had never been infected. It would have led to a happier and more secure twenties.'

Zara's use of the terms 'sick' and 'infected' may seem discomfiting, but it's only because their usage is overdue. And not everyone finds the clarity Zara did through Instagram— something a quick scroll of the app makes painfully obvious. You could encounter messaging as disparate and confusing as:

'Hey you!! You're beautiful just the way you are. And don't you forget it ♡,'—a reminder by Indian-American actress and comedian Lilly Singh.

Great, I'm beautiful, and I don't need to do anything![5]

Further down, another celebrity, an airbrushed model or a fitness expert or, worse, both, might say, 'Fitness is SO important to me…. Not only have I shed half my body weight, but I also *feel* amazing, which is much more important!'[6]

So, I guess it doesn't matter how I look, but fitness is important, it's about how it makes me feel…. *Wait, does she look better than me?*

Still further down: some article about how increasing South Asian representation on the American screen has broken barriers for 'Indians on the global stage'.

Wow, I'm so happy to see brown and voluptuous women making it big. I should start feeling comfortable in my own skin too.[7]

Still further: another article about how these representations only perpetuate stereotypes of being a 'person of colour', and while it's great to see representation improving, it's still not where it should be.[8]

Right...fair...what...should I think...and do.

Still more: some slides about how body positivity is actually very toxic, because it still emphasizes the importance of appearance.

*Ugh. Totally. It shouldn't matter at **all** how I look.*[9]

Still more: we should be talking 'body neutrality' instead.[10] It eliminates physical appearance as a source of self-worth.

Yes. We shouldn't have bodies. Why do I exist?

Social media usage is understandably correlated with increased anxiety and depression.

I think it's impossible for human beings to not care about how they look. Notions of the ideal figure have permeated space, time, and cultures across history. As much as the body is a playground for individual selfhood, a reflection of mind itself, collective ideals of body image also reflect the health and ideals of the society they come from. We now live in a hyper-visual, hyper-verbal, hyper-multiplicative world. Narratives proliferate about everything, including the relationship we should have with our bodies, and the birth of industries like skincare, haircare, and the beauty market at large conflating itself with concepts like 'self-love' and 'self-care'—they're all indicators of how deep the need to look and feel good—by spending money—has become entwined with psychological *'wellness'*. Whatever 'awareness' exists amongst a small and educated part of Indian society also clashes with the stubbornly conservative views that infuse it at large, where not only food and eating, but also the female body, is a site for caste, class, and religious politics. Indian heroines are policed for what they wear and how they behave—god forbid you like the look of saffron on a bikini—and a patriarchal society burdens its women about how they perform their gender.[11] (The average Indian politician is likely to look at a female who uses the internet or is scantily-clad or out late, or worse, drinking or smoking, or, even worse, in the company of men, or, worst of all, all of these together, and say that she was 'asking for it'.)[11]

The Indian body-image is thus shaped by a generational feedback loop: media that reflect societal attitudes, which are shaped by people who shape the power structures that control the media. Religion, caste, sexuality, gender, and age all intersect with capitalism, which insists on self-presentation, feeding inequalities that dictate who gets to feel good about themselves, and who gets to decide what 'good' even means.

In this sense, this story isn't just about women and the lengths they go to, to feel like they belong in a world that bombards them with pressures and contradictory meanings. It is a story about how all of us are vulnerable to the scrutiny of being looked at, and looking at each other and ourselves.

Yes, I'm talking about mimesis again. 🦋

'*Tashan flop rahi, lekin Bebo ka size zero hit raha!*' lilts Janvi Morzaria, the narrator of a 2009 video called 'What is Kareena Kapoor's size zero secret?'[13] '*Tashan* was a flop, but Bebo's size zero was a hit!' popular film critic Rajeev Masand concurred. 'The sight of Kareena Kapoor in a two-piece bikini is about the only thing that wakes you up from your sleep while watching *Tashan*,' says an IMDB review.[14]

'My genre is bad films!' Kareena joked in a first-season episode of *Koffee with Karan*. She was being self-deprecating about the number of flops she'd had leading roles in, despite coming from a lineage of Hindi cinema's earliest and most successful actors.[15] Dressed in gaudy pink, her brash candor remains her most lovable trait. After she played Geet, the bubbly female lead in *Jab We Met* (2007), opposite her off-screen boyfriend Shahid Kapoor, 'I began to love her,' said Monal. 'That's when she started having an influence on me, and when *Tashan* came out, she was even skinnier.'

Kareena was so skinny that she was picked up by Sony Vaio as the brand ambassador for their new, thinnest-ever range of laptops in 2009.[16] 'The whole size-zero thing in India has to do with people being slim and lightweight,' she said at a press conference. 'And I am slim and lightweight.'[17]

'And so is this laptop. I think this new laptop is very chic and sexy and people associate me with these qualities.'[18] (A year later, a Mumbai-based bakery named a pizza after her.)[19]

If it now strikes us as perverse that a woman's body was equated to aspects of precisely manufactured devices, it is because capitalism in the noughts hadn't yet morphed into the loopy, self-referential, hyper-aware form it takes today, where both the problem and the anti-problem can, at least theoretically, battle each other to occupy equal space. Back then, the problem—'You need to look good, and here's how!'—was still in the making, so that the anti-problem—'You actually don't need to look good, or listen to other people's definitions of what 'good' is, and here's how!—could now be a credible position.

Tashan cemented the Indian import of the thin, tall, and fair heroine, which was a colonial twentieth-century construct of female beauty. As European rulers cemented their superiority over the people they ruled, their fair skin and slender frames came to be associated with purity, morality, virtue, and discipline.[20] Foreign brands and satellite TVs brought these images into Indian homes after 1991, mingling with native notions of femininity, beauty, and desirability. A dialogue from *Bajrangi Bhaijan* (2015) is revealing of the native caste and class notions of fairness: 'Doodh jaisi gori hai, zaroor Brahmin hogi.'

She's fair as milk, she must be a Brahmin.[21]

But the new 'Western' looks and short skirts also inflamed entrenched old worries about 'Indian' traditions and values. The female performer was historically associated with prostitution, both in India and in the West; here, it was taboo for an upper-caste Hindu woman to work on stage or screen. Her sexuality was to be protected, not paraded for entertainment—and what is a woman but her sexuality—so her 'purity' had to be the sole preserve of the Hindu caste-order. (Nothing is more important to caste than endogamous, or intra-caste, marriage.)

The 'Gori Miss' in early Hindi cinema was thus an actress of foreign origin, made to play the high-caste, high-class Hindu woman. Given names like Sita Devi, watching her on screen allowed 'the male Indian spectator to "possess" an English beauty', reversing 'the power relations that prevailed in British-dominated colonial society'.[22]

So, when upper-caste women started to act in Hindi cinema, they had to occupy a high-pressure, ambiguous space, thinly balancing this new freedom with being inherently 'Indian' and projecting an 'ideal womanhood'. You can see why female actors in Bollywood are representations of national anxieties about our 'culture', the expectation that Indian women must preserve 'Indian morality'.[23]

What we see on our screens is important because it is from there that we get our ideas of what is normal, what is accepted, what is desirable—*how to be*. Psychologically, we come to see celebrities and stars as the 'ideal other', with the identification carrying multiple layers: worship, admiration, aspiration, and desire.[24] And as we also look to each other to learn what to want and how to be, it is easy to understand how the screen sets the bar for life itself.

For Lopa, college was a 'cultural shock'. 'You had all these third-year senior girls who were sitting in hot pants in the mess,' she said, 'and they were very comfortable with their own skin. I mean, it was humid as fuck and they still looked good. Then I was like, "Oh my God"; that was the moment I became really conscious about how I look.'

The most commonly crushed-upon girls were thin, tall, fair, and looked and spoke a certain way. 'So, you understood that this was the beauty standard you have to mould yourself into,' she said. 'Even the most crushed-upon actresses then, Katrina Kaif and the likes, looked that way.'

My collegiate diary entries affirm her suspicions. I wrote, in June 2012, after all my weight loss anointed me the 'second-hottest' girl on campus: 'I monitor my body and enjoy its new contours and shadows: these are words I've now come to associate with it. It wasn't so two years ago…it fills me with a glow and relief, as if to say, "Lucky we got that of the way." I'd be lying if I said looking pretty had nothing to do with it. It also happens to be my only declarable accomplishment in life.'

I understood the mechanics of beauty and power early. Maybe too early. Maybe too well.

Two other women, however, soared to greater fame than me as a result of chasing size zero. One of them is Payal Gidwani Tiwari, Kareena's yoga trainer at the time. 'We made history,' she said to me on our call. 'We were all over the news, all over the place, we got a lot of fame and just took a flight up! The book happened after that,' she explained, referring to *From XL to XS,* and her other publications after *Tashan.*

I'd slid into Tiwari's DMs after her yoga business moved online through the pandemic, triggered by a Bangladeshi woman insisting on being coached by her. 'Everybody till date says that [if] you gave Kareena Kapoor a size zero, you can give me one. Day before yesterday, somebody was telling me they could not work out for a week.'

'*Oh my god*!' Tiwari went into sing-song, imitating the client. '"*That means I'll never be a size zero like Kareena Kapoor*!" If it's like this now, more than ten years later, just imagine what it was like back then.' Tiwari teaches clients from 'all over' from her home in Mumbai, continuing her success of teaching 'everyone in Bollywood'.

'Yoga was brought into the industry by Kareena. It was only after her that Shilpa Shetty and all the others came up,' she said. Kareena 'sparked the trend', as the Sony Vaio ads put it.

But there remained one actress who managed to subvert it: Vidya Balan. 'In the case of Kareena Kapoor,' writes Tupur Chatterjee in film magazine *Synoptique*, 'we find a significant aspect of her stardom dedicated to her size zero figure, and the subsequent positioning of this as a desirous goal for young females in the country…. Balan seeks to subvert this by championing a more curvaceous body type, which is often positioned as "authentically Indian"'—even though Balan starred in provocative roles such as B-movie porn-star, Silk Smitha, in *Dirty Picture* (2009).[25]

With a touch of regret, Tiwari told me, 'I remember getting a call from her secretary then, but [Balan] did not start classes with me…. It was fine the way she was, she pulled it off. But even at this point if you tell me to go and teach Vidya Balan, I will jump for it. I see her on screen, it's such a beautiful face. I think, "You might have to do something about yourself."' And even Balan, for all her subversion, did not escape the emotional toll of being 'different'. She's revealed that she was once drinking ten glasses of water a day to hopefully lose extra kilos. And when she did lose weight, Balan was trolled by meanies on the internet for condemning oppressive beauty standards but eventually living up to them. There's no winning.[26]

No Indian heroine has shrugged off the weight of national pressures on their bodies. After Aishwarya Rai won the Miss World beauty pageant in 1994, she, like her predecessor Sushmita Sen, came to represent India on the global stage. Their victories implied the assertion of a new confidence among Indians about their bodies.[27] But soon after Rai gave birth to her first child, she also received negative press for her weight gain, especially as the Indian ambassador at Cannes.

Such scrutiny exists on a spectrum of less crude to very crude. In the 'What is Kareena Kapoor's size zero secret?' video, the narrator plots Kareena's career in Bollywood against her weight.[28]

'The sensex of her weight was highest' at its start, she croons, perhaps naturally so because Kareena is from a 'khaati peeti Punjabi family'.

'Kareena's weight, like her career, has gone up and down.'

It was the rumours of starvation—not just among young Indian women, but her own—that led Kareena to clarify how she achieved the size zero figure. In *Don't Lose Your Mind, Lose Your Weight* (2009), authored by her dietician Rujuta Diwekar, Kareena wrote, '[Diwekar] told me [dieting] wasn't about starving but about eating well, eating right, and eating regularly.'[29]

Diwekar was the other woman, after Tiwari, to shoot to fame after size zero. She wrote other blockbuster titles, including *Women and the Weight Loss Tamasha* (2010), establishing herself as India's leading celebrity nutritionist with her 'common-sense' approach. This involved 'simple, local, seasonal' foods which have 'a name in your local language'.

Along with her diet, Kareena's fitness routine was held responsible for her results—in the proportion of 70:30, to be precise. Yoga Sutra was key. It became 'the new fitness mantra for actresses' after Kareena went from 65 to 54 kilograms.[30] 'She used to wake up every day [to work out], she was very disciplined,' said Tiwari, who believed that people who talk about size zero tend to 'go about it the wrong way'. 'You have to keep exercising, 150 minutes a week is must. Be sustainable, eat normal, get all your vitamins and nutrients. Crash diets don't work. You'll always be a yo-yo.'

Sana, an engineer-turned-political-consultant, was thirteen when *Tashan* released. She felt like 'doing something' after a childhood of being the fattest girl in her class, teased as moti-moti and Bhabhi-bhabhi and getting her clothes customized and stitched because 'when we were kids, there was no Plus Size concept, especially in a city like Varanasi'. 'Kareena did yoga, 100 suryanamaskars a day, so "*Why not me?*", I thought. I didn't do 100 per day, but that was the motivation,' said Sana. '[Kareena] lost so much weight just because of yoga and diet changes.'

Sana was also careful, though. 'I was at home, and my parents were like, "Diet mein utna kuch change nahi karna hai."' 'Normal Indian' meals were to be had, with two rotis (no oil), boiled dal, and green veggies for lunch, and always boiled lauki for dinner.[31]

In later videos, Kareena too exhorted 'Indian food tradition' and following a diet of 'dal chawal and sabzi like a proud Indian', with 'nothing in low oil or boiled or anything like that', and valuing, respecting, and practising 'our ancient food wisdom'. 'When people start starving, I find it fearful,' said Diwekar in 2010. 'We didn't inspire them to do so.' She dubbed size zero a 'creation of the media', when, in fact, it is 'just a garment size found on a retail store rack, not meant for a body—anybody'.[32]

It turned out that Kareena's diet and workout routines were also a creation of the media. 'We did follow Hatha Yoga,' clarified Tiwari on our call, 'but there was a lot of calisthenics and functional training put together with it. We even did high-intensity workouts. So, all of that happened together. But no weights involved whatsoever.' As for her diet, Kareena ate 'very normal, maybe an egg in the morning and a slice of bread. It wasn't drastic, but her calorie intake was definitely reduced'.

In her videos, Diwekar warns against cutting down on

Indian carbs like poha, idli, and dosa following the 'Western trend of avoiding carbs from bagels, pizzas, cupcakes, muffins.' By doing so, she said, 'you not just disrespect the oral wisdom of sampradaya, but you also just trampled upon your common sense!'

The familiar Indian complex about powerful Western trends rears its head again, along with a tail-wag towards the answers lying in our own culture. Sampradaya is a Sanskrit word that can be translated to 'tradition', but the idea that 'Indian tradition' is 'simple' or 'common sense' or monolithic might be the biggest media-invented myth here.

Less than a third of India is vegetarian, but the country is seen as predominantly so.[33] Vegetarianism is a trait associated with Hinduism, even though not even all Hindus are vegetarians—estimates say that only a third of upper-caste Hindus, who anyway form less than 20 per cent of the population, are vegetarian.[34] Meat is important to Kayasthas, the high-ranking warrior caste, who might hold that 'vegetarianism is for rabbits'. Brahmins from Bengal and Kashmir eat meat too, while South Indian Brahmins may not even tolerate onions or garlic in their dishes. Iyengar Brahmins have food rituals that prohibit the person cooking from entering the kitchen without bathing. They publish vegetarian recipe books, while meat- or beef-eating citizens may be razed for doing so openly.[35]

Despite my mother's warning before I left for college, and like several other rebellious upper-caste kids from the '90s, I did sample meat. After accidentally tasting chicken broth in Goa once, I thought I had nothing more to lose. So, I ate more non-vegetarian food over the next three years, justifying it with my new size zero body's protein requirements. One time, I ordered a Subway salad with salami and found Appa standing right next to me. I quickly discarded the slices in a dustbin nearby and ate the rest of it with him.

I quit meat after an overnight realization that although I was curious, especially about whatever was forbidden by my family, animals were never meant to be on my plate. I didn't enjoy the taste either. I went back to relying on six egg-whites a day and Whey protein. But not everyone can afford these luxuries; for a majority of the Indian population, meat is the cheapest source of protein.

But I don't know that meat-eating should be defended. It's supposed to be bad for the climate (but what isn't, am I right?); it is impure for some Hindu castes but not others; and it may be unimaginable to traditional Buddhists, because their first precept is to not harm. But India's neo-Buddhists, most of whom are non-vegetarian, follow Navayana Buddhism, which rejects traditional Buddhist tenets like the existence of karma and rebirth, and also the Four Noble Truths, which are the basis for why other beings should not be hurt.

So, on the one hand, you have meat as a source of cheap nutrition for a disadvantaged part of the population, who also seem to follow a religion that advocates no harm, or as little harm as possible, but nonetheless eat meat freely.

The only way out of the moral conundrums that meat-eating presents is this: meat-eaters must acknowledge that their decision to harm, for personal benefit, carries an equivalence with the choices others make to prioritize their own self-interest, even at a systemic cost.

In other words, where do we draw the line on self-interest, and balancing individual needs with collective responsibility, for ourselves, and where do we draw it for others? If one justifies harming animals for nourishment or comfort or the natural order of things, can you truly condemn billionaires who hoard wealth at the expense of the climate or labour systems? Most of us believe we'd do better than the person we're criticizing if placed in their exact situation, but there's not much reason to think we would. It's quite possible we'd behave just as poorly, shaped by the same pressures, history, and incentives.

By the way, double lives are not all bad: one is responsible for a major contribution to Indian and world cuisine. The now famous Eggs Kejriwal was named after a man even more afraid than me. Devi Prasad Kejriwal belonged to the Baniya caste and was forbidden to eat eggs at home. So, he'd frequent the Willingdon Sports Club in Mumbai, ordering this dish so often that they named it after him.

Keep hiding from your families, readers!

The more I lost weight all over, and put on admirers instead, the more I started to worry about another part of my body: my boobs. One boyfriend would only refer to them as 'tits'. At my thinnest, I was wearing an A-cup. My friends and I fleetingly discussed cosmetic surgery when I also told them about my cheeks. Unlike the rest of me, they still jiggled when I spoke and became so round when I smiled. Although a trustworthy male friend repeatedly assured me that I'd surpassed the 'threshold for hotness', and should stop worrying, I couldn't stop obsessing over the minutiae of my appearance.

For my friend Nina, these minutiae weren't her cheeks or breasts—she was appropriately endowed there—but her legs and thighs and buttocks. 'No matter how much I exercised,' she said, 'I couldn't change my big calves because I got them from my father.'

But we were prompted to see ourselves differently by another agent of capitalism. A 2004 Dove ad alerted us to the universality of our predicament by discovering that only 2 per cent of women found themselves beautiful.[36] It would be hilarious if it wasn't so sad. The award-winning viral 'Real Beauty' campaign realized how shitty women felt because of beauty standards, and decided to tell them, finally, that they needn't have taken them so seriously after all.[37] No wonder every other brand since then has strived to make beauty products not about looking better, but about a feeling, a form of love that the female self is 'worth'.

What women are shown—'skinny body, straight hair, fair skin'—'puts too much pressure on them,' said L. P., a former brand manager at Dove, who requested anonymity because he is not authorized to speak to the media. 'Trying to conform to that beauty ideal can lead to a lot of mental and physical issues,' he said. 'The idea was to change, over time, the way people look at both advertising and beauty.'

Dove decided to only cast 'real women from every walk of life' in their Real Beauty ads, never celebrities or models, building on their approach in Western markets, where ordinary women had been providing the brand testimonials since the '50s and '60s.

The campaign more than doubled brand sales in India.[38]

A 2021 iteration made more of their original insight to showcase the painful ways in which a woman's appearance affects how much love she receives. The #StopTheBeautyTest ad portrayed a range of Indian women being judged by potential in-laws—and in turn their own families—for their weight, skin colour, and height. If this seems like an exaggeration, listen to Monal describe how her mother assessed a potential bride for one of her cousins: 'She was like, "Arre ladki kitni moti hai." "Ladki toh kaali hai." I'm like...she's a lawyer! She could have been the first bride for our house.'

But even after arguing with her mother about how hard it is for a woman to be highly educated in India, and how she shouldn't judge potential brides with these scales—'she started laughing,' said Monal. 'I saw [my mother's] attitude towards body-image hampering me and my sisters.'

She remembers her mother's criticism of her teenage body still. 'I started putting on some weight around puberty. I didn't look fat or anything, but she would keep telling me to exercise, what to eat, and it all made me feel like shit because I was doing so many other things in life.' But, like the rest of her generation, Monal could hardly tell her mother then how she felt.

These internalized critical ideals are #not-just-surviving-but-thriving within women, according to Kyra, who runs her own nutrition and fitness-coaching business online. Her clientele shot up after the first nationwide coronavirus lockdown, when 'sitting at home obviously made people fat'. As restrictions started to lift, she was approached by women with requests for rapid weight loss. 'They're rarely ever doing it just for themselves,' she observed. 'There's usually an event that's about to happen, like if they're looking to get married, or know someone who is getting married.' After one of her clients went to a wedding and was complimented for her weight loss, Kyra got twenty-five more leads from the same event.

'The obsession is very big. Women send me the pictures of different Instagram models saying, "Look at her body. I want that," or "I want to wear clothes like hers,"' she said. Despite the fact that there are so many more role models and body types to be inspired by today, Kyra believes these requests come from 'generations of fat-shaming'. 'It's only recently that you see plus-size models and inclusivity on-screen. But even now, my own grandmother, who loves me a lot, is capable of body-shaming me in an instant.'

Freely commenting on other people's bodies and salaries and children's school performance is such an accepted part of Indian culture that it was only a few months in Europe that showed me how rare it is, otherwise, for such private details to emerge in casual conversation between acquaintances and extended circles. The lack of space and competition for resources in India probably translates to an entitled, envious kind of surveillance of each other's claims to these essentials, measured against standards that are shown to be deserving.

Kyra believed that the thin and fair woman has been glorified so much that 'it will take time to change, and may not ever change', but more 'normal' women in leading roles—'irrespective of age, height, weight, skin colour, type of hair, marital status,' she said—might help. She cited the second season of *Bridgerton*, where Indian actors were cast as Indian women on a British TV series, as an effective example of representation and inclusivity.

But this may not come naturally to all of us. Nina was discomfited by her own resistance to new role models. 'Women now comfortably wear things that a fat woman wouldn't conventionally wear in the past,' she said. 'It made me go "Oh, wow," and then I was like, "Wait, why did I react like that?" But I started seeing so many posts that I stopped having that vulgar initial reaction. I get it now, and I love it.'

If even '90s kids, who were the first to rebel against the previous generations' norms, take a minute to 'unlearn' their social conditioning about feminine desirability, perhaps the elders in our families deserve some sympathy. Or, at least, some patience—until they die, or the world ends, whichever comes first.

Extreme diets—like avoiding boiled dal or veggies or lauki for a day, perhaps may still be spotted and frowned upon by Indian families. But it is rare to hear anyone being criticized for discipline. Indeed, through more than a decade of counting calories and not eating pizza or maggi or sugar, et cetera, my line of defence towards adult scrutiny was a citation of such impressive statistics as my resting heart rate (only fifty-six; that's in the 'athlete' range, by the way) and my VO2 Max (forty-four, at its best, which falls in the 'severely fit' range for females).

All you need to know about VO2 Max is that I went to the lengths to understand, monitor, and conquer it.

Of course, after we all found out it's not kosher to think so harshly and obsessively about every inch of our bodies, Kareena too had to answer some questions. She now admits that it was excessive, and would not want to do it again. But in a 2018 interview, when journalist Rajdeep Sardesai asked her if she had any 'regrets' about her size-zero phase, the *Tashan*-green-bikini projected on the screen behind them, she said with characteristic playful impudence, 'I think it looks quite good, guys, what's wrong? Why a debate?' She laughed. 'There's nothing wrong, I mean it was super fit. Rajdeep, you should go that way.'

Just like Aamir Khan, who had put on weight for *Dangal* (2016), Kareena said she'd found it an exciting challenge to do something for her character and role. In her 2012 *Style Diary of a Bollywood Diva*, she wrote: '*Tashan* wasn't about a statement wardrobe, it was about making a statement: "*There's nothing Kareena Kapoor can't do.*"'[39]

And let me tell you this. Working out and seeing your body change gives you a sense of control that approximates a *high*. Research corroborates that women do not easily give up this sense of accomplishment, even though compulsive exercise is one of the behaviors associated with eating disorders.[40] This version of body consciousness can still escape notice today, because several influencers and brands peddle the merits of 'taking control' of our health and fitness.

'I became a Cyborg for 10 days!' vlogs a YouTuber in a paid ad for Ultrahuman HQ, which I hurriedly skip now. 'We Are Cult!' I scream, though, in my Cult.fit class the next day, keeping an eye on my Garmin watch to check for heart-rate and calories burnt in real time. I try to do this four to five times a week.

Nina too found that the need to lose weight eventually

'became like a game or a goal that you want to achieve,' she said. 'Which is nice. That's a nice place to be, as long as you're doing it for things like that.' Even though she vividly remembered the green bikini scene from *Tashan*, she couldn't attribute her obsession to become thin to it. 'It came from within,' she said, after her clothes stopped fitting her at the age of fifteen.

'I also started going out more then, and I thought, "Oh, I should be able to wear a dress or a skirt." I had almost no plump friends. I wasn't ever made to feel bad for that,' she hastily clarified, 'but I think I just saw the contrast and thought, "I could look better."'

That looking better so automatically meant getting thinner—whether it was coded as getting fitter, or healthier, or more disciplined—has to do with how, even if we feel we're not influenced by what we see on-screen, we are influenced by our friends and those around us, who have internalized what the screen shows. This trifecta of self, screen, and other is what makes the size-zero phenomenon not simply about women and body image in India, but also about people and the ideals they're shown and aspire to. Contrary to the idea that only women experience objectification, men from my generation also started to dislike being thin around the same time we started to chase it. Instead, they had to follow in the footsteps of Aamir Khan and Shahrukh Khan, who, for *Ghajini* and *Om Shanti Om* respectively, suddenly surfaced with sweaty six-pack abs.[41] Just as we were sacrificing rotis, they were adopting creatine and whey.

We are all obfuscated to ourselves when we believe that what we're doing is self-chosen and for pleasurable reasons, rather than interconnected systems of power shaping history, which we have never had much control over.

But I am dubious about this hard-earned awareness too, and the effectiveness of telling you about it.

Like I said: I still think twice about outfits that reveal my stomach, and selfies that show my 'wrong side'. Having just entered my thirties, I have added another dimension of obsession to my body-image: skin-care. There may be more layers to this in the future, but for now, I have a simple five-step routine, starting with a base (which went from rose water to aloe vera gel to Cetaphil's Gentle Skin Cleanser to now The Minimalist's 2% Salicyclic Acid facewash), followed by a serum (The Minimalist's niacinamide serum, but I'll occasionally experiment with brands for novelty), a primer (so that no makeup clogs skin pores) and foundation or concealers, if I'm going out, followed by lipstick, eye-shadow, and my latest new trial, strobe cream. It's exciting to get ready, to watch my face prettify as I stand in front of the mirror.

I love dressing up.

There was a time when I believed myself to be 'someone who didn't care how she looked'—what else is the advantage of a great personality?—but that was probably because I was also doing whatever I could to actually look good, whether or not I knew that's what I was doing.

And I'll tell you this, based on my limited experience of aging: I fret over the slightest changes to my face, although I'm less intense about my body, and I worry about not being able get fit as quickly as I used to be able to earlier. It is apparent to me, and perhaps acceptable too, that I'll never not care about how I look.

PLEASE GET MARRIED BEFORE I DIE?

'True love begins when nothing is looked for in return.'

—Antoine de Saint-Exupéry

It is fashionable to hate this show now, and, indeed, it is some people's idea of a radical opinion that it is 'not that great', but, to me, this is about as interesting as having strong opinions about the culinary value of Maggi Noodles.

The sitcom I'm talking about is *F.R.I.E.N.D.S*, of course, and much before it became so popular that the cool kids felt the need to distance themselves from it, and even cooler kids in turn decided that *F.R.I.E.N.D.S* is 'actually a good show', what it was is one of India's first cultural imports from America, which I consumed just as I was turning thirteen or fourteen.

It was educational, certainly.[1] Of particular importance to this essay is an episode from season five, in which Monica and Chandler first reveal their relationship. They're still pretending to the others that they're just friends, but, after a delightfully constructed game-theoretic play of admission involving the famous 'they know' and 'we know that they know' and 'they know that we know that they know', Chandler, in mounting frustration, blurts out that he loves Monica. Monica staggers out of the bathroom, where she was hiding, and says, 'I love you too.'

The next day I turned on Star Plus at the usual 7 p.m., fully expecting them to get married. But that episode was about something else entirely. To my mounting surprise, Monica and Chandler continued to have a long, quotidian relationship thereafter, with several ups and downs and other incidents, before finally getting married two seasons later.

It was not a given. The marriage following the 'I love you' was not a given, and as I mulled over my certainty that it would be, it became obvious why: every Indian film or television serial until then had employed the declaration of love in service of marriage, which was always meant to be the 'happily-ever-after'.

I am unable to think of a mainstream Bollywood film from the '90s and '00s that subverted the example, and more scholarly writers than me conclude this too. The heterosexual couple is at the heart of Bollywood, which is often equated with Indian cinema as a whole, by Indians and the world at large. The country's largest film market is its most visible medium, and its defining pictures are directed by the marquee banners of Yash Chopra and Karan Johar, et cetera.

Their films portray the 'big fat Indian wedding' as the culmination of all the trials that separated the lovers, from family and compatibility to appropriately-sized, but not insurmountable, cultural or class differences—but not caste, if you remember. Although there is more nuance now, the generations that grew up on these films unquestioningly are still emulating its protagonists. Bollywood actors' real-life choices inspire real-life couples: ever since Anushka Sharma and Alia Bhatt wore pastel shades on their wedding days, brides started to want 'a slightly modern take' on their traditional bright red coloured wedding dresses.

'Tomorrow, when you get married, you probably don't

want to be *Jodhaa Akbar*,' said designer Tarun Tahiliani in October 2023, referring to the luxuriant 2006 film, a historical romance drama.[2] 'You don't feel that need anymore. You want to be a *modern* Indian bride. There's nothing wrong with going over-the-top, but most of these girls just want to look like themselves.'

Having had the fortune to attend some not totally fat-free Indian weddings, I can confirm that a bride rarely looks like herself at one. Couples spend up to a fifth of their lifetime earnings on their Big Days, some quarterlife of which is allotted precisely towards not looking like oneself. (In some cases, loans taken to host the dream 'Instagrammable' wedding can take more lifetimes to repay.[3]) The rest of the funding is spent on inviting and feeding a few hundred guests over days of ceremonies; the usual North Indian wedding, for instance, has a sangeet, for which the couple's friends and cousins assiduously prepare hashtags and dance choreographies; a wedding proper, in which priests perform shlokas and rituals that might contradict the modernity so earnestly being constructed elsewhere, such as at the reception or 'cocktail' evening, where, once again, the 'arranged love marriage' concept dresses up the caste-based glue that has brought the couple together.[4]

There are more than ten million such 'big days' per year, making India home to a quarter of the world's weddings, in an economy worth $210 billion, as of 2023.[5] More importantly, the product has come full-circle culturally. It is now an export, a commodity in Western markets, popularized by diaspora Netflix content such as *Wedding Season* (2022) and the notorious *Indian Matchmaking*, so that foreigners are actually willing to pay for the experience.

'You haven't been to India until you've been to an Indian wedding,' reads JoinMyWedding.com, which promises 'the ultimate cultural immersion' for travellers looking beyond the usual attractions. For just $250 per person, you can attend an Indian wedding for two days and 'learn first-hand what it really means to be Indian', from 'people who know better than anyone—the locals'.[6]

Weddings have always been sacred to these locals, marking not only the arrival of the individual but the coming together of two families and cultures. But market forces have introduced elements of the profane, making the Indian wedding the globally recognized dick-swinging contest it is today. 'The big Bollywood wedding, its conspicuous consumption dictated by the need to package and present oneself as a globalized Indian who flamboyantly embraces 'tradition' *as a matter of choice*, is symptomatic of a neoliberal subject governed by a regime of consumption where, in order to show that one has 'arrived', every event, including something as conformist as a wedding, must be presented as uniquely individual,' writes researcher Jyotsna Kapur.[7] She traces the 'arranged love marriage' to the film *Hum Aapke Hain Koun*, in which Salman Khan is asked what kind of marriage he wants, arranged or 'love'. His hybrid answer provided the perfectly Indian script for millions, who understood that individuality needn't be sacrificed for collective needs—because it isn't a sacrifice if what you want is what everyone wants too.

And all everyone wants is 'a suitable boy' or 'a good girl' for you.

This is someone of equal social standing: the same caste and class, with similar educational qualifications, from a 'good family background', not broken or in disrepute; the boy should be taller, the girl should be fair; nowadays both of them can work after marriage. Couples meet through their parents, or portals like Shaadi.com, JeevanSaathi.com, or BharatMatrimony.com, where selection happens through traditional filters, but marriage happens only after a period of dating, hopefully even love.

Boy meets girl. Free market meets existing caste, class, and gender strictures. Love, minus the neanderthal aspects of the arranged marriage, equals a neo-happily-ever-after.

Overall, the for-profit restaurant at the end of the Indian universe serves marriage in grandly plated weddings, which are a smorgasbord of self-actualization, the flavours avoiding dreaded extremes of both tradition and modernity for something truly fusion, as seen, for example, in the case studies showcased on WeddingSutra.com, which is the 'most popular and trusted resource on Indian weddings'.[8] Couples submit their weddings to the site, ostensibly to fulfil their primary purpose—to be seen—and see we shall: 'Payal and Shubham's wedding came right after two family weddings. They wanted their wedding to feel different and exciting, with cool modern vibes mixed with a touch of tradition.' Their mehendi ceremony 'emanated a boho tropical vibe', while 'things took the unconventional route' with the *Haldi Pro League* ceremony, in which teams wore bands that challenged the other, as in, 'Team Katarias: aa dekhe zara, kis mein kitna hai dum'. The couple's grand entrance featured an 'energetic dance performance' by a cheerleading squad, which included a few white people and a drone show. The successive banners on the entrance read, one by one, 'Because Two People', 'Fell in Love', 'Till Eternity'.[9]

I must sound obnoxious, but, in truth, I have genuinely enjoyed similar weddings in my milieu, even as I noted their arduous attempts to cultivate something that would pass off as a personality. But the more vulnerable admission is this: I tried for the longest time, albeit unconsciously, definitely neurotically, to have my own perfect 'arranged love marriage'.

I never wanted a big fat Indian wedding, but I did chase

long-term, mainstream love that would not upset anyone.[10] The quest's beginnings were innocent, unadulterated by striving for some end goal, but that changed as soon as I turned twenty-five. As with everything else, the achievement complex took over, goading me towards a socially successful form of love, which meant marriage at-or-before-thirty.

There was the boy whose name and CV would guarantee that our kids would turn out intelligent. I would be at peace in my family, as my mother always wanted to be. It became my life's project to find love for marriage. A series of boys was subjected to my ruthless SMART goals. I tried to date S, whom I spoke to on Twitter for weeks, only for him to ghost me and for me to drop my phone in his toilet when we still met after that. Then, there was Arin, and we adored each other enough that he thought about solidifying his fluid sexuality and lowering his marriageable age, because he was a few years younger than me.

Sure, I've had romantic encounters with several somewhat eccentric men. Sometimes I feel squeamish about this 'pattern' of getting along fabulously with queer men, or even the 'tall, thin, and slightly effeminate' type, as a friend of mine put it in more uncertain terms. For what did it say about me? What was the nature of my own masculinity and femininity that my counter was found in that profile? And what are 'masculinity' and 'femininity', really? What does it mean to be queer? Was I queer?

Queerness is rooted in the act of questioning. (I don't need to remind you of the title of this book, which I fought hard to keep.) The word is a literal synonym for strangeness, for the 'peculiar', for standing apart from what is deemed normal. To be queer is to live in the space of inquiry—to probe the assumptions and the scripts that society hands us about gender, love, identity, and a well-lived life. To be queer is to prioritize authenticity and self-determination.

But soon, just in time for marriage, there was *A One*: a friend from college, whom I knew I should marry within weeks of us dating, who wasn't 'slightly effeminate', whose family I met and spent time with, with whom I moved cities and lived in with for two years—before it all came crashing down. As the distance between us grew, I found myself rapidly crushing on a few exes and male friends, wondering with discomfort and confusion if I was actually also polyamorous?

Queer men, unstable relationships with friends and exes, questions about my gender expression (was I perhaps non-binary? What is womanhood? What is masculine, what is feminine?): these were all classic signs of *something*, I'd learn, with seemingly endless inner work, but...until then....

The mental health professional I consulted during the unravelling that followed the rupture of my almost-marital relationship wondered, in relation to my questioning—my flowering, my blossoming—'but can you really live that life here, in India? Open marriages and polyamorous relationships are not widely accepted in this society. And what if you want to get married later?'

Instead of being concerned about my mental well-being, even in the midst of an apparent nervous breakdown, this professional was reminding me, with the worst timing ever, that I had to think about another divergence from family and conventional society first. God forbid she enabled me to first find my truth and stay true to it, or even acknowledge that these pressures to 'settle down' to prove 'normalcy' were what could be blamed for my state in the first place.

No. Let's figure out, in this moment, the practicalities of whether my current decision will allow me to get married eventually. Most important!

Thus I embarked on my single life precipitously, moving out of the apartment I shared with *A One* into a new, writerly room with a view, before which homeowners in the cosmopolitan city of Bengaluru proved even less supportive than this doctor. One landlady told me she couldn't sublet to a lone lady because 'what if something happened' to me? 'My family will get the blame,' she said, explaining her culpability in me going about my life. Another landlady wondered if I was 'really Brahmin' when I told her, in all foolish honesty, that I often had friends and visitors over, some of whom were men.[11]

This prejudice against single women in India can be traced to a time before 'love' was imported here, when it was the dusty old days of just 'arrangement'.

My great-grandmother, Parvati, was betrothed to her husband-to-be at the age of seven. My grandmother, Rajamma, was no more enlightened when she married my grandfather at the age of seventeen. My mother got married at the age of twenty-two to a man she'd known for six months, which, at the time, was an unusually long courtship. Through it, she spotted several red flags—at the hotel where they first met, when my father belittled his father-in-law-to-be for not carrying enough cash to settle the bill; later, at the wedding venue, when the event wasn't on a floor of my father's choice; at the reception, when my mother was delayed because of her make-up artist.

Still, Amma went ahead with their marriage because 'it was just what people did in those days'. And she stayed in it even when it got grotesque, not only because divorced women are stigmatized, but also because— get this—it would be harder to marry me off if I was from a broken family.

The irony should sink in: part of what kept my mother going through her failing marriage was her steadfast belief that I should remain able to seamlessly get into my own someday. Through it all, it was the institution of marriage that had to be deified, not any individual's feelings. Not mine, not even hers.

Society must be upheld. And to do her part, on one afternoon in the twenty-sixth year of my life, my paternal grandmother (who, by the way, was married off at the age of fifteen) tabled another fine proposition: 'Nee Rohithaye kalyanam pannikalame,' she said.

You can marry Rohit itself, no?

She was nonchalantly referring to my first cousin. Now, consanguineous marriages are not uncommon amongst south Indian families, apparently. I'll leave the gory after-effects for the upcoming end-note, but know that an estimated eleven percent of the Indian female population is married to a close blood relative, such as cousins, uncles, and brothers-in-law. That figure is much higher in South Indian states like Tamil Nadu (27.9 per cent), Karnataka (26.6 per cent), and Andhra Pradesh (26.4 per cent), where intra-family marriage is seen as a method to keep wealth within the family, and reduce the burdens of dowry. Such marriages are not prevalent in North Indian states, however, where marrying within one's gotra, which are sub-divisions of castes, is prohibited.[12]

'Though it may involve incest, it implies more than the sexual nature of incest,' Wikipedia says about the phenomenon. 'In a clinical sense, marriage between two family members who are second cousins or closer qualifies as consanguineous.'

What the fuck, patti.

Do you blame me for trying so hard to marriageably fall in love on my own?

Every time we speak still, my grandmother brings up my bound-to-be impending marriage. She lowers her voice and asks coquettishly, 'Kalyanam pannika maatiya (Won't you get married)?'

'Na irkamaatein di. Pannikoyen (I won't be around much longer. Do it, please)?'

Sometimes she will change her approach, assuring me while really reassuring herself. 'Nee paren, adta varshon inda narethuku onnaku yaaro kadachuduvan (You see, this time, next year, you'll have found a man).'

I have argued with her: should my life and marriage happen because she is going to die, or because I have found someone I like? Should I be left with shoddy results because she was in a hurry, or should I do it when it feels right to *me*? I have assured her I am not opposed to the idea—I'm not! Just stop hounding me about when and with whom! I'm not going to marry my cousin! Why don't you just live my life if you want! Why did you give birth to my father and why did he give birth to me if all of you just wanted to live my life for me!

I tried to make her see how well I've been doing for myself: the writings, the book, the freelance business I ran gainfully for many years, the multiple successes in disparate fields, the many friends I have, the fact that I am, actually, hoping and working to meet the right person—but:

Each time I tried to get her to see me as an adult, to talk about the issue with respect and understanding, she would just start cackling, like I'm an idiot or like the point is rhetorical.

What does it matter if I like anyone? The marriage must happen before she dies.

The last time we spoke, I'd had enough. Suffering from a cold, I fielded her phone call still, and before she could even take a breath, she started off, brushing aside some immensely good professional news to follow up on my marriage. I snapped, 'You know what? If we all were to live by timetables, you should be dead by now. You're eighty-six. Why are you still alive and calling me?'

And they call us a disrespectful generation. Weeks—months—years—trying to be heard, while being respectful, polite—never to be seen nor heard—but the moment you have a valid human reaction, you're doomed.

Fuck that shit.

This situation is typical of savarna households, usually worse. Nishant C, a Tamil Brahmin who lives and works in the United States, last travelled home for one reason: to explain to his family that his relationship was not at the marital stage, as close to death as his father believed himself to be. (It really is the same threat being used everywhere.) Kids avoid visiting or calling home altogether, knowing how inevitably the subject veers towards 'marriage-marriage-marriage', as one friend exasperatedly put it. The conversation is rarely broached to understand the goings-on of the child—now a full-grown adult—but to impress upon them that parental goals are still unmet, and further services, like grandkids, are yet to be provided.

Nowhere is this 'generation gap' more savagely depicted than in *Natchatiram Nagargiradhu*, a film by Pa Ranjith, whose anti-caste oeuvre radically diverges from mainstream Bollywood. In it, an upper-caste character has fallen in love with a woman outside his caste, and has gathered the courage to travel back home and tell his family about it—just as they are finalizing a bride for him (with or without him). His mother listens to his news with disbelief, and proceeds to completely lose it. In the very next room, with all their relatives outside, the mother threatens to kill herself by hanging from the fan if her son does not get married to the girl of their choice.

Obviously, he caves.

Therein lies the destabilizing shine of Pa Ranjith's mirror for the savarna wedding and family, which, unlike the mirage constructed by Bollywood and its nepo-babe protagonists, isn't an unbothered and moisturized compromise between individual and collective needs. The compromise is hardly unexacting, if ever 'happily-ever-after'.

Indeed: nothing was ever unexacting or utopian about the arranged marriage. In his 1916 thesis 'Castes in India: Their Genesis and Development', B. R. Ambedkar wrote that girl marriage was one of the mechanisms of preventing the 'surplus woman' and 'surplus man', who'd threaten the Hindu caste hierarchy with their unattachment.[13]

'As she does not know to whom she is going to be married, she must not feel affection for any man at all before marriage. If she does so, it is a sin,' wrote Ambedkar. 'So, it is better for a girl to know whom she has to love, before any sexual consciousness has been awakened in her. Hence, girl marriage.' Widow remarriage and sati (the practice of a widow immolating herself after her husband's death) were also about ensuring women do not become 'surplus'. Love is evil in this system. These are the pillars on which caste-society is built.

For the un-surplus man and woman, though, the birth of a child is essential. Their obligatory marriage is about propagating the system, and is officiated through customs and rituals that are considered sacrosanct and permanent. The Shastras and other Hindu scriptures do not even recognize the concept of 'divorce'.

As I learnt all this, my unravelling continued, and the patriarchal knot that had bound my life became loose, visible: so that's why my grandmothers had gotten married so early. This is why my mother had followed in autopilot, and couldn't let go for years more than she should have. This is why she would rather have suffered in private than be free in public. This is why they wished the same for me. This is why any association with the opposite sex invited a moralistic furore in Indian institutions more than any mere indiscipline should ever. This is why I couldn't even get a flat as a single woman for so long. This is why my father worried about me, an unmarried woman, living alone before marriage. It wasn't that he loved me or cared about me—no, not really, perhaps not—it was also that I wasn't protected from prying male forces in the way that a Brahmin daughter should be.

Forget polyamory; forget relationships; forget love. All of those ideas became, in one fell swoop, separate for me from marriage, which is probably a natural outcome of maturing. You learn that marriage has always been an economic contract, its primary concern the merging of estates and wealth. Its conflation with love was a nineteenth-century development, birthed in romantic literature—*yearning,*—and the rise of urbanization and consumerism.[14] So, this anyway manmade construct has always been a bit distant from 'love', and in India, marriage was an instrument of caste.

'What do you mean, if I want to get married later?' I could have asked that doctor.

It is offensive that that should remain the question to answer.

But she might find me aggressive.

Let us be contained and sane.

How do you recognize and honour romantic love without sullying it, in a system that never had any place for it?

Any awareness of caste, its functioning and its implications, should produce grave conflicts in the thinking Indian's mind, one of them being the above. That burden of awareness, which can grip the conscience in a stranglehold, and, left unaddressed, drain it of hope and power, demands a character of equal strength for any resolution.

'When I moved from India, I knew I was running away from impositions of who I needed to be as a woman,' said

Aarohi Ramesh, a Telugu-Brahmin woman born in 1994 and brought up mostly in the city of Bengaluru. Growing up, she too had a different life outside home than inside it, where her parents had an unhappy marriage that often saw her used as an emotional pawn. 'I studied chemical engineering in my undergrad, and wanted to go abroad for my higher studies initially because all my friends were doing it. But I started thinking of it as an escape chute,' she said. After almost not going because a family astrologer ordained that a hefty educational loan would make her less marriageable, Aarohi managed to obtain a scholarship to Canada, where she met Ayush.

'He happens to be from the same community as me, Tulu Brahmin. We bonded over our mutual frustrations,' she said. 'He had also moved out of his home at a young age. He was not compatible with his family and their religious outlook. We were compatible [with each other].' After a period of living together in Canada, the couple was contemplating marriage just as the pandemic struck, allowing them to postpone the trip their parents wanted for the wedding. 'That was also when both of us were reading a lot of Ambedkar, reckoning with all the social privilege we had accumulated—and what the fuck were doing about it?' Aarohi said. 'We started questioning whether we wanted to get married by a priest, whether we wanted to literally uphold these patriarchal, Brahminical systems through their rituals and customs.'

Their exciting new idea was not well-received. 'My dad got really upset,' she said. 'He was like, "If she's not *dharmically* initiated into the marriage, what's the point? Her son is supposed to do my last rites, so it has to be approved the right way."

'And I was like, "What the fuck? What makes you think I'm going to have a son?"'

Aarohi spiralled, wondering if she should even get married,

considering how that went for her parents. But the couple loved each other, and after some research on anti-caste weddings, they settled upon a Mantra Mangalya ceremony, which was conceptualized in 1966 by Kuvempu, a poet from Karnataka. 'We used his rationalist framework to take our vows, and sent a video of it to my parents,' she said. 'I kind of eloped, basically. It was a big thing. I later found out my father contemplated killing himself, and I went from being the shining example for all my cousins to pretty much being excommunicated.'

Aarohi had already been estranged from her parents in the months before the wedding, and it got no easier afterwards, when she couldn't announce it to anyone. Her double life from childhood continued until her next visit home, where she only met her parents twice and didn't stay with them.

'There's a lot of pain there,' she said. 'My mother's mental health has deteriorated to a point where she's not able to understand and reconcile with what these things are. My father and I are not as close as we used to be either. But we are at least trying to have a relationship, to see each other as individuals and not hold on to previous conditioning.'

Despite the 'several books and therapy' that her decisions elicited, though, Aarohi claims to be more fulfilled by the battles she chose to fought. 'When I escaped abroad, I could have just continued being "normal" and not rocked the boat with my family.' That approach would also have been more typical of her generation—even among the percentage that possesses any burdensome awareness.

'I've seen a lot of people who have caste-consciousness get married to someone from the same caste,' said Vidya Iyer, a twenty-nine-year-old woman from Kerala.

But should the standard for Brahmins who are truly against caste be to deliberately marry outside it? Would that be love?

For another woman I spoke to, a '93-born Maharashtrian Brahmin called Ananya Deshmukh, it wouldn't be. 'Knowingly or unknowingly, I seem to be drawn to similar people, this intellectual type of person. I may be sapiosexual—I probably am, in fact,' she said. Her first boyfriend was 'basically Sheldon from *Big Bang Theory*', whom she may have chosen simply because her extended circles consisted of such Brahmins, or because she subconsciously veered to them because she knew her parents would never approve otherwise.

Ananya knows what to look for on the dating apps because 'I have had to do it, you know,' she said. 'Not only my parents, but the entire household and extended family have brought up the topic of love jihad, how Muslim men create converts of Hindu women by making them fall in love and get married. Similarly, they used to say, "SC/ST ladke Brahmin ladki ko fasate hain (Men of the scheduled castes and tribes 'trap' Brahmin women into marriages, so that they can upgrade their own caste-status)."'

'This might not be true—or it may be, I don't really know,' said Ananya. 'But they have built up these stories so that I have my guard up, ki mujhe Brahmin ladke se hi shaadi karni hai (I have to marry a Brahmin man).'

And because she already knows this, and is also looking for romantic, non-arranged love, women like Ananya have to develop proxies and filters. 'I have a friend, a Chaturvedi; so, a north Indian Brahmin,' said Ananya. 'She had to break up with her Muslim boyfriend because ghar wale nange kar dete.'

The inter-faith couple would be skinned alive. Because the Charturvedi knew this, she needed a way to identify suitable Brahmins on Bumble and other dating apps, so Ananya advised her to 'smoothly slide in the topic of "have you had a thread ceremony?"' The Upanayana is 'the most important ritual for a Brahmin male, signifying his entry into adulthood, and formally ensuring his rights and responsibilities as a Brahmin'. The sacred thread donned by the end of it, going over the boy's left shoulder and under his right arm, signifies his 'readiness for learning, studying the Veda and performing rituals'.[15]

Ananya thought this would be a surefire method to identify them. But how Chaturvedi would bring this up in casual conversation is the bigger challenge.

There are profiles on dating apps that don't even bother with such progressive niceties, straight up declaring, 'Interested in only Gaur Brahmin boys.' In the north, some men may refer to their 'Royal Rajput blood' or post a picture of their Royal Enfield bike with a sticker mentioning their caste, as in 'Munde Jattan De (Jatt Boys)'; the South Indians may use a picture of Parashuram, the mythological figure, to indicate their Brahminhood.[16] Although matrimonial sites and traditional matchmaking services, typically used by parents and older generations, offer caste and religion as explicit drop-down-box filters, their presence on new dating apps indicates how inured younger generations are too.

Awareness of social conditioning and politics does not immediately imply action that will challenge it. V and D had both just gotten married (to their respective partners), and V, tipsy one evening, confessed her guilt at not being able to stand up to her family's expectations, unlike her friend D. D had refused to adopt her husband's last name during their wedding ceremony, quietly repeating her maiden name until the priest gave up. Listening to V talk about her shame and fatigue at not being able to stand up to her family made me realize that everyone's gone through some version of what I have; navigating family expectations in India oscillates between some level of rebellion and reluctant submission, with no path offering perfect comfort or resolution.

It wasn't long ago that caste consciousness was so absent in India that upper-caste Hindus unquestioningly accepted their rituals and customs as the norm. Meghna Trivedi, a writer born in 1988 to a Kashmiri Pandit father and a Kshatriya mother, got married to a Bengali Brahmin. Through their wedding, it was only when the pandit asked for their gotras, the sub-division they belonged to within their castes, that she became somewhat cognizant of it. 'But it wasn't something that mattered to me,' she said, 'because it didn't make any difference to my life, since we were both upper-caste.' Her newfound awareness came from pop culture and the internet. 'You now have a *Dalit Desk*, *Mooknayak*, Anurag Minus Verma, Yashica Dutt, and I was attending these Twitter spaces and listening to how people are mistreated because they are from a certain caste,' she said.

She could then also join the dots about why she was schooled not to be open to some advances, as a girl. 'After all these years, I still don't know whether he was an SC, ST, or OBC,' Meghna recalled. 'But I remember going back home and telling my mother about him. I had tiny butterflies in my stomach, and it's really sad to say this, but that's how their conditioning was.... The first thing my mother mentioned was his caste.'

With conditioning this strong, and social ties still drawn along similar outlines, it takes a hero to colour outside of them; and not everyone need aspire to be one. Most people just want 'normal', peaceful lives—not that there's anything wrong with that—and the majority of Indians—more than 90 per cent—still marry within their caste, despite a growing stated willingness to marry outside it.[17]

Still, some might say relationships are changing 'like anything', especially in hyper-urban parts of India. There are varieties you would never encounter merely ten years before: open relationships and marriages, more singledom, quicker separations and divorces, lives built and lived with friends ('free of the stress and drama of marriage').[18] From 2011 to 2019, the number of single people between the age of fifteen and twenty-nine years increased from 17.2 per cent to 23 per cent.[19]

As a former member of this cohort (by one year), and still single (arguably), I am privy to the multiple possible influences behind these changing attitudes.

PERSONS IN THE PLAY: India's Lonely-Hearts Club, and/or People Who Don't Want to Make the Same Mistakes Their Parents Did by Getting Married and Having Children Unconsciously, and/or People Who Are Taking the Time to Heal and Find Themselves First, namely,

    SINGLE LADY 1 [30 y/o]
    SINGLE LADY 2 [30 y/o]
    ALL THE SINGLE LADIES[20]
    ONE SINGLE MAN [33 y/o]
    SINGLE LADY 3 [35 y/o]

THE SCENES OF THE PLAY

    Just this one, actually.

  TIME: Ephemeral
  PLACE: The 'New India'
  ANIMAL: None
  THING: No objects were harmed through the staging of this play
  FIRST PERFORMANCE: Hidden from the judgemental eyes of conventional society

  ALL THE SINGLE LADIES: ALL THE SINGLE LADIES! ALL THE SINGLE LADIES! ALL THE SINGLE LADIES! Now put your hands up.

SINGLE LADY 1: So, must we carry on the entire conversation like this?

SINGLE LADY 2: Seems a little undignified. But such is the fate, the very calling, of the single ladies.

SINGLE LADY 3: Do you think they realize what—

SINGLE LADY 1: Your right hand is not up.

SINGLE LADY 3 [*Both hands up now*]: Do you think they realize that this is a metaphor for the expressly inconvenient life that single women in Indian society have to lead?

SINGLE LADY 1 [*Sighs*]: Who is 'they'?

SINGLE LADY 2: Well, my parents were not happy together. I told them so.

ONE SINGLE MAN: Neither were mine. How did you tell them?

SINGLE LADY 3: Neither were mine. But what are you doing here?

ONE SINGLE MAN: It doesn't say anywhere that this sub-tract on singledom is supposed to subtract men from it.

SINGLE LADY 2: Doth that meanst youst getst to keepst your hands *up*—as *we* speak?

ONE SINGLE MAN: I believe my task is merely to put a ring on it. That is, if I like it, of course.

SINGLE LADY 3: Ha! Well, anyway, my parents were not happy either.

SINGLE LADY 1: And because you had no model for a loving, long-term relationship, you can't realistically imagine the effort it takes to be in one as worth it now?

SINGLE LADY 3: If only it were that obvious. But alas, I'm not even single. I'm happily married.

SINGLE LADY 2 [*Flustered*]: What are you doing here? You have a 'single' in your name.

SINGLE LADY 3 [*Embarrassed*]: Is that true? I suppose I had better put my hands down.

SINGLE LADY 1: Hmm. This is awkward. The writer seems to have fucked up.

SINGLE LADY 2: Such a basic detail…

SINGLE LADY 3 [*Hands down, visibly relaxed*]: Let's not be so fast. Who knows, maybe I'll add some diversity of perspective? Only time will tell. Until then, let's have some empathy for the fuck-up: to be a writer today is to embark on a fragile career path. There is a lot of pressure. One cannot simply write. One has to protect oneself from the government, the economy, the climate, social media, one's own readers, who demand simple prose and mediocrity. The biggest protection one needs is from oneself. Still, should one undertake the impossible task of writing still, that too an entire book, one must look ahead and prevent the possibility of failure—even death—which may come a-knockin' from the book's explosive contents, or creative fatigue, or the lack of adequate sales, or incessant self-criticism.

SINGLE LADY 1 [*Relieved*]: Doesn't one?

SINGLE LADY 2: Oh, yes…there's also AI.

ONE SINGLE MAN [*Excited*]: Where?

SINGLE LADY 3: As I was saying, my parents were unhappy. Caste and class and gender or all these political terms were never my identity. I only know I had that privilege of ignorance because I was upper-caste, of course. But the first thing that defined me, or what I thought defined me to others, was that I was from a broken home.

SINGLE LADY 1: Would you believe this? Despite her unhappiness, my mother wouldn't consider a divorce because then *I* would be from a broken home, and then *I* wouldn't be able to get married and have my own broken home.

SINGLE LADY 2: Better to *be* a broken home than to show it!

SINGLE LADY 3: I knew an uncle who once told me that I should be grateful for even receiving a rishta—a marital prospect—from IIM Ahmedabad, no less. Back then I'd told them I wasn't so keen on marriage, and he'd said, 'You should feel lucky you are being approached proactively (because you are from a broken family).'

SINGLE LADY 2: To be approached proactively is never the way of a *rishta*. Only when a man approaches reactively, out of some unbearable external pressure, can an arranged marriage flourish.

SINGLE LADY 1: For then there is yet the possibility of a twist, the ultimate redemption arc, of finding love where there wasn't meant to be any!

ONE SINGLE MAN: Exactly!

SINGLE LADY 3: We said 'finding love where there wasn't meant to be any'. Not 'finding men where there aren't meant to be any'.

ONE SINGLE MAN: I see you aren't convinced of my worth in this room. My parents kept fighting too, you know—

ALL THE SINGLE LADIES: ALL THE SINGLE LADIES! ALL THE SINGLE LADIES! ALL THE SINGLE LADIES! Now put your hands up.

SINGLE LADY 3: I am clearly not the only broken record. It's not like that 'identity' has left me, by the way. Even now, it would take some royal immorality by my husband—he'd have to kill someone, or cheat on me—for us to break up. Because otherwise, I know that everyone will just point fingers at my mother and say that I walked in her footsteps as a single woman, you know? It doesn't matter that my father was the asshole. It is the woman who has to 'adjust' and hold the house together and keep holding it together forever.

SINGLE LADY 1 [*Agitated*]: I'm worried that we're skipping to Chapter 6. But maybe you're right: I know men feel the pressure to keep it together all the time too, but the family–well, a well-kempt family is the woman's responsibility. And a daughter from a broken home feels the need to prove that the brokenness of her childhood isn't responsible for any brokenness in adulthood. You must get creative and confuse people about the cause of brokenness, always!

SINGLE LADY 2: Well, in my case, the lack of models of a happy marriage definitely has something to do with my singledom. My parents were not the type who wanted to get married, I think, but it's just what people did at the time. I was an only child, and as they started to get into their careers more, I had to fend for myself a lot. They still need to separate. It's been thirty-three years of the same trauma. I am now this hyper-independent woman and so used to taking care of myself that I…cannot deal with men. Or rather, men can't deal with me. They're intimidated by me.

SINGLE LADY 1: Ah! That is the classic case of a Woman Trapped in Her Masculine Energy, which would ward off any 'real man', if Instagram diagnoses are to be believed. The solution for you, according to @ThatGoddessEnergy, would be to balance your Masculine and Feminine sides, to ground yourself in your Divine Femininity, so that you can start attracting what is really meant to be yours: a man who will care for you without making you feel small. According to @ThatGoddessEnergy–she has 57K followers–some 'practical ways to increase your feminine polarity' are going shopping, spending time in nature, praying, booking beauty and spa treatments, spending time with amazing women, through charitable pursuits and painting. She also offers 'practical ways to increase *his* masculine polarity': ask for his help, ask for his opinion, come on to him, let him decide, enjoy time away from him, workout with him. She also has reels about how women can 'kill intimacy with a masculine man'—by being controlling and nagging, for example—and 'how to set boundaries as a feminine woman'—never over-explain—and so on.

SINGLE LADY 2: If only it were that obvious.

ONE SINGLE MAN: I wonder if there was a man who could weigh in here….

ALL THE SINGLE LADIES: ALL THE SINGLE LADIES! ALL THE SINGLE LADIES! ALL THE SINGLE LADIES! Now put your hands up.

SINGLE LADY 1 [*Straightening both hands*]: So, have you given up on relationships?

SINGLE LADY 2: It's not just me. For my research, I spoke to scores of other people our age, who told me they've given up on relationships.

SINGLE LADY 1: In as many words?

SINGLE LADY 2: In as many words, because (a) dating apps are scam swamps. People don't believe they can seriously be used to 'find someone'. Somebody could just use your pictures and do anything with them. It's so easy for your profile to become content, to get memed….

ONE SINGLE MAN: Are we allowed to use footnotes down here?

SINGLE LADY 2: Least I could do with my hands up top. And (a) might seem farfetched, but I have had such things happen to friends, you know. One of them now says, 'I don't want to date anymore. I just want to get married.' So, she is going the route of matrimony. People feel it is safer because of the involvement of parents. (b) The pandemic—remember that?—also seems to have exhausted everyone. Simply making ends meet and managing yourself and your family is enough, if you can do it. When you can do more, you want to just have fun. We don't necessarily find the rigours of making a relationship work in the long-term that fulfilling anymore. And (c)—which I believe is the most crucial indicator of our times—is that people are too...*aware*. They've consumed too much content about 'red flags' and 'toxic patterns' and they're unable to give themselves up to the fundamentally uncertain and risky endeavour of getting to know someone with no guarantee of it being worthwhile. A heightened sense of judgement, of self and other, is always threatening to interrupt. They've become too self-protective. Like you and me, they've learnt 'unconscious patterns' and 'trauma responses' and 'attachment styles' and what they should 'heal' and 'manifest' so that the 'law of attraction' starts 'working automatically' for them.

SINGLE LADY 3: Romance is dead.

ONE SINGLE MAN: Long live romance.[21]

SINGLE LADY 1: What is the future of relationships then? Is there one?

ONE SINGLE MAN: Single Lady 3 is married. She's got to believe in it!

SINGLE LADY 3: For me, a relationship is about working towards something—some goal—together.

SINGLE LADY 1: Come to think of it, you *can* see a celebration of singledom in mainstream media in a way that hasn't happened before. Instead of a happily-ever-after, the ending of Barbie, for example, has Ken and Barbie going their own ways to become 'whole people' themselves first. Miley Cyrus's chart-topping 'Flowers' is about the end of a relationship like 'gold', until it starts to burn. 'Started to cry but then I remembered I...I could buy myself flowers, write my name in the sand. Talk to myself for hours, say things you don't understand. I can take myself dancing, and I can hold my own hand. Yeah, I can love me better than you can.'

SINGLE LADY 2: Beautiful. See! The future of relationships is finding in ourselves what we have always looked for outside. And maybe living with other people who don't believe romance has to be the fulcrum for life.

ONE SINGLE MAN: That is the song that should be playing then—

ALL THE SINGLE LADIES: ALL THE SINGLE LADIES! ALL THE SINGLE LADIES! ALL THE SINGLE LADIES! Now put your hands up—

ONE SINGLE MAN: I must say my bit, or I will explode! This is what happened to me at home the whole time. My parents kept fighting, and anger and conflict became so ugly that—

SINGLE LADY 1 [*Sardonic*]: You skipped to Chapter 6.

ONE SINGLE MAN *realizes his error and starts hyperventilating, and then he realizes he's hyperventilating. He starts taking forced, deep breaths, locking his head in his hands and putting it between his knees.* SINGLE LADY 1 *gives him a paper bag, which* ONE SINGLE MAN *doesn't know what to do with.*

SINGLE LADY 1: It's what they do in those English films whenever someone wants to puke, right? Or can't breathe? Perhaps it only works on flights.

ONE SINGLE MAN [*Gasping*]: All I want to say is that I believe in love and relationships. I want to be able to say what I think and feel. We were always vilified for expressing ourselves as we felt, and now even more so, because 'men are privileged', right? Men are never supposed to have problems, right? Anyway, what I wanted to say is that it's not like I want a big, flashy Indian wedding. But that's also not because I have problems with the institution of marriage. I may not do certain rituals, but I can't pretend I'm going to have a certain type of reformed wedding for caste-related reasons. I don't always know how to reconcile the personal with the political. I'm not a rebellious person in that way—and I don't use that term pejoratively—but I just don't have that streak in me to overthrow things, unless it directly harms me not to. I don't know if this is 'privileged', and as privileged as it may be, I find it natural to think about love outside of politics. I believe my future relationship exists. It not only exists; my future relationship has a bright future of its own. I imagine a partner with whom I'm compatible in various ways. She understands my humour, and I understand hers, and this is a must because I crack a lot of bad jokes. We should both be financially independent—

SINGLE LADY 1: You know, there's a whole internet sub-culture that believes a goddess can and should be provided for by her king only. But I have a friend, who certainly believes himself to be a king, whose goddess does not want to bear any children. 'If she's not going to fulfil her biological duty,' he says, 'why should I provide for her [and fulfil *my* biological duty]?' He has resentment while saying this. I cannot imagine he truly loves her. What about the generations for which women have performed unpaid labour at home? The arguments are mani—

ONE SINGLE MAN [*Gasping*]: If I may just… finish…. My hope is that I find someone to love and stay with throughout our lives. At the age of sixteen, my default answer to the question of love and long-term commitment was 'No'. At the age of twenty-two, it occurred to me that I might get married at forty-three-and-a-half exactly, because by then I would have exhausted the activities, such as travel or esoteric projects, that a significant commitment to another would prevent. Most of my generation initially saw marriage as a relic of our parent's generation, with long and unhappy examples, but what if we read into their unhappiness more deeply than we should have? Let me explain. I have started seeing a woman. We have a long-distance relationship. I never imagined I could be in one, much less be happy in one, but investing in ours has bequeathed me with a new kind of fulfilment, and who is to say that a thirty-three-year-old marriage won't naturally include its own spells of deep unhappiness as a necessary but sufficient investment? How could it not? Yet there are those who decide to stay; surely every relationship that lasts outweighs its cons. Believe me: I would not so readily trust in marriage were it not for some positive models, like that of my brother and also my cousin. My cousin, in fact, is a child of divorce, a most bitter one with a battle over custody. He grew up very angry. I was surprised when he found someone he wanted to settle with. They had a kid a week ago. I was impressed. It gave me hope. It gives me hope to see two people happy in each other's company. I have seen what comes of those who shrug off the concept totally. I recently had to care for an octogenarian family friend, who never married and lived alone most of his life. He was too comfortable and set in his own ways. His rigidity made it impossible for anyone to co-habit with him; I got a taste of that in our time together. I do not want to be like that. Love boils down to the joy of companionship. My grandmother remained with my grandfather through his late years, despite his illnesses, and, even today, her children and her grandchildren happily and regularly visit her, of their own accord. She likes to watch movies, and I am the only one she goes to the cinema with. I would try to visit her every week, at least for a coffee. She lives in the same neighbourhood as us, but is quite independent. She doesn't want to live with us, but likes having us in the vicinity. She is a model for me on how to build a life: to love well, to love so well that you are deserving of love, to be someone who is good to be around. Heck! Even if I don't meet anyone I want to settle down with, I need to be someone people want to be around. That doesn't mean changing who I am as a person. It simply means being a decent human being.

And there are no downsides to that in my book.

SINGLE LADY 1: Well, this is *my* book, and I have only one question for you: What if you find the person of your dreams, someone you love impossibly, who loves you back, with whom you have chemistry and compatibility, but your families disallow you from being together because you come from different backgrounds?

ONE SINGLE MAN *can't take it anymore. He starts seizing up, his limbs twitching, until, over a few minutes, the life goes out of his body.* SINGLE LADY 1 *and* SINGLE LADY 2 *start living together, while* SINGLE LADY 3 *goes back home to work with her husband on some shared goals.*

ALL THE SINGLE LADIES: Whoa, oh, oh, oh, oh, oh, oh, oh, oh.

[Curtain]

Modern life is too political for that question to go unanswered. Even the man who omitted caste from his Bollywood adaption of *Sairat*, the Marathi film that portrayed two inter-caste lovers getting murdered by their families, has been made to reckon with it. In *Rocky Aur Rani Kii Prem Kahaani,* Karan Johar centres the question of marriage around two charismatic individuals, who hit it off instantly. But they are worried about their long-term compatibility.

Marriage, after all, is the coming together of two families, and Rocky's and Rani's are diametrically opposed. Rocky is a stereotypical 'PUPY'—a Prosperous Urban Punjabi Youth—whose family is loud and business-minded, even if oddly matriarchal. Rani, meanwhile, can talk about an unfulfilling sex life with her cultured, intellectual Bengali parents; her father is a dancer, his femininity ridiculed by the boisterous men from Rocky's family, while Rani's mother is a sentient English dictionary. Rani's family looks down on Rocky's, and Rocky's disbelieves that a modern daughter can adapt to their traditions.

It's a story that manoeuvres the tensions between the comfortably progressive and the comfortably conservative with the main characters' charm, problem-solving, and teamwork, aided, of course, by a writer's room aware of all the cultural fault lines through social media, including which resolutions are cancellable and which are not. The movie shows off a self-deprecating awareness of its express purpose, like when a character under scrutiny about what's okay to say declares, 'Inter-caste marriage toh honi chahiye!'

Inter-caste marriage should happen, of course.

And it did for the first time on Indian TV screens in the second season of *Made in Heaven*, an original series by Amazon Prime. In the fifth episode of this season, an upper-caste man is about to marry a Dalit woman, both intellectuals who meet at an Ivy League college. But the episode's brilliance is not just in its luxurious portrayal of their Buddhist wedding, but in all the conflicts that lead up to it: how the upper-caste family's initial rejection of the Buddhist ceremony is read by the Dalit woman as a distaste for her background, a theory the man avowedly rejects; how the woman is plunged into self-doubt about seeing 'caste' everywhere, her anxiety heighted by her own family's suggestion that she might be 'too radical and intellectual'; and the man finally discovering that his fiancé's understanding of his own family is not far off the mark.

Bollywood should catch up soon.

But when I watched *Rocky Aur Rani Kii Prem Kahaani*, I was also struck by Rani's relationship with her father. They share an emotional intimacy rare among the Indian parent-child of opposite sexes. Rani is able to *talk* to him; he listens and has the vocabulary to understand her, perhaps as a result of his comfort with his own femininity, which he is also made fun of by the more hyper-masculine side of Rocky's family.

And now we're back to it, the main concern, the fundamental question: masculinity, femininity; fatherhood and motherhood; unstable relationships, emotional unavailability, psychological wounds.

My father and I had many intellectual interests in common: we bonded over mathematics, chess, the ways of the universe, mystical and spiritual concepts like karma yoga, meditation, past lives, astrology, and Reiki. He was a practitioner, and he often cured me of migraines in my childhood, my head resting on his lap with his hand on my forehead for hours. And with my brothers, he plays every sport. He is the medicine man at home, familiar with what should be taken and in what quantity for whichever illness. He could be silly and playful, breaking out into mimicries of celebrities or friends mid-conversation. But anger, irritation, and critically were equally his reactions, not only to minor inconveniences, but also his children's ailments, whether their own fault or otherwise.

Aggressive expressions of aversion were also his only known language for care and affection.

By the time I was a teenager, our relationship had grown pregnant with differences. I never shared my true feelings and interests with either parent, but at least my mother knew which class I was in, and bothered to keep up with my education.

My father was out of touch with fatherhood, and as my girlhood blossomed, I only felt more distant from him: I had to hide the music I listened to, the boys I sometimes spoke to after school, my increasingly 'English' cultural tastes, and what I really thought of him.

Because through my life I was viewed as the responsible elder child, the one 'having everything together', I really believed myself to have grasped the mix of structure and chaos within myself. Yes, I was the rebellious party girl, the almost-black-sheep, but I was too academically gifted to really be one. I had proven through my achievements that I could command literally anything of myself and follow through to perfection. Everyone was hoodwinked. Everything was under my control.

That is until—

There's a lot about the psychological detriments of an absent father on the daughter, and it has been my fate to not only live through all of them, but also elect the most powerful material on the subject. And as is common with modern media, the pop-psychoanalysis of rather serious phenomena distorts what is multi-faceted into snackable, rule-based ideas.

If it were only that obvious. Maybe it is. Ananya said, 'I have friends, Sanjana, who lost their father at a young age, and for them, ladkon ka validation bahaut important ho jata hai (The validation of men becomes very important).'

KnowYourMeme has an accessible definition of 'fatherlessness': fatherless behaviour is a slang used to call out people who act in a way that suggests they have daddy issues, or were raised without a father...usually categorized by a rebellious or otherwise unorthodox style of clothing, reflective of a lack of parental control. The term gained popularity in mid-2021, as a slur towards sexually provocative women, or members of the LGBTQIA+ community.[22]

It is difficult to digest that my sexuality and several relationships were not necessarily a pure expression of the affection and attraction I felt for various people. Some of it seems to have been driven from a need for the validation that a father figure should have provided me. A cliché, no doubt; nothing but a popular theory; but one that has been proven true through my life and crushing experiences.

The slightest validation from certain types of men seemed to cause my heart to race. I thought it was attraction, and the culture has even defined love as obsession, infatuation, and encourages ignoring anything less. One of the boys I started liking through the end of my almost-marital relationship was a writer and editor who doted not only on my words but also validated my other talents and achievements. 'There's nothing you can't do'—my heart would skip a beat hearing that from him. Yet, even through the attention and the poetry he gifted me, he wouldn't acknowledge any romantic feelings for me.

Consciously, I didn't care for praise. I was a writer-marketer-engineer defined by the objective standards of excellence in each field, after all. But these 'objective' standards were all internalizations of external definitions of success in everything—art, science, or love.

Despite—or perhaps because of—this extreme conscious will to engineer the perfect romantic arrangement, there also seemed to a compulsion for far-from-ideal romantic behaviour. Walking away from those who liked me, or were available and consistent, towards those who spelled 'trouble' in capital letters. Men with a poor relationship to their emotions, their femininity, poor habits, mirroring, perhaps, my own wounded masculinity, the inheritance, perhaps, of a less-than-perfect fathering. The rigid insistence on control, on achievement. The externally formed sense of self masquerading as a confident, stable, internally-derived foundation. A search for a partnership not always driven by authentic ideals of good companionate love, but a rigid need for intellectual affinity, towards some set oucome, sometimes at the cost of emotional hygiene.

Limerence is the psychological term for what feels like intoxicating yearning but is really more like the mind hijacking itself. Where the child felt emotionally deprived by the parent, there the adult spins a story of love around a similar adult figure, as if this time, finally, the outcome will be different. Layers of projection—parts of oneself that should be owned and integrated in adulthood—dispensed onto others and sought through romantic attachment: parts like my own femininity, my own comedic, creative, ambitious sides.

This is what the queer men and the funny, intelligent but emotionally inequipped types were supposed to be: proxies for the talents and qualities I had to develop and enact myself. I was the woman, I was the funny, the intelligent one, and I had to mature and cultivate my own inner father, my own inner masculinity, who would validate me, support my femininity— not be at war with it—in adulthood.

Psychotherapist Susan Schwartz writes that fathers often have difficulty relating to a daughter's emotional life. Even if they are physically present, the daughter may feel unseen and unknown, and this causes her to take on the burden of this failure as her own. Her sense of lack would seek fulfilment in sports or scholarship or financial success, and her own energy compensates for the father's emptiness, compromising her ability to value herself for who she is. She may find it difficult to set boundaries later on, after becoming used to her feelings being invalidated. Male figures may unconsciously always be viewed through the lens of authority and control. Research finds that children raised in a father-absent home are more likely to go to prison, commit crime, become a pregnant teen, abuse drugs or alcohol, or drop out of school.[23]

Here I am: a paragon of independence and female achievement, still having gotten there from at once chasing and avoiding the internal masculine, which never should have been fulfilled through achievement alone. It needs love, psychological growth, inner strength.

What, then, is love?

What is its function, what is its core?

It is not infatuation, it is not projection, it is not marriage. What is it?

One story from the Pali Canon involves a king, King Pasenadi, who asks his queen, Queen Mallika: 'Who do you love most in the world?'

If this were a Bollywood or Hollywood story, the queen might have said without hesitation, 'Why, I love you the most, my king.' But this is the Pali Canon, and the queen says, 'Myself.' The king too nods and agrees, he loves himself the most. There are many directions this anecdote can go, and the Buddha apparently makes it about why you must treat yourself and others well—but to me, it reflected a truth about romantic relationships.

Romantic love goes through many seasons over a lifetime, as many as people who are constantly changing, which we are. I've been shocked to learn that my love of others is often not my love of them as Others, but about the reflection of myself I see in them. We claim to love others, but what we love is the way they make us feel. If that feeling changes, why should we be in love with them still?

What we can say for sure is this: any love lasts so long as there is mutual obligation. That definition is tangible, and it is this: love is a contract. When someone stops meeting your needs, you stop loving them, later than sooner, perhaps, despite all your claims to loving them unconditionally. If you loved them unconditionally, you might be in love with them even if they've never spoken to you—fandom, stalker-ish—or even if they've cheated on you—low self-esteem? Complicated history?

What I'm trying to say for sure is this: we only love ourselves, and all our outward love is an expression of our self-love.

WORK, WORK, WORK, WORK, WORK

'It is difficult to get a man to understand something when his salary depends on him not understanding it.'

—Upton Sinclair

Post-Independence India, from 1947 to 1991, was what they called a 'dirigiste' economy—highly protectionist, with extensive state intervention and economic regulation. C. Rajagopalachari pejoratively called this era the License Raj, a play on the 'British Raj', when only four or five licences would be doled out for big developmental projects in steel, electrical power, and communications. Licence owners could run large, practically state-owned enterprises without competition or the expectation of generating profits. As a result, the government often incurred losses, leading to a financially burdened state with sub-par infrastructure. By the 1970s, the Green Revolution had modernized agricultural production, but Indira Gandhi's government wanted to further nationalize the economy. All the external financing added up with the public sector's inefficiencies to create significant debt, high inflation, sluggish growth, and a deteriorating 'balance of payments'—which is the fancy term for inter-country Splitwise.

So, in 1991, the International Monetary Fund and the World Bank paused further loans to India, calling for drastic measures to address the economic crisis. And after a first failed attempt in 1966, to avoid defaulting on its loan payments, India finally opened itself up to foreign participation in the economy.

'Thus began a historic new era,' my voice-over shall say, over crowded stills of Indian streets, people in Levi's jeans milling outside McDonald's, shopping at malls in DLF and Palladium, looking at their Nokia N73 smartphones. 'Urbanization. Technological advancement. Rapid economic growth. A rising new middle class. Globalization. And an influx of narratives that would forever change Indian consciousness.'

'Pepsi entered the country. "Sanjanas" got named. And more of India started climbing up the ladder, not only socioeconomic, but also psychological. The promised land of self-actualization was within reach,' I will say, looking into the camera for this imagined Netflix series based on my book—which would really be a dream come true, speaking of self-actualization.

'For status wasn't just about defining yourself through the right brands and products. It was about the role you occupied in this global Indian economy.'

Roll Title Sequence. I continue in broad, dramatic brushstrokes: through the Industrial Revolution, work became centralized in factories and mills for the first time. Then World War II happened, and everything was disrupted. The economic machinery of Western countries was dedicated to war's ends, leading to quite a few innovations, actually.[1] And after the war, this machinery was redirected at what would become modern corporate culture, with the rise of white-collar work in finance, marketing, and technology. 'The Company Man' was now an archetype, the stable, well-to-do sorta fella whose identity revolved around his one employer, who would provide for him and his family forever in exchange for the shareholder value created by his labour. In response to this conformity, the '60s and '70s birthed the counter-culture, challenging the mainstream obsession with work as purpose. For them, it was about communal living, self-expression, and authenticity. Still, the '80s also witnessed the rise of neoliberalism and individualism, and mantras like 'Greed is Good' legitimized the pursuit of success and wealth as makers of identity.

By the '90s, a few films had identified and voiced the psychopathic ambition of the zeitgeist, how self-definition's canvas was consumerism, how work had become self-worth: Bret Easton Ellis's *American Psycho*, Chuck Palahniuk's *Fight Club*, and over here in India, the Shah Rukh Khan starring *Baazigar*. All three stories depict a male protagonist's loss of self and humanity in his attachment to conventional status, achievement, and material possessions. There is an image of oneself that is more desirable than the actual self. Women are adjacent in their rise to power, instruments that either serve or deter. The end goal they seek, through a hazy awareness of the emptiness of their lives, is dominance.

The consumer had become the consumed.

And then the internet and social media came, we got chewed up and spit out, the mood all changed. Big Tech companies centralized and pulverized a global population's attention by incentivizing them to create for free, with the possibility of going viral and gaining a personal audience, while advertisers tried to catch everyone's attention every now and then. In this playground of brands and people, with each trying to become and outdo the other, the battle over the selfattained an all-time peak—so far.[2]

Much before these effects were obvious, a 1999 book called *The Sovereign Individual* predicted them: capitalism would become more unstable and unequal. A small group of elites would stop belonging to any nation and exist only online. There would be a 'new digital form of money' consisting of 'encrypted sequences...unique, anonymous and verifiable... tradable at a keystroke in a multitrillion-dollar wholesale market without borders', which basically describes Bitcoin more than a decade before it was invented. In this new digital economy, the losers who did not 'excel in problem-solving or possess globally marketable skills' would turn towards angry nationalism and bitter nostalgia.[3]

And the winners? They would be 'sovereign individuals'. Such people would work on their own terms and trade their skills internationally. In India, this class of people is a sliver, pejoratively reduced to 'influencers', which doesn't quite capture how professions that could not exist merely a decade ago do now. People making some kind of a living from their writing, comedy, dancing, art, or lifestyle would never be understood or respected by earlier generations, until recently. Shows like *Shark Tank India* reflect the new, normalized ambition to pursue your own entrepreneurial dream, whether by starting a D2C skincare brand or a VC-funded tech company or by becoming a creator. The usual degree or two and managerial job had, in just a few years, suddenly become passé.

These many ways to be successful became more commonplace after the pandemic; before that, social media was still 'risky', but the lockdown and remote work made being online for work and for pleasure mainstream. But we know all this. Social media platforms and their infinite web of opportunities can feel like a drug: full of reward, full of peril. Being able to carve one or two of several career paths is a recipe for existential disaster, with the freedom of choice leading itself to a near constant state of optimization paralysis, where you're wondering about the opportunity cost of whatever you have chosen, if you should be doing something else, if there was another #BestLife you could be living, if the combination of things you're doing is even legal or ethical and how to manage your multiple personalities without losing your mind. Managing yourself as a brand and watching everyone else's brand seemingly bloom from the privacy of your bedroom can stoke cauldrons of insecurities. Even if your life is 'The Dream', you are colonized by the algorithm, which is lodged in your mind and always running on the present moment, seeking to best document, share, or monetize it somehow. No wonder we live in an age where it's both possible to realize your artistic vision but also for anxiety and depression to be at record high levels.

Why, to build my audience as an upcoming author and Twitter comedian, I posted several times a day consistently for months, trying not to give away too much of the book while also occasionally promoting it and pErSoNaL bRaNdInG myself as a 'writer', while also actually writing, and holding down some three-to-five other marketing jobs that paid my bills, because writing a book or magazine articles or whatever in India pays about enough to sustain a pet's needs and lifestyle. It's hobby money. And although we do live in an age of democratized access to storytelling and creation, it's only the top few percentiles of creators who make enough to only live off of that work. The rest of the pyramid does have to do other paid work.

But the demands of the online creator economy are reflective of the general financial experience for '90s-borns: a 2023 global survey of more than 22,000 Millennials and Zoomers revealed that financial pressures were delaying what were the usual markers of adulthood for many previous generations, such as buying a house or a new car or starting a family. Half of Gen-Zs and millennials reported living from pay check to pay check, as even the most prestigious jobs became unreliable post-pandemic.[4] A better source to confirm this might just have been that meme comparing 'my parents at twenty-nine' to 'me at twenty-nine'.

My parents at twenty-nine? 'Let's buy this house and have two children and decorate the backyard as a nice garden for our little family.' Me at twenty-nine? 'I will never financially recover from this purchase', and the purchase is a loaf of bread and milk.[5]

So, the high salaries that supposedly graced my generation were cancelled out by lifestyle inflation, a high cost-of-living, and our increased tendency to spend more than save, which every new generation kind of veers towards.[6] Side hustles are today thus as much about making an extra buck and expanding your professional game as they are outlets—and stressful ones at that. Being online made about half the respondents feel like spending on things they didn't really need, and about four in ten felt more inadequate and lonelier, but also unable to quit the pressure to have an online presence today.[7]

Except for the rare, evolved individual, most elites are evermore trapped in the matrix, submerged in a constant sense of infinite possibility, burdened by the weight of their own imagined, hidden, or lost potential, ruled by the feeling that their inner creative genius just needs to be unleashed for their legacy to be built, with a few hundred thousand followers to show for it. If you're not spending every minute tending to this beast, you're not living well—but, luckily for you, Andrew Huberman or Joe Rogan or Rick Rubin or the Indian Productivity League, comprising of BeerBiceps and Raj Shamani and Ankur Warikoo, will educate you about how to stay on the hype-train, perhaps with a five-minute creative protocol or some sperm-saving methods to focus.

No amount of awareness of the illusory nature of these games seems enough to escape it.

Yeah, okay, late-stage capitalism sucks, but I should have

begun by saying I'm grateful to work. Because I can work, I can make my own money and buy my freedom from difficult personal situations, instead of needing to be rescued or relying on people who can hurt or control me, like my own family. Only working allows you to create the conditions to stop working in the future, however ironic it is that you need money to be free from money.

For those who have had some success within the system, it is difficult to think of an economic model with a more fair premise than capitalism—you get paid in proportion to your ability to contribute to the economy and advance yourself as much as you can. You have the incentive to work hard, and can rightfully do whatever you want with its fruits. You don't owe anyone anything. Developing a sense of self based on products and material possessions is also easy and natural because unlike people, objects can never leave you. Objects can never break your heart. You can project parts of yourself onto them safely and endlessly. Brands are the ultimate providers of status and belonging, acting immediately and fitting snugly into Maslow's hierarchy of needs. And unlike in communist systems, you're not being asked to slave towards some common goal with nothing in it for you personally, neither glory nor financial reward nor the opportunity to self-actualize, however superficially. Capitalist systems also don't quickly implode into violent regimes, their mechanisms of control being more insidious and long-term, by which time it may be impossible to fix or reverse, both at societal and individual levels.[8] Depending on your ability to maintain a certain distance, healthy or unhealthy, from your true self, you can become immensely 'successful' in practical terms. And if you have any problems with it all, just say so—capitalism will mutate and absorb those criticisms into its fold, like so:

Yes, okay, capitalism is fair, in theory—but it's based on creating aspirations that objectify the self and feed on human insecurity? *Okay, no problem…. Just rebrand those aspirations that sold you those products to feel young and beautiful into products you need to simply love yourself—as you are! But with the products, of course.*

Capitalism is built on heteronormative ideas that objectify women and marginalized communities who don't conform? *No problem! Just start including them and making them aspirational, especially on the days of the calendar marked to celebrate them!*

Capitalism is built on exploiting the natural environment and fellow human beings to maximize profit for a small, elite group? *No problem! Just share a single-digit percentage of profits towards environmental and charitable goals, create lots of noise around it, and skirt the issue for as long as the world still exists!*

And keep telling the people who work for you for far less than what you make off of their labour that their status and sense of self depends on it!

This actually works!

With capitalism, you can also be anti-consumerist and in a consumerist way. *Here's a tote bag saying 'GREED IS NOT GOOD' to that effect, free with all orders above ₹5,999/- of your entire being!*

Anyway, for all this hyper-awareness of how the system keeps you ensnared, you still have to make peace with it in order to survive. It helps that I have worked on and on at fashioning a self that can succeed in the neoliberal marketplace: ambitious, competent, technologically forward, well-spoken, hardworking, structured, charming, authentic, interesting, but never so personal or problematic or authentic about my struggles as a woman that the people who work with me don't want to anymore.

Just feign a sense of destiny. 'Leave your emotions at the door.' Submit enthusiastically to the mythology of whatever role you're playing in whatever company you're a working for. Remember: you're not a junior assistant brand manager. You are changing the way India lives, works, and stays clean.

But really, facetiousness aside—it's so hard to stop sarcastically praising the institution that has you in a vice-like grip—a degree of conscientiousness, and performing at just the right level, brings in a salary that allows you to make practical, potentially life-changing improvements. A few years after the divorce, my mother bought herself a Maruti Nexa with her own hard-earned money. It might have been the first substantial expense she made for herself—imagine! With her own money! And the few times I borrowed it, she'd tell me to be very, very careful, that the car was her 'uyire', her life. It was a symbol of her hard-won freedom. Being able to make her own living was the only thing that secured her eventual escape from abuse—financial, emotional, mental.

Hans Rosling, the author of *Factfulness*, wrote that household technologies like the washing machine, piped gas, running hot water, the microwave, etecetera were more important inventions than the internet. These devices reduced the time needed to manage a house from roughly sixty hours per week a century ago to a single-digit number of hours in the 2010s. Industrialization and the markets allowed women, immigrants, and the marginalized to get jobs, have fewer children, learn languages, write books, and lead more flourishing lives. 'Critics of markets say "you can't eat GDP", [but] you can't eat, learn to read, go to school, leave a bad marriage, or do any of the basics needed for a good life without the wealth and time created by the market economy,' wrote Rosling.[9]

And in India, it is a feat that women, including those of my identity, can work at all—even to this date.

'In 1900, an ambitious young Tamil Brahman would probably have hoped to become a high court judge, but by 2000 he—or even she—would more likely aspire to be CEO in a major IT company,' write the authors of *Tamil Brahmins: The Making of a Middle-Class Caste*.[10] The switch in possible genders over the period of a century is pertinent: 100 years ago, even in elite urban families, Brahmin girls were rarely educated beyond primary school.[11] The ideal was to marry the girl off before the onset of menstruation, as kanyadana—the 'gift of a virgin'—and parents failing to do so were considered sinful. Scriptural authorities may not have been unanimous in this regard, but it was enough for prepubescent marriage to become the norm for Brahmin girls from the sixth or seventh centuries.

But as Brahmin men got more educated and employable, they started to prefer suitably educated Brahmin women. The Brahmins' pre-Independence lead in academic achievement and employment continued into the 1980s and, indeed, the present day. Even as their presence reduced in government services, due to quotas for marginalized groups, Brahmin men turned to prestigious private fields like engineering, medicine, or law, guided towards employability by their parents and elder males in the family.[12]

So, for Brahmin girls, improving their marital prospects to such eligible bachelors was the crucial motivator behind more education.[13] Through the twentieth century, they started to complete school and college so that by the end of it, they could match Brahmin boys, but were ideally not 'over-educated'. Men liked 'home-loving' women who were worldly and cultured, perhaps talented at Carnatic music or Bharatanatyam, but who would ultimately manage the house and teach the children, and were not more qualified than the groom. Sons were encouraged to take up high-status managerial and professional career paths, while daughters were taught to value their careers also for the sake of marriageability, more than their own intellectualism or employment. For this reason, teaching, commerce, working in government offices and banks were seen as appropriate professions for women.

These attitudes did not remain confined to the twentieth century. At home, my aunt, a high-school teacher, was always praised for having a suitable job unlike my mother, a lawyer, whose returning home at 7 p.m. or 9 p.m. occasionally was a source of misery to our family members. Even in the late-'00s, Meghna Trivedi had to convince her family to let her pursue journalism over a more stable and salaried career, such as teaching. 'My uncle was a bit hesitant because it remains a not very clear path,' she said. 'It's not easy to find jobs, who will marry you, very different lifestyle, and all that.'

Meghna had gotten into the Asian College of Journalism in Chennai, the country's most premier institute in the field, but also the Indian Institute of Journalism and New Media in Bengaluru, which was slightly less prestigious. Her family had 'typically North Indian apprehensions' about sending her to Chennai, because the water there didn't suit a relative who'd once visited the city. 'They didn't even let me go for the interview at ACJ,' she said. 'So I had to give that up, which was kind of a bummer.'

Similarly, Aarohi Ramesh, born to Brahmin parents in Karnataka in 1994, was altogether prohibited from pursuing journalism. 'When I told my dad I wanted to be a journalist in sixth or seventh [standard], he was like, "What's wrong with you? As a woman, you'd have to travel too much."' To his credit, he also shot down his daughter's more unrealistic dreams, such as astronomy and becoming a professional swimmer. He pushed her towards pragmatic careers in chartered accountancy or software engineering. 'That way you can earn enough, have a family, and give it all up for them,' Ramesh quipped.

I suppose I should feel lucky for the intellectual territory I've gotten to traverse over my education and career. After all, my ancestors weren't even allowed to stay at school once they hit puberty. (Although I too wasn't allowed to attend a more premier college in North India over a slightly less premier one in Goa, because the former would be too far from home, even if the latter was India's party state, which seemed to not factor in my family's considerations, *despite* my history.)

'No mature married girl'—cannot even begin to unpack the absurdity of that phrase—'was permitted to risk her moral reputation through an encounter with a male stranger, or even the rumour of one, outside the safety of her own home,' wrote the authors of *Tamil Brahmans*. 'If [young wives] were accused of immorality before cohabitation, their husbands' families might refuse to accept them, and the public reputations of both families would be damaged.'[14] In *The High-Caste Hindu Woman,* Pundita Ramabai writes that in the year 1887, 'the silence of a thousand years has been broken...', referring to the rarity of a high-caste woman like herself writing in the public domain.[15]

And yet, it was the modicum of freedom they allowed their women that enabled Brahmins to become a 'modern', middle-class caste. Forgoing child marriage should have levelled them with other castes, as a process of 'de-Sanskritization', as it were. But by colluding with globalization, at least superficially, wherein both genders were allowed some say in their marital and economic futures, even if few women actually pursued careers long-term, the Brahmins were able to navigate the new world economy successfully, consolidating their power over other castes.[16]

If conditions were this dire for the most elite group of women in India, the others have ostensibly more to complain about. In pre-colonial times, women's work in India varied across regions and communities, but was mostly agricultural and related to the household. Before private property, when land was still loosely owned by tribes, the role of the woman at home was at par with the man's hunting outside. But as land was consolidated towards patriarchs circa 1000 BCE, control over its surplus production gave the man more economic power. The woman's domestic activities became less important. Women could now only share the wealth with the man, with no real control over it. Around this period, as Aryans established control over non-Aryan tribes, the latter were incorporated as slaves into the emerging *varna* or caste system. Lower-caste women were treated by polygamic Aryan men as workers, concubines, or wives, which pit them against Aryan women in the household. Between 400 BCE to 100 CE, writers of the Dharmasutras started advocating for Aryan girls to be married right after puberty.

And then came the Laws of Manu, casting the Hindu mind in favour of strict chastity and monogamous marriage, which mainly only applied to the female. Brahmins, rajas, and other nobles could still fuck around and find out, but the morality imposed on female sexuality would curb women's rights and their upward movement for aeons to come.

The forces against an Indian woman remaining in the workforce is comparable to a gravitational pull: unless she attains escape velocity and keeps maintaining or exceeding it through all the other upheavals in her life, she risks being sucked back into the vortex that wants her home, at the mercy of others' plans for her. But before we explore this vortex, some salient facts about women and work in India:

- Women in India have traditionally worked in labour-intensive, low-paid, informal sectors without social security.

- The female labour force participation rate (FLFPR) was recorded at 24.1 per cent in 1955, eight years after independence.[17] By 2000, this number was 31 per cent, after which it steadily declined year after year until the pandemic, when it hit an all-time low of 26 per cent.[18] (Some sources put this at 19 per cent.)[19]
- This put India's FLFPR in the same league as war-torn Yemen. Through the first lockdown in 2020, only 7 per cent of men lost their jobs, compared to 47 per cent of women who lost their jobs and did not return to work.[20]
- More girls than boys were left out of school during the pandemic, with parents willingly resorting to child marriage to save costs.[21]
- Although women constitute about 48 per cent of the Indian population, they contribute to only 17 per cent of the GDP, much lower than the global average of 37 per cent. India's working women contended with the strongest gender bias across Asia Pacific countries.[22]
- The reasons why more women should participate in the workforce are obvious. When women work, it's a boon to any economy; countries simply develop faster when more of their population enters the workforce. A 2018 McKinsey report found that increasing India's FLFPR by just 10 per cent could increase GDP by $550 billion.[23]
- But the gender gap in the Indian workforce grew over the years despite India's increased economic growth over decades, a simultaneous decrease in fertility rates, and increased educational attainments among women.

This presents a paradox that begs us to ask: what causes women to be persistently excluded from paid work even as the Indian economy otherwise grows? What explains the drop across rural and urban regions, through class, religious, and age divides? And how can the conditions for women to work improve?

- Indian women expend ten times more hours than men on unpaid domestic work, which is three times more than the global average. During the pandemic, their share of unpaid work grew by nearly 30 per cent. Women were three times more likely than men to have faced long-term job loss after the pandemic.[24]
  - Women across age groups spend more hours per day than men on household chores or caregiving. The average Indian female aged between fifteen and twenty-nine spends around 5.5 hours a day doing unpaid labour, whereas a male spends about fifty minutes. Another 2019 survey found that only about 29 per cent of men took on domestic work, if at all, for an average of just 1.5 hours a day.[25]
  - The value of this unpaid labour across rural and urban India was estimated to be over 22 trillion Indian rupees in 2019.
  - 'We're never going to have gender equality until we also have couple equity,' said economist Claudia Goldin, who won the Nobel Prize in 2023 for her work on why the gender pay gap persists.[26]
- Indian women who became mothers always find it harder to re-enter the workforce, and they are forced to take pay cuts if they even do.
- As Indians become wealthier, families prefer to keep women at home because it confers them status. It's considered emasculating for the wife to contribute to the family income, and educated, ambitious women are often resented for wanting a life outside the home.[27]

o Consider, for example, the attitudes revealed by Indian TradWife content—a TradWife in general promotes traditional gender roles, such as women taking satisfaction in running the home, cooking, breastfeeding, etc—and, according to Based Brahman Memes, an ideal wife loves her children, and is 'excited about her fourth child', 'is a natural beauty, needs no makeup and hairstyles,' is 'soft-spoken and obedient', doesn't go to the gym, beauty parlour, or use social media. The 'Liberated Feminist', on the other hand, is 'loud and generally disliked', 'eternally depressed and always complaining about mental health', is 'worried about losing followers on Insta', and 'got pregnant while celebrating her third abortion'.[28] In other words, the Indian TradWife is the Brahminical ideal of the pativrata, or husband-worshipper, while any other kind of woman is a slut, mentally ill, and deserving of hatred.

o You could argue that these are fringe takes on the internet, not to be taken seriously. But a Pew research report found that 87 per cent of Indians think that 'a wife must always obey her husband'. Women were only slightly less likely than men to agree with this sentiment. Throughout the report, on various matters like splitting of household responsibilities and who should earn, Indian women were not much more likely than men to express egalitarian views on gender roles.[29]

• If, after all that society lobs at her, a woman overcomes both herself and others to make it to the workplace, she continues to battle sexisms small and large, from skepticism about her competence to outright mental and/or sexual harassment.

- In combatting these, in fighting for either simple dignity or her right to survive independently, a woman risks losing her womanhood.

What follow are real stories from real women with real problems—not mere 'first-world' issues that should be summarily dismissed. 'Privileged' though these women may be in some form, they are the only ones that get to go to a formal workplace at all, sometimes because they have no choice not to, sometimes after overcoming inhuman barriers. If this is privilege, then I only want more of it, and a better version of it. These are also issues that will encumber any new entrant to the workplace from more marginalized communities.

They are also limitations imposed upon a woman's selfhood.

It may sound familiar, having been talked about since the 'liberated feminist' ever became a thing, but the problems persist, perhaps from not being taken seriously enough.

Unfortunately for female writers seeking originality, this repetition of subject matter is necessary.

If you're reading this, it's because I'm somehow still alive. But this isn't a handbook on how to survive in a mostly male-dominated world in mostly male-dominated careers. It's a picture of living in that world daily, of the subtle and loud forces stoking feminine rage and stifling it in the same breath, to the point of engendering madness and autoimmune diseases. For someone who has never gone through these experiences, it's not going to be relatable, and it might even make you resentful of all the 'complaining'. But for those who have witnessed and felt this, it maybe the confirmation, affirmation, and release they need—to know that they were never insane to begin with, but may have been driven towards it.

At the time of writing this, I've been a software engineer at a FAANG company. I've worked in marketing at what is considered its 'mecca', a global consumer goods company that invented the word 'brand', but also in independent media, and for multiple start-ups and tech companies. I have also been a writer and journalist, with by-lines in Indian and international publications. I ran my own mostly one-person marketing agency built off of my personal brand online.

In short, I am a storyteller, a creator, and an entrepreneur. Through this cross-section of experiences over about seven years, I was sometimes belittled and made to question my basic thoughts because my existence as a woman in many of these spaces was an anomaly. Even if nobody had intended this, which they sometimes explicitly did, my past traumas—seeing my mother insulted for her intelligence, my father's criticism of our smallest mistakes, and my parents' expectations that I excel all the time—had made me hyper-aware of all my flaws—real, imagined, potential—which I'd then attribute to being a woman. Competence and womanhood, an intertwined psychological complex that demanded release in whatever endeavour I undertook. That is the burden of trauma: you become suspicious that you're about to be attacked for the same reasons you were attacked before, manifesting an unsavoury past until you heal, heal, heal.

At the start of this career, on my first day as a developer at a Big Tech company, I was assigned a relatively simple task, which I nonetheless took some time to complete, new systems and spaces all considered. A male programmer from IIT Kharagpur commented to a co-worker, 'She took so long to write that little code? Come on.' You could argue that insensitive co-workers are to be found everywhere, across human history and culture, and that learning to deal with them is Work and Social Relations 101. It just has to be undergone. And I agree. Snarkiness isn't necessarily proportional to gender or identity (although who get to express it publicly, and get away with it, is identity-based).

But when social conditioning instils certain perceptions about skill levels based on gender and identity, it takes an enormous amount of effort to stand outside of those perceptions, to rearrange reality in the opposite direction, both for ourselves and others, and to maintain one's mind and dignity while doing so.

In a 2022 report titled 'The Enduring Sexism of India's Tech Industry', Indian women in tech, in both technical and non-technical roles, spoke about their struggles to be taken seriously at the office.[30] Their image and potential chances were affected by anything from wearing heels, to carrying a backpack or having a certain tone of voice. Organizing cakes and office parties inevitably fell upon them. 'Most "bros" are scared of women who hold strong opinions,' said one software engineer from Chandigarh, who wasn't believed when she pointed out flaws in an algorithm that was biased in favour of men. Women who were from oppressed castes or rural backgrounds were further made self-conscious about their English, or willingness to attend team outings at pubs. The result is women walking around with a constant alertness about their behaviours, worrying about whether they're being misinterpreted, trying to prevent it all the time.

A less obvious consequence of being a bit of a rarity in the workplace is being fetishized and chased by the other sex. Managing male egos remains an unsavoury part of the job description. I needed to be in their good books to succeed, so I staved off their unwarranted attention tactically, trying not to offend them too much. Later I found out that one such senior manager was asked to leave the company for causing his female subordinates mental harassment. I myself never thought about reporting him—I simply didn't want the trouble, and assumed that dealing with such people was a skill I'd have to develop.

I wasn't wrong. I encountered his type multiple times: men endearing themselves into a woman's career as a means to gain control over her, or just to get her attention. And after all that ego management for survival or self-actualization, women get branded as opportunists who give themselves up sexually just to get ahead.[31] Sometimes it feels like there's just no winning. Perhaps this damned-if-you-do-damned-if-you-don't power dynamic that women become trapped in explains why younger generations look up to someone like Monica Lewinsky, who was severely shamed for her involvement with a man twenty-seven years her senior, who was also the president of the nation, who received much less wrath than her in the aftermath of their affair. Lewinsky has since then become an icon of resilience, reclaiming her narrative by bringing up the politics of shame and the double standards that women face, where they risk being blamed for either being too passive and/or too complicit. She's inspired 'siren-core', a movement that questions the vilification of women who, knowingly or otherwise, become embroiled in toxic power plays with men in positions of authority.

Once, while applying for a marketing role at one of India's most successful tech start-ups, I made the mistake of answering a male interviewer's question honestly. The start-up was known to be unpleasant for women to work at. There was no woman on the board, and a female friend who'd worked there warned me going in. 'We can anyway never display doubt,' she said. 'It proves what they already think: That we're not fit for the job.'

But I needed the job, at least as a backup. I was coming from a toxic old boys' club masquerading as a business journalism outlet, where the CEO frequently referred to his own 'mind palace' and colluded with his right-hand COO to outsmart employees working for them and execute their own ideas instead. He once called me 'diffident' for okaying whatever copy he wanted to use instead of fighting for the one I had suggested. It seemed alright for him to call me underconfident, instead of wondering that I perhaps did not care enough to argue over an email he instructed us to do his way in the first place.

Now, at the tech start-up, all six interviews were conducted by men, one of whom showed up late and barely listened as he looked at his phone. Another interviewer was the head of marketing, who was impressed with my work experience but concerned that I wanted to switch jobs for a 'big and interesting' new challenge.

'Sanjana,' he said. 'I understand you. Your mind processes information at lightning speed. I get it.'

I didn't say anything. He continued, 'All that is okay for someone at the early stages of their career. Now you should settle down and impart what you have learnt. Tell me, why did you leave your previous company?'

'I wasn't treated very well there,' I said. 'Sometimes it's hard to work as a woman in India.'

'Hmm,' he said, coughing uneasily. 'Yes, yes, I tell the women all in my team now, that there are so many of them that I should be the one who's scared of them!'

What a strange thing to say.

Why should anyone be scared of anyone?

If this was his way of putting me at ease, it only confirmed my wariness about gender (and how attitudes about it vary by age and generation) at the average Indian workplace. At a workshop I attended a few weeks later, I found out just how commonplace my feelings were across industries and roles for women at every level in an organization. Put together by Creative Equals, a global diversity and inclusion consultancy, I met women in their twenties, thirties, and forties, predominantly from a creative background, who were there to not only talk about their craft, but also about how they'd all been cast out of the workplace through the pandemic.

In our first call, we covered why: how male bosses had ill-treated us, how our families had been unforgiving.... I'm running out of synonyms for 'belittled', 'not taken seriously', 'caregiving', and 'managing the household'.

It was heart-breaking.

I kept in touch with the women. One of them—let's call her Rhea—later told me about how she was a naturally confident young woman, never shy about taking the stage or starting conversations with new people. 'But I suddenly stopped being like that,' she said, referring to a series of early-career experiences. 'I was made a team-lead in one of India's top advertising agencies, and I was the youngest person to hold that position. And I was female. I was constantly reminded of these two facts any time something happened, like, "You can't handle this situation because you're too immature" or people saying, "I can't accept her as my boss or manager." Even some other women of the organization didn't support me.' In an office with 200 people, only twenty were women; two of them were older than her and contenders for the same position. When someone younger got it, after all that they themselves had been through, perhaps the women became resentful. It was finally a rumour that made Rhea eventually quit.

'Someone told the HR that I'd slept with my manager to get the position,' she said, dryly. 'Whatever followed was so mismanaged. Instead of even checking with my manager first, who is my senior, the HR casually said they wanted to have an "informal chat" with me. When I asked them if this was information they were acting on, they said they just wanted to hear from me first. Something so damaging to my own career was nothing but gossip that probably didn't even reach [my manager's] ears.'

If office politics is to be accepted as part of corporate social life, their own gender is usually working against the women involved. God forbid when a woman is talented, unapologetic, and doesn't care to people-please. Remote work has also been a double- or triple-edged sword here.

Research finds that women, non-binary, and LGBTQ+ professionals were less likely to report harassment at the workplace, and also to feel that their organization responded well. About six in ten Gen-Zs and half the millennials had experienced harassment of some form at work, via inappropriate emails, unwanted jokes, gender-based undermining, or physical advances.[32]

Still, as is the paradoxical nature of life, it was also technology and remote work that had enabled alternative incomes, more free time, lower costs, and, in my case, my third career—my unlived life as an independent writer, creator, and entrepreneur. Working for myself, and doing well, restored some of my dignity by not prostrating me towards people who could abuse their position. The marketplace evidently recognized this as a privilege, with companies in the US only allowing employees to work from home if they agreed to a pay cut—which a surprisingly high number said they'd agree to.

In India, hybrid work remains a more common option, with more people wanting it than are actually able to avail it.[33] White-collar jobs in tech and financial services tend to be the only careers that offer it at all. After the world was thrown into a four-year impromptu mass experiment with remote work, studies are mired in contradictory results. One found that it both decreased and increased worker productivity; basically, it depended on the sector and managerial methods in use.[34] While some working women—or their households—benefited from remote work, women also bore greater penalties. Both men and women were more likely to suspect that women are shirking when engaging in remote work, perhaps because co-workers know that women are more likely to have additional responsibilities at home.[35] Women also felt less empowered to ask follow-up questions and received less feedback while working remotely, while men remained more likely to be 'in the know', receiving accolades and mentorship both remotely and on-site.[36]

Still, women working remotely also faced fewer microaggressions and experienced higher levels of psychological safety.[37] More than a third of women with children said that jobs with flexibility had allowed them to remain in the workforce.[38] But this very flexibility also became a factor behind the gender wage gap.[39]

Nothing is either completely good or completely bad; every system has the potential to carry forward the worst tendencies of the ones that came before it.

If masculinity is inherently about providing and protecting, and femininity is about nurturing and care, the one-sided, patriarchal arc of human economic history has distorted both roles. Psychologists recognize that all individuals are inherently androgynous, possessing both masculine and feminine qualities. But when men abuse their husband-father-provider status by controlling women, stereotyping them as weak and inferior, or denying them their autonomy and wholeness, they rob themselves of their own wholeness too. Meanwhile, women have to fight extra hard to don their provider-hats, often causing a blow to their femininity in the process. The feminine principle, rooted in being, creative play, and receptivity, is disdained in a society obsessed with 'getting', productivity, and monetizing every human act.

We're all neurotic max now. Both genders are out of

touch with their androgyny, and neither completely trusts the other. Women struggle to let go of their hard-earned independence, to be 'taken care of', because they associate this with the risk of being subjugated or demeaned. Men resent women because their own femininity was never freely allowed them, and to see women get all the 'mercy' and 'victimhood' is frustrating.

Both are suffering from having internalized a societally elevated, somewhat corrupt version of masculinity. It isn't easy for anyone to reclaim their femininity. It is always going to be an act of heroism. It will call for hours of inner work and repeatedly unlearning the maladaptive forces that influenced us, growing up, and redefining what we were taught to value.

And yet, for every unpleasant workplace story I can tell, I can also share one that has made me believe in humanity and the kindness of people. Mentors and colleagues who didn't belittle me, who saw my potential both inside and outside the workplace, who cared about me as a whole person, and made me want to show up and give a '120 per cent'.

In 2003, a Canadian documentary film called *The Corporation* asked a simple question: if the modern corporation were a person, what type of person would it be? Over three hours, through interviews with well-known critics like Noam Chomsky and Michael Moore, it concludes that the corporation would be a psychopath. Psychiatrist Robert D. Hare points out the prevalence of the diagnostic criteria of psychopathy in the contemporary profitable corporation, such as the 'callous disregard for the feelings and safety of other people', 'the incapacity to maintain human relationships', deceitfulness in return for profit, the incapacity to experience guilt, the failure to conform to social norms and respect the law, and the inability to accept accountability for one's own actions.[40]

In 2020, the makers released *The New Corporation: The Unfortunately Necessary Sequel*, whose subtitle reviewers questioned because the detrimental effects of corporate conduct had now become mainstream knowledge. Even as businesses turn to social justice causes to respond to the cultural pressure to actually do good for society, most young people believe that companies don't really have a positive impact on the world, and have no real ambition beyond profit. Nearly forty percent of these survey respondents said that they had rejected assignments or employers due to ethical concerns and a mismatch in values.[41]

The idea of 'bringing your full self to work' started gaining currency around the late 2010s. 'In today's work environment, the lines between our professional and personal lives are blurred more than ever before,' writes Mike Robbins, the author of *Bring Your Whole Self to Work*.[42] With political beliefs increasingly dictating our relationships, and some divisive event happening every other day, knowing what your workplace and colleagues stand for may be an important aspect of feeling safe at work for some.

There are costs to hiding parts of ourselves where we spend most of our time. And although authenticity takes courage, it is worth it, Robbins insists, outlining five principles to help you do this.[43] But—I'm sorry to tell you the truth here—every time I have been authentically myself at work, I've faced some repercussions. Every time someone else has authentically been themselves, I have been wary too.[44] Imagine adding some new colleagues on WhatsApp and watching their Ram-Janmabhoomi-Pran-Pratistha-status on the day of the new Ayodhya temple's inauguration. They, in turn, might judge me for being single in my thirties, coming from a broken home, dating multiple people, 'writing' and 'questioning the establishment' part-time.

I might be better off not revealing these aspects of myself to them somehow—which means being conscious of what I share on WhatsApp and social media, straddling multiple personalities that are typically reserved for different audiences, who have all now collapsed together on these platforms. But building this has therefore also enforced a kind of integrity in my persona, as it were, forcing me to architect a lowest-common-denominator version of myself that is appropriate and entertaining for all these audiences. This has been challenging, but also necessary for my well-being.

Despite the increasing emphasis on good mental health and diversity and inclusion at the modern workplace, anecdotal experiences indicate that being totally transparent in touchy areas can backfire. A friend who was diagnosed with ADHD and put on medication for it sometime after the pandemic found his performance under increased scrutiny as a result, with co-workers blaming his condition for any backlogs, or resorting to it to sabotage future opportunities. I remember more than one 'ice-breaker' event at an office outing becoming inappropriate and uncomfortable, as the booze was flowed free and people asked risqué questions to 'get to know each other'.

At one such #CompanyOffsite, an ice-breaker event involved all the new hires being asked to name their three office crushes to 'the seniors'. Before I could get to mine, somebody had the gall to ask me if that problematic senior manager who insinuated himself into my career was one of my crushes. I cannot begin to articulate the dystopia. Get hit on by the dude in senior management at work and play to his ego so that you get to keep your job, and then get asked inappropriate questions by catastrophically tone-deaf and half-drunk colleagues who think you courted that kind of attention, and whose idea of a good time it is to bring it up casually, in public, at an office party.

Disgusting.

And a bit sad, the emptiness of the lives of those who've submitted themselves to the system without awareness. Their personalities are shells of the whole people they could be. When your mental forces have been colonized into believing that what is important is not how much control over your time you have, how well you love your family and friends, but the accumulation of achievements and a currency that lets you buy things you may not really need, beyond a certain point, of course you define yourself by your ability to buy them.

For work to genuinely be as necessary to society as the upper echelons deem it, perhaps we all need to become comfortable with what in India is considered 'impure' or menial labour: serving people, cleaning shit, cooking, washing clothes. If this were considered more prestigious, it wouldn't be so exploitative of the castes who are currently forced into doing it by dint of their birth. As Kancha Ilaiah Shepherd writes in *Why I am Not a Hindu,* corporate India runs on 'casteized capital'.[45] The anglicization of the upper-castes enabled their integration into the global techno-economic market, while lower castes remained alienated from it. 'The Brahmins and Baniyas never realized the fact that the manipulation of capitalist markets to suit the needs of their own culture and ideology is detrimental to the national interest,' wrote Shepherd. 'If their selfish interests are served, they couldn't care less about serving the country and its people.'[46]

Indeed, most 'innovative' Indian start-ups are directed at the 'top 5 per cent', solving problems that feed the insecurities and desires that have mainly been created by those who'd profit from their existence. Predatory EdTech companies peddle loans to gullible families, selling them dreams of 'cracking' an education that by design will likely exclude them. Grocery apps consider it the pinnacle of problem-solving to shorten delivery times from thirty minutes to less than ten, and to segregate orders based on 'pure vegeterianness' (while trying to make it look like this has nothing to do with the country's sociology). Health-tech companies enable elites to get more and more grisly about their every bodily statistic, as though such minutiae wouldn't have diminishing returns to both 'users' and society at large. (Are you really going to '10x fitness' by analysing every piece of data there is to know about your body, or are you just being brainwashed about the importance of that data by someone whose livelihood depends on it?)

In *Bullshit Jobs: A Theory*, anthropologist David Graeber unpacks the myth of the highly productive, highly paid corporate worker. Over half of societal work done is 'bullshit', he writes: 'Huge swathes of people spend their working lives performing tasks they secretly believe do not need to be performed.'[47] But, as part of the conditions of employment, the employee must pretend otherwise. Big corporate meetings and presentations are manifestations of neo-feudalism, he argues, their chief purpose to justify the existence of those jobs rather than make anything real. Meanwhile, actually difficult and socially useful work—caregiving, cleaning, the essentials—are paid the least.[48]

In a culture that only respects ambition and consumption, the highest-status jobs are the most hollow, while lowest-status jobs are arguably more useful. Work, and self-worth tied to work, become functions of performance, status, an elaborate illusion.

There have been alternative visions for capitalism. Conscious capitalism is about prioritizing social good along with profits. Moral capitalism is about having the markets operate under moral imperatives, like fairness, ensuring worker's rights, 'environmental stewardship', et cetera. De-growth is about reducing production and consumption and focussing on sustainability and well-being instead. In *Small is Beautiful*, E. F. Schumacher advocates for small-scale, decentralized economies that promote quality of life over constant growth.

'Right Livelihood' is one of the tenets of the Buddha's Eightfold Path to enlightenment, seen as part of a rounded, fulfilled life. Buddhist economics questions whether reducing labour—say through automation, so as to profit corporations, or to increase leisure, so as to benefit workers—is ideal for either party in the capitalist system. Work, when properly designed, fulfils the same relation to higher human faculties that food does to the physical body: it is a form of nourishment, meant to enliven and provide purpose. 'For the modern economist, this is very difficult to understand,' writes Schumacher, 'who is used to measuring "the standard of living" by the amount of annual consumption, assuming that the man who consumes all the time is "better off' than the man who consumes less.'[49] But the Buddhist-economic view considers consumption as a means to well-being, not an end in itself.

'The less toil there is, the more time and strength is left for artistic creativity.'

Through everything I did to achieve the highest levels of success in whatever discipline I undertook, I really did believe I was doing it to 'be the best', out of a pure love of excellence. After getting there—to the 'top'—and staying there for some time, and seeing how equal I was to the people and places the culture had pedestalized (and also how fucked up they were), the veil was gradually lifted. There's no such thing as 'being the best' anyway; most definitions of 'top'-ness at whatever are also constructed by other people, mostly men, and are based off of limited ideas of intelligence and success, drawing from prestige, fame, money, chauvinism—all defined externally and adopted unquestioningly at large.

People are mostly making shit up. The so-called most successful are pandering to the mean. Insight is elusive. It demands a depth and courage that people find easy to live without.

But even after you see through the system and grow disillusioned, you can appreciate its mechanisms—you might have to, to survive. *Of course* you need it to puff up the ego and construct an identity around work; glory and status must compensate for the lack of *soul*-meaning. Capitalism needs egos to survive, because its deeper method is endlessly creating new desires, making them high-status and aspirational, so they can be channelled into consumables and commodities. And as the rate of societal acceleration keeps increasing, so does the rate at which these desires—and the identities attached to them—form and dissolve.

It not only takes egos to succeed, but also 'weak egos' that easily and periodically become attached to new forms of status. Jonah Peretti, the founder of Buzzfeed, wrote about how the system exploits susceptibility, because without people wanting to identify with the latest new fad—whether it's ADHD or being 'neurospicy' or using niacinamide for skincare or even being anti-capitalist—you would not have industries. (Yes, unless you are working for the radical left or living in some commune or practising caregiving or free-ganism or climate activism, your anti-capitalistic social media posts while you work at some normal job are just as consumerist as any venture capitalist's promise to really benefit society at large. And that's *fine*! It's okay to not save the world, or make it even a slightly better place. Nearly everyone who isn't a monk is possibly a net negative on civilization in the terms that we define these things in. And you are most people. Just thought you might need to hear that.[50])

Basically: marketing would not work if it did not cultivate dualism. And anything dualistic is a bit false.

So, it's interesting that I, a marketer and also a Buddhism-enjoyer, a creator of dualism and an advocate of non-dualism, continue to survive in all the 'contradictory' systems I am a part of.

But that is the meaning of maya, the nature of maya.

I am one of the techbros, one of the girlbosses, one of the arthoes. I am all of these things and not any of these. I detest the lack of drive and gatekeeping that seem habitual of legacy creative spaces (yes, the stereotype is true), who might benefit from some of the processes and professionalism common to businesses, for instance. But I dislike the grand military metaphors and self-important mission statements that too many #hustlebros cloak their agendas in. (Seriously, it's very cringe to unironically believe you're changing the world—like who isn't? What is the world if it's not changing already? And that your solution will be 'universally good' and won't also create its own problems (yes, the stereotype is true)).

But I also love having beautiful gadgets and being able to buy art and jewellery and therapy and make up and good clothes and not having to rely on anyone—a boy or my parents—to take care of me.

I love doing more than just one thing. I love intellectual curiosity.

Paul Graham has an essay in *Hackers and Painters* called 'How to Make Wealth', and in it he argues that wealth creation, especially in start-ups, *should* be proportional to talent and value added.[51] When talent and skill is concentrated and rare, such as in the CEO or in someone whose unique abilities drive the company's success, it is justified that that person is paid a hundred times more than anyone else. This is about as anti-communist, and anti-non-dualism, as it gets, but I kind of agree. Reading this made me leave the big company I was at, where I thought I worked and produced at a higher level than the average employee—and was also made to believe that I did, remember? They need to puff you up—but getting compensated the same as everyone. Four years hence, I do believe I am employed in conditions that need and reward my unique set of skills (yes, okay, skill set). And the desire to build upon this skill set to get more and more 'alpha', gives my life meaning.

Besides, a start-up may even 'solve for' Marx's key issue with capitalism, which was that man, because he is detached from the fruits of his labour, becomes self-alienated. This is true. But in start-ups, workers actually own part of their company and are, in a smaller way than being the sole owner, still working for themselves; they are directly and fairly tied to the fruit of their labour.

Perhaps technology is fusing both ends of the economic spectrum, creating hybrid spaces where individuals can be both owners and workers, consumers and creators. You reap the rewards of your labour not just solely for producing another's profit, even if while being part of a larger, questionable system.

And with AI, whose promise is to elevate human creativity and reduce rote, alienating labour, we're faced with the final medley of individualist, capitalist innovation and Marxist ideals of shared wealth. As I wrote in my piece on Big Tech and people's fear of it—never forget to plug—'According to Altman, AI will improve performance and reduce costs in multiple aspects of daily life.[52] "Imagine a world where, for decades, everything—housing, education, food, clothing—became half as expensive every two years," he writes.' The OpenAI CEO envisions a utopia where technology allows humanity to flourish, with basic needs all taken care of, plenty of time for leisure, work as discretionary, and equitably distributed capital, i.e. phenomenal wealth for everyone—and if it wasn't coming from someone on the opposite end of the economic spectrum, Altman's vision would be mistaken for Marx's wet dream.

Technology is therefore post-dualism, where wealth generation and equity were never at odds in the first place. #Abundancemindset #blessed

If you're able to detach from work and self-worth being equivalent, the system of meaning can actually be good for you, even while creating problems for society, which, let's face it, is true of any system. Maybe late-stage capitalism, or the most socialist versions of it in, say, Scandinavia, et cetera, are the best we can do. You'll certainly find support in evidence for this. In *Women Have Better Sex Under Socialism: And Other Arguments for Economic Independence*, Kristen R. Ghodsee analyses how socialist policies positively impact women's lives. Drawing from studies in post-socialist Eastern Europe and Scandinavia (and we can start there to see if those conditions for success could be replicated, to what extent, or whether some other model can work elsewhere, etc), Ghodsee examines quality-of-life indicators such as economic equality, job satisfaction, and even sexual fulfilment to find that women face fewer pressures, economically and emotionally, when the state offers robust social service and support. They are less dependent on male breadwinners and have more agency about their work, their relationships, and sex lives.[53]

I can attest to this. There is a reason social justice movements, from anti-racism to feminism and queer rights, have used capitalism and class advancement as a legit means to undo ancient systems of oppression that would otherwise keep people where they are. Yes, the same systems have several problems; it doesn't change the fact that the environment is still being ravaged by our existence and need for profit, but—

I sometimes think that to expect consistency, or any real meritocracy, in people and systems is to operate from the point of view of a child. I am still frequently bothered by the implications of not 'picking a camp'—establishment or anti-establishment—but I know there isn't an easy resolution for anyone alive. You're sipping bottled water and dining out when you can and trying to lead good lives with your families while sharing god knows what politically correct worldview in circles that have come to recognize them as signals for good thinking and/or virtue, with little correlation between the signals and actual good behaviour. There is no real sacrifice happening anywhere. And if it is, that is where we need to pay attention—not the vapid and/or murderous media and beliefs and behaviours we more easily douse ourselves in.

Anyway, a bottom line: a tough life—tougher than the one I've already had—is not for me, a woman of many talents and tastes and certain refinements. The richer I get, the more secure and capable I become of being myself, of writing, of having good sex, or being of any help to anyone at all. In his paper on capitalism and 'schizophrenia' (as it pertains to 'accelerated identity formation/dissolution'), Peretti also wrote that a valid, 'robust' anti-capitalism movement would use the tools of capitalism to promote messages that resist it.[54]

I'm not doing that, evidently. I'm just saying: it is a pyramid scheme all the way up, but it seems worth participating in fully, as much as you can.

Then you do whatever you want.

6

WHAT IS LOVE? BABY, DON'T HURT ME

'Where love rules, there is no will to power. Where power predominates, there love is lacking.'

—Carl Jung

English words pronounced in 'Gujju style' sound funny: 'cheese' becomes 'cheej', 'fees' becomes 'phees', 'fish' becomes 'piss', 'hall' becomes 'hole', and so on. This is to the great benefit of that genre of Instagram comedy that has people imitating an accent after an automated female voice says something like, 'Your Gujju accent is so sexy. Say it again?'[1]

These features of the Gujju accent are also the source of one of my father's most troubling jokes. On the nineteenth birthday of my younger twin brothers, the entire family happened to be in the same city, a fate I'd tried to avoid for a few years by then. We decided to get dinner at an upscale restaurant. This was Sai Palace in Andheri East, which, for my middle-class family, demanded an occasion. Spending some ₹2,000 at a dinner for five people would have been unthinkable for my parents in their youth.

At the time, I was in the middle of a class of nervous breakdowns, the first of its kind to grace me after a lifetime of perfect strangulating mental self-control. I was thus allowed to speak my mind, for once, with the expectation that my father would listen and not aggravate the situation with his retorts.

It had led, finally, after twenty-nine years of emotional martyrdom, to what we'll call The Great Confrontation and Reckoning. It spanned eighteen days, one of which ended in this dinner.

Fawther and Brother #1 bonded while ordering dinner. Brother #1 is a fan of rap music, like many people his age and, quite spontaneously, Fawther cackled about how 'Gujjus' would pronounce 'rap' as 'rape'.

'What is wrong with you?' I said, as they laughed and Amma and Brother #2 looked at the menu.

'What is the big deal? You have a problem with everything,' said my father.

It must have been the activated PTSD that brought back his nightly pastime for several years, which was storming my mother whenever she returned from work with insults, equating her wish to be good at her job and to keep it—the only job that provided for four children, three actual ones and the one that she had married—as a desire to be raped. Even such a husband and father insisted on 'respect', which he believd his existence entitled him to.

'What do you mean "what's wrong with it"?' I snapped.

'I have to be myself somewhere, no!' he said, hands flouncing.

I still don't think I'm up to the task of condensing all that is wrong with that sentiment. 'Just imagine if I used words like "behenchod" and "madarchod" at the dinner table,' I said. 'Would you be okay with it? You think it's okay to make "rape jokes" casually, that too in front of women? In front of your own daughter? How can you be so uncouth?'

Amma saw that Appa was about to escalate, so she intervened, 'Don't you have any maturity? Can't you keep quiet for once?'

'She's not well,' Amma added.

I had to be unwell to demand an absence of misogyny at dinner. 'She just needs to say it properly, then,' he paused. 'And if it's really wrong, people can think about it and change.'

He looked me in the eye while saying that. I softened inwardly.

'Yes, at the grand old age of sixty. After I've been saying it "properly" for years. While you can be as improper as you like. What a bloody achievement.'

For many years, I hated my father with the low-key persistence of a fan turned on and forgotten in some untidy back room of the house. Sometimes I'd become conscious of it, and if it was during a workout, I would channel my anger into my burpees or at the boxing bag. I might have clinically reasoned how beneficial it would be if he died, so that we would all be put out of our misery—especially him.

A father with no positives to offer could at least not pile on negatives, I thought, because with him, the latter could come at any time, like accidental bludgeons to the head.

I used to look over my shoulders while walking on the road, worried that I would be struck.

Once, Fawther was so upset about my mother being 'late' from work that he took my eleven-year-old brothers to a mall the night before their exams were to start at school, just to inconvenience and spite Amma. Leaving for college at the age of eighteen was both my only ticket to freedom, from oppression and abuse, but also a paranoic bane: who would stop them from fighting, which always intensified when I wasn't around?

Who would remind her not to take his shit?

Who would protect my brothers from his terrible influence?

Who would suggest she deserved a better life, for the sake of everyone unfortunately involved?

He took this fundamental self-concern to be 'interference'. I had a need to 'be the panacea for the world's problems', as he once put it on WhatsApp. He thought I was chasing a moral high ground. Instead of seeing a hurt angry, scared daughter—his own—he saw arrogance. Projeting upon me his petty need to have the upper hand in the family, he saw my indignity as unwarranted 'modern' feminism. He made fun of Amma and I for liking the movie *Mary Kom*. One summer, two years after the divorce, when I was in another city interning at a magazine, getting my first by-line before I began my corporate job in marketing, I received a call from my mother.

'He is saying he is going to call the company and tell them you were expelled.'

I couldn't believe it.

In a minute, I whirled through the possibilities: would my father actually do this? What would he get out of getting me fired? Had he completely lost all obligation and affection towards me? How could he make such mistakes and penalize *me* on top of it? What had I done to deserve this? Was I cursed? Why couldn't he die already? Would any company take a man calling them like this seriously? Would they care that I had been expelled from some college ten years before? Surely, they'd hold the degrees I'd earned afterward from more prestigious institutes in higher regard. And how I had won the job at the end of my internship, after a presentation to the leadership on the brand's growth plan. The marketing director had swiftly followed with, 'We'll see you next year'—so convinced were they of my intelligence and tenacity. This had never happened before in the history of the company, I heard. The other interns would hear three months later, if at all.

No, a random phone call from my father wouldn't crush me.

Worst case, I might be judged for being associated with such a loose man, whose idea of a good plan was to pick up the phone and try to get somebody fired while claiming to be their father.

No, I couldn't lose it. It was my only way to clear the loans, to make a living, and to buy my freedom and a life outside this house.

It was the only thing I was outside this mess.

'The happier you think you can be, the unhappier you think you are,' reads a line from *Veronika Decides to Die*.[2] I'm probably fifteen years old, and I don't know that I'll remember the line forever, but it strikes me as profound and true even then.

I didn't finish the rest of the book because it seemed too depressing, but I might trace my touch of melancholy back to that time.

Now, we all know that is what books and stories were to me all along: a way out of the mess. 'Probably the greatest of wounds—not to have been loved just as one truly was—cannot heal without the work of mourning. It can be either more or less successfully resisted and covered up (as in grandiosity and depression), or constantly torn open again in the compulsion to repeat,' writes Alice Miller, in *The Drama of the Gifted Child*.[3]

Magical thinking. That is the cost borne by sensitive, perceptive children who adapt to their parents' needs at the expense of their own. The 'gifted' child—not necessarily in intellect, but in their attunement to the energy around them— learns to adjust to what their caregiver needs of them, causing a schism with their own authentic self. This split in childhood results in adults who, though seemingly successful and high-functioning, are haunted by a hollow ache and a lifetime of compulsive compensations for lost love, via achievement or self-sabotage or drugs, that all mask the unacknowledged wound. Grandiosity over achievement may continue the illusion that "I was loved", but it is really just a defence against depression, a real pain from the loss of one's true self.

The only way to heal from that wound is to face it, to 'deeply mourn the situation of the former child', and repeatedly reprogram yourself. The mess I was trying to escape wasn't just around me, after all, in the atmosphere of the many rented houses our souls trawled through, or in the heavy interactions I grew up seeing and hearing. It had percolated deeply.

It was in my body.

But books, like my dreams, my career, my body, and the exceptionalism I tried to hand-carve upon every aspect of my life, were under my control. They were entertainment and wisdom amidst adults who seemed to provide neither.

In some sense, they became my real parents, my identity.

That was the 'Real Me'—everything I was outside of home, in reality and in imagination. Whoever I was at home was a burdened burden that nobody saw or appreciated or understood.

So, when Brother #2 defiled a magazine I bought in Germany during my exchange semester at B-school, I erupted. His scribbles with a blue ball pen on the cover of an elegant February 2017 edition of the *National Geographic* set my insides on fire, as the magazine's subject matter might: BOOZE. For the next four hours, in what might have been the sixth rented house our mother lugged us through every other year, I raged at him, belittled him, and abused him like my father might have done to me once—or worse.

After the fight, while watching *The Trial* by Orson Welles on a mattress in the other room, I texted a friend and told him what happened in brief. I always felt the need for a confessional after succumbing to such fits of rage. They meant

I could no longer pride myself on being the only one in the family who had kept it together. They suggested that something was wrong with me too. It meant that despite my efforts and best intentions, I had my father's worst qualities within me.

As much as I disdained and tried to avoid his fate, I had internalized his harsh and critical tendencies. In Jungian psychology, the 'monstrous father complex' is born from a father figure who has embodied power, judgement, and control in destructive ways. I had an 'inner tyrant' imprinted on my psyche, a relentless, punishing voice that mirrored the father figure in my life. Even when the father himself is distant later, the tyrant is active, critical of every thought, anxious and loud about inadequacies, framing life as a test that one is bound to fail. Left unhealed—a long task—it permeates other relationships too, especially with the men in one's life, and with one's own inner masculinity.

My younger brothers were often the butt of this hurt I didn't then know how to manage. They were the only people I was allowed to feel superior to, according to the familial dynamics we were embedded in. Even that didn't last long, as Fawther soon used Brother #2 as a pawn to feel supported and excused for his bad behaviour. I have a vague memory of locking my brothers up in the bathroom, when I was barely a teenager and they were very little, for 'disobeying' me. Sometimes, I got away with flinging contempt at my mother. We hurt each other many times over the years: I was annoyed by her insistence that I too conform to societal expectations, from what I should study to when I should be married, even though conforming had brought her little satisfaction. I resented her overreliance on me, my having to absorb and solve her problems.

But she also never reacted or seemed to take my anger too personally. She had become the stoic bearer of everything around her, grief or rage or resignation. I'd like to think she held her awareness of my bottled hatred towards all of them with some understanding, knowing it was caused by the life and childhood I'd had.

But the person behind it all seemed to never bear the brunt of his actions. Whenever I stood up to him or defended my mother or told him what I really thought of him, he'd instantly call me arrogant, abrasive, bipolar, mentally ill, destined to fail, or 'unable to find and keep someone'.

My heart cannot bear the irony.

My pages are wet with grief.

For the longest time, he would not listen, he would not apologize, and he always made it worse.

All of them were ignorant of the Real Me—a brilliant achiever, sincere and hard-working, a beloved friend, an artist, a sufferer beyond compare, single-handedly bearing pain as a panacea to the world's problems.

No, in their eyes I was meddlesome, a pesky bitch who thought too much of what she thought, wielding her ideas of right and wrong and good and evil like a weapon, daring to shoot at an otherwise peaceful 'home' with the words on her tongue. Maybe they were better off without me, who knows. I could never take my suffering home, and rest easy in the arms of a loving, caring, and trustworthy parent who themselves was not suffering. They seemed more unconscious than I was.

And because I only let myself suffer for a cause, I never even suffered properly.

Even my pain was unlived by me.

When I did discover it, it metabolized in billows and belches, the stench of its politics nauseating every passer-by, stretching the fabric of my mindbody to the seams. I knew I'd befallen some tragic fate in this birth, which was compounded by how much I felt I'd had to do to survive.

All he had had to do was try. Try anything: getting another job, or forgiving himself for his perceived inadequacies, or practising self-acceptance. Nobody expected him to be the provider of the family, but was it so much to ask that he at least acknowledge my mother as one, and not torture her, and apologize for his mistakes, because that would be proof of his sanity, and therefore not my burden to prove mine?

Was it so much to ask that he just deal with his emotions somehow?

I don't know, man, there are so many ways to be a nice person—just thinking about being one counts—but there is no evidence that my father thought about it. If we ever so much as got late while going somewhere, or countered his idea of what to do, god damn us, he would perceive it as an attack, doubling down on his right to be a menace and also accepted for it.

Every promise he made to stop shouting, he broke. Amma put up with it for twenty-six years. For twenty-three, I tried to run away it. Their every fight was an axe that cleaved my head in half. One time, when they were visiting me in Bengaluru, Amma told him that I wasn't trying to 'pick a fight' or 'talk back' to him, I was trying to stop him from shouting at her so that I wouldn't get any more headaches.

Their divorce happened because there was no other choice.

It was not my fault.

But he didn't see it that way.

But I was young, and saw no other way to help them or myself.

It helped, or at least it was 'the right thing to do at the time', Amma said five years after the act. But it created problems of its own. Later I read about this mental model called 'second-order thinking', thirteen years after I first thought about my parents needing a divorce at the age of thirteen. And I thought: who knows, had I educated myself sooner, had I 'thought' better, we might have been able to avoid the following unintended consequences.

Through the divorce, Amma worked with Persis, a waif-like lawyer who specialized in helping women get out of abusive domestic situations. I met Persis a few times, approved of her, and then helped Amma shift from one rented house to another, although not as many times as my brothers, who were still so young that they only lived with her. I at least had colleges and jobs and other lives.

Every time I visited home, I noticed my brothers leaping into new shapes and sizes. Sometimes Brother #2 would have put on weight; sometimes Brother #1 would ask me to stand next to him to see who was taller. Both of them eventually reached my height but, just as inconspicuously, I noticed one day that Brother #1 was cackling on the phone with Fawther, about this or that cricketer and cricket match, and then, the most dreadful set of words—'Hindustani Bhau kya bolta hai na! 😆'

'The way Hindustani Bhau talks! 😆'

Hindustani Bhau, or Vikas Faatak, was this crass YouTuber with 3 million followers across social media, who specialized in hurling abusive content at those who were 'against the country' from the confines of his car.[4] His most famous line, 'Nikal laudé, pehli fursat main nikal!'—literally 'Leave, dickhead, leave at the first opportunity!'—was coined as a response to Javed Akhtar, an Indian Muslim lyricist who sparked controversy by suggesting that Indian artists should leave the country if Pakistani artists were banned. The video grew viral through 2019, and the phrase became a popular reaction meme during India-Pakistan cricket matches, plastered on Facebook pages.

Later I found it scrawled on a post-it note in the bedroom, in Brother #1's handwriting: 'Sanjana, nikal laudi, pehli fursat main nikal.'

I don't know when he wrote it or after what fight, but over the years, my relationship with Brother #1 had grown to mirror the tragic and abusive dynamic that my father and I shared. Fawther had inflamed our antagonism by painting me out to be a 'crazy female' who riled my mother up against him and created problems, not for the injustices he meted out to us, but—just—because—

I'm crazy, aren't I?—

The sorrow and the disgust that swirled through me when I read that note repeated itself over the years almost every time Brother #1 and I met—such as when I returned home from the hospital after my mother's second surgery for her pierced eardrum, courtesy of Fawther's furious right hand one night in October 2015. This was the day of the second ear surgery.

If what followed were an instruction manual, I would call it 'How To Turn Your Children Against Each Other By Refusing to Take Accountability as a Damaged and Narcissistic Patriarch'.

'Bonus: Cause *Lasting* Damage! To Not One, Not Two, but *All* Family Members!'

In the hours after Appa hit Amma in October 2015, it was Brother #1 who called me at some 4 a.m., saying that Appa had slapped Amma and that her ear was bleeding. From a city thousands of kilometres away, I instructed my then twelve-year-old brothers to take her to the hospital, and, in a state of detached calm, thrust into responsibility, untrusting of my father's sanity once again, I called the nearest police station. Upon hearing that the cops were involved, Fawther sprang into action and ran from the house. He disappeared for the night.

When I reached home two days later for her surgery, at a modest clinic Amma seemed to have found herself, Fawther had the audacity to stand close to me and apologize, either in actual or feigned tears. But I didn't care.

He was not a serious person. I could not look at him; I didn't say a word to him.

Eight years later, Amma's hearing called for another round of repair. I didn't hold back this time. This second surgery arrived after two years of a stable meditation practice, including two ten-day Vipassana courses, lots of therapy and inner work, and a year of healing following the Great Confrontation.

How could you raise me like this, you don't even know or care how I am, I am thirty years old but you don't know what you have done to me, you tried to get me fired, you could not even smile in my graduation photographs, how can a father want to see his daughter fail so badly, how damaged did you have to be to actively wish me harm, how could you not see that your mistakes were the only reason I did what I had to do, how could you think I even wanted the role I was thrust into in this family, I don't even want to *be* part of this family, I am *not* part of this family, how could you, even now, shove me away as I speak so that you can watch some cricket match, how could you spit that 'I'm living in the past' when, for twenty-seven years and counting, you haven't gotten over a brother-in-law not keeping his promise to get you a job and, as a result, hating him and everyone else in the world instead of trying harder yourself, how can you not see that I am what I am despite you and not because of you, how can you not see the enormous amount of pressure I have lived under to merely survive because I have had nothing and nobody to turn to, because I could never let myself be like you, how can you not even feel like apologizing, how are you the worst man I have ever known, how is your ego so big that you expect complete impunity after everything you have done to me when, in fact, I need to scream and shout to be heard, and when you finally do hear me you call *me* crazy, and you expect that I should not even tell you how I feel even at the age of thirty. Why did you give birth to me if you wanted me to just be roadkill to the hit-and-run case that was your marriage, and before you call me 'insane' one more time, why don't you think about why I am only so 'insane' here, and so 'sane' outside?

I have had to prove my sanity outside this house, through endless achievements and socialisation, just so that you, my own family, would not bury me deep.

Even on the day I got fired from a job, you came crawling to me and continued your schtick of asking me everything about which job to keep, and which house to live in, and how to split money with this idiot I expressly asked you to live away from for your own good, which also you decided against 'for the sake of the kids', who, thanks to this decision, are now constantly and casually exposed to the most lazy, misogynistic, and divisive presence, influenced by him to hate their sister, when, for a fact, you too have never really cared about me, you love them and not me, you only wanted me to excel academically so you could show me off to your colleagues and friends like I was some special crockery to be saved up for occasions, and this perfectionism is also why you wanted me to get married before the age of thirty, despite your own failed marriage, instead of encouraging your daughter to be herself, to learn to think for herself, but, worst of all, even though I stood up for you and fought for you and tried to protect you from your own poorly chosen fate, you let me get ostracized in my own family by letting this 'father' and his sons think that everything that happened here was my fault.

It was you I was trying to help, and even you did not help me.

Who have I got?

Devourers for parents.

Amma apologized for emotionally draining me, while also occasionally saying, as if in defence, 'so many families are divorced', as though they weren't also suffering, as though the extent of our trauma was somehow disproportionate to the shit we'd been through.

Fawther, meanwhile, sat upon the sofa with the neglected look of a man waiting for food to be served. At moments, I glimpsed the hint of a tear, when he was reminded that he'd sabotaged himself and his own family. But at other moments, he persisted in slipping his retorts in, and at one time called all his errors inadvertent.

And here, finally, is that unintended consequence I could never have foreseen.

But perhaps it would have been the same in a different way if my parents had stayed together—god.

We could call these my inadvertent errors: on the day of the Great Confrontation, and on the day of the second ear surgery, as I fought Fawther, Brother #1 intervened on his behalf and defended him, and when I asked him to stay out of it, accidentally flinging my teary snot at him while gesticulating that he leave the room, he told me to get help from a 'psychiatrist or doctor', and that I should 'only come back to the house after becoming okay', while defending the psychologically, emotionally, and occasionally physically abusive patriarch, believing that I was the one stirring up drama for drama's sake.

He had forgotten that I was the one he'd called on the night of violence. He probably never registered that the more I defended Amma, the more Fawther hated me, so that by the end of my first college degree, Fawther refused to pay my fees. Brother #1 definitely did not recall the night he was born, when we brought the twins back from the hospital, and Fawther refused to take care of them. How he snored, his backside face-up, his mattress on the floor beside the bed, while Amma and I cradled her sons into the morning. I remember the dimly lit bedroom of the 1BHK we were living in then. It continued like this throughout their childhood: Appa refusing to pay their fees, or help in any way by say teaching them or packing their bags or takings them to the doctor. Amma did all the work—cooking, cleaning, educating, and rearing kids—and also all the work outside it too, as the only breadwinner. I *was* roadkill.

She had been forced to become five people rolled into one, and was still being abused by her husband for it.

I had ignored Brother #1 for years; he was too young and traumatized to know what he was doing, laughing and fraternizing with the resident misogynist, a neglectful, abandoning, unproviding father. But that day, on the day of the second ear surgery, he had been more than eighteen years old for two years, with no sense of right or wrong, casually siding with a maniac, with no feeling for his ostracized sister and bandaged mother. His mother paid all his fees and raised him and cooked for him and served it to him on the sofa, while he played sports and video games with a man-child called Appa, who was no more useful than a playground friend.

So, I become angry, very angry that all my attempts at processing my emotions and becoming a better person and not being horrible to the people who'd repeatedly been horrible to me had gone unnoticed and unappreciated, and I spoke to him in the only language they understood, because they never understood the language of adulthood, of properness. I insulted him for siding with his father and for not appreciating the women in his family, I teased him for his academic performance and for being unemployable like his father, and my mother, roused back into anger from his indifference through her surgery, alerted now to how much pain she had caused me, also told Brother #1 to shut up, and kicked him. Brother #1 fought back. Through it all, Brother #2 was mostly silent. Behind his diplomacy, Amma and I though he discerned right from wrong, which made him safe. But I suspect his body is carrying everything.

I just wrote this poem called 'The Bigger Man'.

You hurt me
So I hurt you

And so on, and so forth
I could stop

As I have done before
But you wouldn't notice

That I was the bigger man
So I hurt again

And get hurt
Because I don't want to be

The bigger man
anymore

I am a woman
Who takes my pain? God?

It's supposed to be in the same vein as that other classic poem about the difficulty of the parent-child relationship and

intergenerational trauma: 'This Be The Verse', by Philip Larkin.
They fuck you up, your mum and dad.

The misogyny in Fawther's psyche leaked into the people around him, so that Amma and I were drained of our femininity in standing up to it. The man of the house was never strong enough to create a safe container around him, one that could hold our truths with dignity. So, I became cut off from an entire function of my psyche, its essence, my femininity—forced, like my father, to become one-sided, incompletely masculine, incompletely feminine.

Traumatized masculine energy had traumatized us, and despite my best efforts to gain consciousness and not be triggered in its presence, or to respond mindfully in the face of its triggers, I did succeed, but I also sometimes failed.

I hate that in my worst moments I perpetuated the abuse I was dealt with. But if I am that weak and human, so are the people who hurt me, and my mistakes and flaws goad me into mercy for myself—and them.

Those failures do sting me, though, and working through them without deflecting them, as I might have before, onto substances and achievements and busyness, feels like the work of lifetimes. In one such lifetime, I mourn the loss of my one-time innocent relationship with Brother #1, whom I had always loved terribly. In his school days, Amma would sometimes be frustrated while teaching him after a long day's work and homemaking, burdened already by the hatred from Fawther. I'd try to teach him differently in those moments, coming up with analogies that might simplify his problems, or reminding him he was capable of learning something if he set his mind to it.

In one lifetime, I wonder about the karmic clusterfuck my family finds itself in: what did our souls do in past lives that we have inflicted so much pain on each other in this one? All of us are trapped by our roles in the family. We are all blaming and hurting each other, we are all the same, I realize and shudder.

In another lifetime, I doubt my relationship to all my emotions—anger, confidence, honesty, love—because in what should have been my own home, these were all left unexpressed and suppressed, or demonized and interpreted at their worst. Intellectualizing and questioning and articulating my feelings was thus not a casual, quirky pastime, but a default way of being I'd developed.

The absence of unconditional love in my family, the shame that cascaded from small mistakes, the toxic cocktail it made with perfectionism in fuelling our 'good' behaviours—all of this became associated with love.

In Kancha Ilaiah Shepherd's *Why I Am Not a Hindu*, I found some of the earliest and most lucid clues to suggest that my family's story was not an isolated phenomenon in Indian culture, totally the blame of a bunch of flawed individuals (us); no, it belonged to a pattern that has long been studied as the 'Brahminical patriarchy'.[5]

The first time I likely saw that term, it was on a signboard that had been foisted upon the founder and CEO of then Twitter, Jack Dorsey, when he was visiting India in 2018. After meeting with ministers and Bollywood celebrities, Dorsey sat down with a group of female journalists and activists. Dorsey is seen betwixt these women in a picture that went viral later, smiling inanely with a poster that says 'SMASH THE BRAHMINICAL PATRIARCHY'. The *India Today* piece on the incident ventured that 'Jack didn't know what the word "Brahminical" meant. He must have thought it had something to do with patriarchy, which is not exactly a nice thing.'[6] But Dorsey was probably not clued into the hot-button issue that caste is in India.

2018 us, JD, fr.[7]

My reaction to it was a barely registered dismissal, even though I came from a violently sexist household, of specific Brahminical variety. Through India's #MeToo movement, I scoffed at the stories of abused and harassed women I saw online, on Facebook; so inoculated was I to being seen as 'just another feminist', or 'another one of those woman', or as the 'activist type'. It also had to do with not wanting to be any more 'difficult' or 'radical' than I already was at home. Outside, I wanted to lead an unblemished, successful life, although the unfairness of pretending to have had such a past only complicated things. Chiefly, I wanted my trauma to be special, the source of my writerly fame, the preserve of my moving, searing, intricately funny, and intelligent book about my life and society—not the subject matter of some attention-seeking 'posts'.

Well, here we are.

And I resent everything I've read in preparation for writing about the Brahminical patriarchy, which forms the scaffolding of modern Indian life, not only because they were vomit-inducing and eye-opening texts, but also because the lens was such a forceful departure from the mainstream-quirky-comedic persona I imagined I'd have as an artist.[8] Navigating this stuff makes me squirm. I hate to be in the same bracket as 'obscure' or 'extreme' intellectuals and academics I don't see myself fitting in with, because they don't seem to have a sense of humour, although I agree that this subject is hardly grounds for humour. I just worry about meeting the extreme moral standards they seem to endorse.[9]

I would just like to remain unserious and reasonably self-interested even after all this. Can't I pierce the heart of our social and political and psychological condition without sacrificing a popular, safe, comfortable life?

This can hardly be my ticket to fame.

But here we are. My famous second-last question.

What is the Brahminical patriarchy, and how does it differ from any other vanilla patriarchy, and how can it be held responsible for my life, and how many others are suffering from it?

Caste is transferred from parents to children at birth, and to maintain the hierarchy prescribed in ancient Hindu texts, supposedly essential for social harmony, endogamy—marriage within castes—is the rule. If it all sounds like a recipe for social disaster, it is; the rules of engagement followed in every Hindu cookbook since the Rig Veda. Around 500 BCE, the *Smritis* were published, which said women were 'impure' by definition due to their God-given reproductive capacity[7], which only prolongs life and does not aid eternal salvation. Sexuality was thus corrupt and women were its accursed bearers.

'Lower'-caste women were the only 'valid' sexual objects, meant to serve the sexual needs of 'upper'-caste men. 'Upper'-caste women, on the other hand, were gateways to the entire caste order, their sexuality the key to its unravelling, a matter of utmost threat—after all, it only takes one lower-caste man to impregnate an upper-caste woman before the whole thing comes crashing down.

No, can't have it; so the *Smritis* insisted that Brahmin women get married as quickly as possible, preferably as girls, to a Brahmin man of their parent's choosing, with the explicit purpose of bearing sons for their future husbands, because only sons can perform the funereal rites of a father such that it brings him closer to salvation in his next life. The birth of a daughter is just short of a curse, best observed by this saying in my family—'yenga Amma vaiyathla ponnu poranda maadri'; literally, 'that is like a daughter born in my mother's stomach'. The idiom is used to describe anything from an unpleasant fate to curd gone bad.

I have heard my grandmother use this idiom the most.

The Smritis say that the 'upper'-caste wife should not divorce, because marriage is the primary function of her life, its breakage her biggest sin, and, if she is widowed, she should not remarry, for she would create a surfeit of eligible men for future girl-brides of 'upper'-caste, disturbing the balance of society. The Smritis thus restricted Brahmin women from working, relegating them to the domestic sphere, condemning late-risers and late-sleepers, for all of these are 'loose' qualities that encourage promiscuity and sexuality, tinge purity, threaten social disorder, and are offensive to the very gods. The Brahminical ideal of women is the 'pativrata', literally 'husband-worshipper', whose first duty is to treat 'her husband as god, no matter how cruel' he is. The Puranas contain examples of such women for good measure: Renuka was beheaded for looking at the reflection (!) of the sanyasi who sat on the opposite bank of the river. She was turned to stone for sleeping with a god who came to her in the guise of her husband(!!). But men who slept with a hundred women were still pure as fire(!!!).

There is an active effort in modern Indian conservativism to project caste as a sort of benign 'professional club'. 'The four varnas were never meant to be 'vertical' hierarchies,' said one friend with a three-lined vibhuti on his forehead. 'They were merely supposed to be a horizontal segregation of occupations, a neat way to manage society.'

But if caste were an egalitarian division of labour, why aren't the labourers allowed to decide which club they want to join based on what they like and are good at? Why are there moral values assigned to each club, and punitive discriminations meted out to those who don't conform? You can't even say caste-based violence doesn't even happen anymore.

Why did women have to literally *burn themselves* if their husbands died? There probably weren't even an equal number of men and women at any point in society so that one man dying needed his wife to literally *immolate* herself in order to maintain the ratio. If anything, given that that there have always been a little less women than men, and human society needs companionship and reproduction to propagate, women should have been given the chance to pair with multiple men for the greater good. This is literally why men fight wars and not women—they are expendable, women are not.

Now imagine if I actually believed in all this a way to organize society, instead of just countering the logic that caste is based upon. Multiple regional Indian writers have explored these double standards of Hindu 'gods' and their worshippers. *Phaniyamma* is a novel by M. K. Indira, part of the Navya (literally 'new' or 'modern') canon of Kannada literature, which questioned the orthodoxies of social life in the 1950s and 60s. In the story, Phaniyamma is married off to Nanjunda at the age of nine. Nanjunda dies of a snake bite two months later. The girl is widowed even before she reaches puberty.

Shortest honeymoon ever.

Phaniyamma's culture needs her to practise 'madi'—the ritual purity of widowhood. To become madi, a widow has to wear madi clothes (white clothes) every day after bathing; she needs to remain indoors for one year, eat only one meal a day and fast for the rest; she must pray to god and before the Tulsi plant; she should recite the Gita and the Ramayana every day; she has to work in the kitchen till midnight, and sleep only on the floor; she faces taboos around touching, and if she touches anything 'impure', she must bathe and wear madi clothes again. A widow must shave her head after her husband's death (the English word for it is 'tonsure', I learnt); she must give up 'kumkum', 'sindhoor', and 'haldi', which are all symbols of sexuality and reproduction that can no longer be hers.[10]

'On the eleventh day [after her husband's death], the old men and women of the village mercilessly broke the bangles of the nine-year-old girl. They wiped off her turmeric and kumkum and tore off her mangalasutra.' After her tonsure, Phaniyamma ceased to be part of pujas and religious ceremonies that the other girls are invited to. Quite reasonably, she starts hating her life. 'She realized that until she died, she would have to eat one meal a day and live with a shaven head. But what could she do? This happened to every woman whose husband died ... If there was any mistake, they would be excommunicated by the temple at Sringeri.'[11]

Phaniyamma's condition makes her grapple with the roots of her misery: 'If a man touches an outcaste woman, all he needs to do is to bathe and change his sacred thread, and he's pure again. If a woman even looks at another man, she's a whore. O Lord, why do you play with us like this? The left hand which washes the buttocks is used to ring the bell during your prayers. When we pray, we must join both palms to you. For every task we need the left hand. And we're not allowed to begin any auspicious ceremony with it! How many blind traditions we have... No one ever thinks of changing anything.'

Hearing these arguments, perhaps a little red-faced, one's right-wing Hindu friends might submit that the logic underlying caste is fundamentally unequal, even evil, that is if they have a conscience. But they could further argue that things have changed. 'Yes, it was shitty 3,000 years ago, but stop flogging a dead horse just to be "woke", dude....'

But the Brahminical mind-virus remains responsible for a grotesque degree of violence, owing in large part to its insidiousness. In 2011, a lawyer called Sarah Kathryn French set out to establish that Indian Brahmin women are so prone to domestic abuse and insufficiently protected in their own country that they should be eligible for special asylum in the United States. A PSG, or particular social group, that is at risk in its home country qualifies for such asylum.

After a Togalese woman was granted shelter in the US, because she hailed from a tribe that expected its female members to undergo genital mutilation, the American board of immigration appeals began to hear more cases related to gender and domestic violence.[12] One such case was Asha's, a Tamil-Brahmin woman who was punched in her swollen abdomen by her husband, who left her bleeding and caused their baby to get miscarried. Originally belonging to a wealthy Brahmin family, Asha knew that reporting her husband, a powerful government official who had abused and raped her, would be futile. Her opportunity to flee came when they moved to the United States for his new job, where she obtained a protection order and applied for asylum.

Kathryn French had to meet several conditions to make the case for Brahmin women—summarily, that they faced violence *because* of their Brahmin-ness, and had inadequate provisions to secure protection in India. The argument was built on the claim that Hindu women suffer persecution from their husbands, because they believe that Hindu women are inferior to them. Like the tribes of Tchamba-Kunsuntu, who perform female genital mutilation to control the sexuality of their women, a Brahmin man may abuse his wife to control hers. Because her sexuality provides access to the Brahmin caste to lower-caste men, who are also construed as threats, Brahmin women's movements have historically been restricted. They have been punished for the smallest infractions, such as going out late or being seen on the street alone after 6 p.m.[13] They may also be abused for not bearing their husbands a male heir.

As in my mother's case, she may be expected to become the outlet for the man's sense of powerlessness outside the house, or else....

In the face of such abuse, Indian women encounter obstacles to securing their own protection. Separation and divorce not only demand resources, but are also so culturally shameful that it is unthinkable for women to leave, lest they be branded as castaways, omens, or failures. Although divorce is legally recognized under the Hindu Marriage Act, it does not even exist as a concept religiously, because marriage is a sacrament that cannot be undone—especially Brahmin marriages, which are described in the Rig Veda as the archetypal union that other castes are to imitate. Speaking up about violence or abuse, even at home, is thus seen as complaining, because the Brahmin wife should 'make it work' no matter what.[14]

This is often the attitude even from people who are supposed to help, whether family members or policemen. Even the few NGOs and shelters that cater to abused women first try to reconcile the victim and her abuser, so that they remain in the same house.[15] Indians view domestic violence as a private problem, as seen in a campaign meant to raise awareness about it. The 'Bell Bajao' advertisement, launched in 2008, showed a man hearing his neighbour hitting his wife. He walks next door and rings the doorbell, and the screaming stops. When the neighbour answers the door, our man asks to borrow a cup of milk (!). Instead of calling the police or an NGO for help, the strategy advocated is making a polite request that hopefully interrupts abuse and then letting it be, revealing how stigmatic it is for Indians to take a stance when it comes to 'personal matters'.

And although laws exist to protect abused women, their invocation is so complicated that the process itself is punishment. The victim may have to prove that she was in 'grave danger'; this, in a state of mind where survival alone can be challenging, the victim has to have the mental and financial wherewithal to construct a legal case. Despite amendments to these laws, research found that the number of cases registered by the police and eventually punished by the courts did not increase.

If the law feels like a wormhole, the social contexts of upper-caste women are dug even deeper. 'It is generally believed in India,' French writes, 'that the higher the caste, the higher the seclusion for women, and the lower the caste, the more freedom.'[16] This is corroborated by several writers. In her essay titled 'Brahminical Nature of Violence Against Women', scholar Sharmila Rege writes that a caste-based analysis of violent practices against women would reveal a greater incidence of dowry murders, widow burning, and controls on mobility and sexuality among upper-caste women, while Dalit women are more prone to rape and physical violence at large.[17] Lalithambika Antharjanam was a Malayali writer whose short stories depicted the cruelty that women of her caste, the Namboodiri Brahmins, faced at home.[18] In over a hundred tales written over forty years, she talks about the women who were often under their husbands' control, even when the latter claimed to be progressive. In 'Is This Desirable?' and 'Realism', the wife is married to a leftist intellectual who publicly advocates for equality and increased freedom for women. At home, however, the wife is insulted and deemed intellectually inferior. She may deviate from gender roles—just a little bit!—so long as the nearest patriarch, father or husband, is not upset and can remain in power. The word 'Antharjanam' is a Namboodiri caste name—literally meaning 'one who lives in the interiors'.

Wife-beating, in particular, is a patriarchal practice that exists among all castes, including the Dalit Bahujans. But, as Kancha Ilaiah Shepherd writes, their families are embedded in a manner of egalitarianism, so that 'bad behaviour' need not be the sole preserve of men.[19] Dalit Bahujan women, unlike savarnas, would not be shamed for making abuse public by shouting or hitting the husband back. They may have the support of other women in the community.

But Brahmin women may not be helped by their own families once they're married off, especially if dowry is involved. In southern India, once a Brahmin daughter marries, she belongs 'entirely to her husband's family', so her own may be ashamed to 'take her back'. Havik Brahmin women from Karnataka transfer all their property and possessions their in-laws after marriage, and are not permitted to inherit land herself, making it hard for them to leave an abusive situation. Non-Brahmin Divaru women from the same village, on the other hand, may hold property, and still have a shot at independence.[20]

These passages are not to compare the sufferings of different groups of women, but to dispel the myths that some suffer and some do not, or that only some suffering has to do with caste, and others do not. Women in India are often in untenable positions, abused but unable to flee, with Brahmin women at risk because of their ritual seclusion and control by their own families. Kathryn French concludes that rural Brahmin would especially qualify for special asylum, more so than urban Brahmin women, who could still escape thanks to their higher education and relative economic independence.[21] She quotes the instance of an urban Brahmin woman who obtained a divorce even though it made her family shun her. Her college degree and employment allowed her to support herself without anyone else's assistance.

Sounds familiar.

'The way that Brahmin society isolates single women and widows is disgusting,' said Mira Narayan, the twenty-five-year-old daughter of a single Brahmin woman. 'You're not allowed to wear or do certain things. And I thought [my mother] would understand [about caste] because she's faced its problems, just because there was no male in the house. But I don't know... it's like the two still add up in her head.' Mira's father died in a car accident when she was only six years old. And because 'the dead are never spoken ill of', she remembers her parents' marriage as mostly happy and peaceful. Mira's mother was gradually ostracized by her extended family, no longer included in pujas because she is a widow.

Like my Amma, despite having suffered from Brahminism, Mira's mother still expected her to follow its rules, in all their modern manifestations. She was to be marriageable, and her acne only became a problem when she was old enough to marry. 'I have PCOS, and one of the first things my mother asked the gynaecologist was, "Will she be able to have children?" I was like, "I am going through something and your concern is.... Can we just fix the problem first?"'

Mira's mother would rather she get married to a Christian than someone of a lower-caste, because 'how will they perform the rituals?'

'I was like, "Who told you I want to do those rituals?"' Mira said. 'There's a ritual that asks women to pray for a good husband, and I kept telling them that I don't want to do all this.' Mira is alert to the differences in how she and her brother are treated at home. 'If you're a male in a Brahminical household, your ego will be stroked, you'll be made to think it's your responsibility to climb every ladder in society,' she said. 'For women, it's like... you have to be educated and "modern", be the best at everything, but not too much also. You have to submit and conform at some point.'

Even on our call, with two screens and several kilometres between us, you could smell her distaste for these double standards. She didn't seem all that rebellious to me, in her circular rimmed glasses, which she pushed up her nose while complaining about the twisted gender norms that ran through our homes. 'She teaches my brother that he should wash the dishes and respect women,' she said. 'But she doesn't want me to think that I might find such a man myself.'

'When I tell [my mother] I will not marry someone who's not willing to share the workload with me, she's like, "You can't go around saying these things before marriage. Afterwards you can convey all your feminism, but if you do it now people will call you egoistic and headstrong".'

'Headstrong'—the exact word that people used to describe my aunt, who displayed a degree of autonomy more than Amma. Atthai taught at a school, and also took tuitions afterwards, which was considered the perfectly wifely approach to work. She wouldn't enter the house later than her husband, and also didn't make more money than him. Atthai, who is named after one of the Hindu goddesses, herself seemed to believe she had struck the 'right balance'.

And this is how Brahminism shines: by blinding the people who believe in it to how it harms them. Upper-caste women become complicit in upholding a system that denigrates them because they come to identify—understandably, regrettably—with its basis: the notion of the divine, of God.

It took Amma years to acknowledge that while Brahmin men are equated to gods, women are deemed inferior by the same rules. She developed more awareness gradually, even if it has not translated outwardly into an upending of the habits and festivals that she and everyone she knows has followed for so long.

This, to me, is good progress: there is awareness, and an awareness of contradictions too.

But what happens when these contradictions are too much to bear (that god cares about me, and that this very same god expects me to hand over essential parts of myself to the control of others that he deems higher than me)? What goes on in a more innocent mind, which expects reality, life, and the world to be logical, not self-contradictory?

I don't think I fully understand it, but the case of a Brahmin woman named Bapu is telling in this regard. Born circa 1950 and married into a hostile family that practically usurped the house bought for her by her father, Bapu became increasingly torn between the different aspects that made up her 'self'.

On the one hand, there was devotion to god, particularly Lord Krishna, who she believed communicated with her through her writings and poetry. On the other hand, there was her duty towards her two children and her husband and her in-laws, who are rude and dismissive to her. Bapu is at the bottom of the domestic hierarchy, cooking and cleaning up after everyone from dawn until midnight. She is ritually secluded from them throughout her menstruation, and disparaged for the limp in her leg, despite being richer than the family she married into.

'My husband considers me an enemy if he doesn't get my body or my money,' she wrote in her journals.

Her devotion and her motherhood were both intrinsic to her. But they were also roles expected from a Brahmin woman. As she sought a closer relationship with god, spending hours in the prayer room—'the one space in her house she could claim as her own'—people started to frown. Unlike Brahmin men, who have cultural sanction to abandon their families and devote their whole lives to spirituality, the priests in Bapu's community tell her it is not her place to become a total sannyasin.

But Bapu needs her religion more and more, wanting to distance herself from her shallow family and their obsession with money, to instead be lost 'in the ocean of devotion'.

She ran away to temples in nearby cities again and again, disappearing for days on end until her family would set out to bring her back. They took her to doctors who were diagnosed her as schizophrenic, and subjected her to electroshock therapy. Her sense of alienation fluctuated over the years, even though she was aware that her mysticism and connection to Krishna would never be understood by the 'scientific world'. She was hurt that her in-laws routinely called her crazy, cursing her for neglecting domestic tasks. But she saw her 'god intoxication' as a form of divine madness, as proof of her insight, following in the tradition of other saints who became estranged from their social lives in pursuit of phenomena that others could neither see nor hear. One of her notebooks was entitled 'Mohanam Ramayana'—'mohanam' meaning 'enchanting' in Tamil, but also 'mentally confusing' in Sanskrit.

'Perhaps Bapu was aware of how another might see her project: as the chronicle of an unsettled mind,' wrote Rachel Aviv, the author of *Strangers to Ourselves*, where I came across Bapu's story. As I read it, I kept asking, 'What is at the heart of her condition? What one thing explains all this?'—a question that Aviv is intentionally vague about in each of her six stories on mental illness, which explore the relationship between diagnosis and identity.[22] Once an anorexic six-year-old herself, Aviv's position is that psychiatry is a double-edged sword, offering both explanations for complex conditions, but also potentially cementing their intractability. I'd like to stay away from any unprofessional guesswork, but here I venture what her narrative does not—a layman explanation that rings true: their god betrays Brahmin women.

Bapu seemed to be caught in a 'double bind', a psychiatric concept that suggests schizophrenic individuals experience conflicting messages or expectations within their families. Their inability to express themselves authentically, or having their experiences misinterpreted frequently, creates a divided self. The word 'schizophrenia' literally comes from the Greek 'skhizein' (to split) and 'phrēn' (mind)—a split mind. Between needing to attend to her family, for whom she might have had mixed feelings, and her devotion to god, which was at once encouraged but not *too* much for a Brahmin woman— there was no path Bapu could have chosen that wouldn't have resulted in some inner and outer conflict. She also wasn't the only woman in her family to defy expectations of how a Brahmin wife should behave; her mother had lived independently too, starting a business after her husband's death. And Bapu was keen to not be seen in the same light, embarrassed that 'women in her family couldn't settle down'. She was perhaps afflicted by a double bind that demanded religiosity and devotion but also selfless motherhood and domestication, until they collided with her authentic self, a sense of being autonomous in an exploitative marital situation that made it impossible to oppose the religion that was both her route to salvation and the source of her subjugation.

Bapu's children grew up neglected and 'motherless', and had their own journeys reckoning with their mother's mental illness, which, as is Aviv's point, lay at the intersection of personal biology and history, familial dynamics and cultural norms. Bapu's daughter found feminist literature more helpful in explaining her mother than psychiatry.

'The traditional upheavals in a woman's life—the adjustments required of a young bride, adapting to new sexual and social expectations, or the isolation and shame of being widowed—often led to a fractured sense of self... When I moved into feminism, I saw that my dad shouldn't have done all the things that he did, but it was part of all the things he had imbibed growing up.'

If the conditioning of the 1950s feels too far from today's aggressive progressivism, let's revisit Aarohi's story. It's a rather counter-intuitive example of how trauma percolates from generation to generation. You last met Aarohi in chapter four, as the rare 'modern' Brahmin who married another Brahmin but in decidedly anti-caste fashion. Their choice was led by their investigation of the culture they grew up in, which had thwarted yet another woman's spirit—Aarohi's mother's—to the point that Aarohi bore the brunt of her parent's unhappiness and self-hatred.

Born in 1994, Aarohi grew up in a cosmopolitan neighbourhood in Bengaluru that was home to Muslims, lower-caste Hindus, and a Telugu population alike. But her life at home was singularly orthodox Brahmin. Her father was an orphan who had worked as a labourer since the age of twelve. He'd started his own Udupi restaurant when he turned thirty. 'As if to compensate for not having a typical Brahmin upbringing, he used to be extra Brahmin in his rituals,' said Aarohi. 'He follows all sorts of prathas. He has a very restrictive diet. Doesn't eat anywhere but at home.'

All of these practices—'many of them gender-based restrictions, certain shlokas I had to sing'—were transferred to Aarohi and her mother, who was a housewife. She'd been the eldest of four siblings in a family whose patriarch was then jobless; she was forced into marriage with a less educated and worldly man.

'My mom studied in a convent school and completed her BCom,' Aarohi explained. 'She used to watch movies and have many friends. She picked up many skills. She was a good baker. She wasn't groomed for a life with my father, who wasn't very emotionally aware because of how he grew up, and also had very patriarchal expectations of her.'

The result was severe incompatibility, constant fighting, and domestic and psychological abuse of an unusually melancholic flavour—but Brahminical nonetheless in its root cause. Aarohi's mother suffered from bursts of anger that often left her father, who Aarohi described as 'sensitive and demure', in tears. She herself was often beaten up, used as a pawn in their fights, her closeness to her father an emotional trigger that her mother often pulled on him. During these frenzies, Aarohi felt her mother 'lose her grip on reality'. She believes that is why her mother cannot admit to her past aggressions to this date. 'It took me years of therapy, and several books, to see both sides to the situation,' she said.

Until the age of ten, reciting prayers to her father's liking was how Aarohi and he bonded. Even after she encountered other influences in school and stopped believing in religion, she performed these rituals to please her father. She now sees their dynamic as co-dependent. One of her father's everyday activities involved going to the Raghavendra Matt nearby and listening to 'a bigoted Brahmin purohit giving discourses about the different Hindu texts'. 'I was made to attend—,' she interrupts herself, '—I would go with my dad voluntarily, but as I grew older, I realized how misogynistic they were. My dad was pretty much in a Brahminical cult. It took Hindutva becoming mainstream for me to join the dots, but I basically grew up in this cult and that explains a lot of my psychology today.'

So, Aarohi's dad was into Hindutva before it was cool. And although her mom was once rebellious and stubborn as a child, her marriage had changed her. 'She felt cheated out of life. And they had me within a year of marriage, hardly prepared. She probably felt her life could have been better without me,' Aarohi said ruefully.

Her mother had been a creative person who liked making greeting cards and gifts for her friends, who now depended on her husband even for petty cash and supplies. When she one day decided to get a job as a teacher at the nearest playschool, her mother came back to find her husband seething in resentment. There followed a series of miscarriages, as Aarohi's mother tried to give her husband a son, which he'd always wanted. All the surgeries wore down her body; Aarohi recalled the depressive, almost psychotic spells her mother went through in those times, once accusing her husband of having an affair so he could birth a son and move closer to salvation.

She told me she wished her parents had gotten separated.

But I told her, from experience, that would hardly have guaranteed happiness for families like ours.

I suppose both our stories gave each other solace that there was no easy way out anyway.

Wow! The divinely ordained subjugation of women, the creation of intense inner conflict and madness, the obsession with one's status and the free servants—the Brahminical patriarchy has it all! And we haven't even touched upon how it usurps women of their own sexuality.

It really is a miracle I didn't too strongly internalize those ideas that besmirched the idea of female sexuality. It may have had to do with being a fat child until I turned sixteen, so that my asexual court jester persona was my dominant mask through school. But by the time I 'turned hot' after size zero, ensconced in a campus thousands of kilometres away from my parents, with six times as many men as women, a new dimension of my existence opened up.

With the characteristic disinhibition of my adolescent self, I performed my first blowjob in the back row of a movie theatre in Andheri West, to the (presumed? assured?) delight of my first bf. We later lost our virginity to each other in my bedroom at home, when my parents went to Shirdi for a weekend.

I know! Gasp!

This general audacity fuelled my twenties, which also saw

my first orgasm, my first one-night stand, my questionable first-date putouts, my one lame night of lesbianism with a good friend, my initiation into masturbation and porn, where the lesbianism continued, so that by the time I was in my late twenties, any boy I truly liked might be able to say, 'She was a lady in the streets and a freak in the sheets— of paper. But sometimes in bedsheets too.'

I may be exaggerating for the sake of my character on paper. But these are monumental feats of normalcy for the kind of education I'd received in sexuality and intimacy. Amma was so awkward about sex and the human anatomy that I found out about periods first from school—like many Indian girls, I'm sure—and when I asked her why she didn't tell me, she assured me that she was going to. More than a decade later, through the opening scene of the film *Masaan*, she squirmed at the frustrated lovers on-screen. 'What kind of film is this?'

When *Desperative Housewives* played on Star World once, she stopped in front of the television to tell me that she didn't want me watching 'such kind of shows'. English shows, basically.

'Everyone in school watches,' I'd said—the key, as always, to getting my parents to relent.

It was no different for Mira, whose mother attended her school farewell and asked, 'Why are these boys putting their arm over you?'

'In her mind, dating was about talking and holding hands, max,' said Mira. 'She used to caution me that "boys will take advantage of you", they are sex-crazed, be very careful. There was no consideration of what *I* might want, that I myself might want to explore these things.'

Like my parents, hers were paranoid about kids having sex. Mira's clothing was policed at home—'you can't be seen around boys like that!'—leading to a widely relatable Indian-

WHAT IS LOVE? BABY, DON'T HURT ME   207

woman phenomenon: wearing one thing while leaving the house, with another actual outfit to change into outside. So unsafe if you think about it.

This confusion sown in our upbringings continues in adulthood. 'Now she wants me to go out and meet boys, just so that she can marry me off,' said Mira.

But how are kids—girls and boys—with such bucketfuls of internalized shame supposed to feel okay about sex, their bodies, the other genders?

I first learnt about sex at the age of eleven, when a group of girlfriends gathered near the building lobby to listen to the one girl who supposedly knew what was up.

'Do you know how your parents gave birth to you?' she asked.

'At Isabella hospital in Chennai?' I said.

'Nooo. Like how did your mom get pregnant with you?'

A pause of *some kind* followed.... I wish I had the right adjective for it.... Anyway, my friend lowered her voice but spoke with certainty.

'Lick your ass,' she said.

I was very confused.

The next day, everyone in school seemed different. There was a new club in town, an original #IfYouKnowYouKnow gang, as it were. Girls and boys who *knew* would be recognized by another student holding up a 'C' to the forehead in their presence—'C' for Corrupt.

You were Corrupted once you knew about sex.

If it was like this in a moderately upscale school in Mumbai in the new millennium, it was probably worse in most parts of the country. Meghna Trivedi, who grew up in Haryana, said that 'women from the North [of India]...we're very repressed. It's unheard of to have sexual encounters before marriage. Even otherwise, it's frowned upon.' Like me, she was exposed to her anatomy, her 'nether regions', by a boyfriend, who was like, 'How do you not know this?'

'And I was like, "I was dancing for the annual function in the ninth standard when they taught this chapter,"' quipped Meghna—like it would have made a difference to attend anyway. Because of the attitudes around her, 'none of us had guy friends,' she said. 'Even if you are seen talking to boys too much, you'd be judged. Till now, no male friend has ever entered my house. At my own wedding, my mother told me to only hug my female friends, not my male friends.' But by then, Meghna was old enough to know that she wasn't answerable to her mother or her husband about this.

Coming from such environments, watching anything remotely explicit at home involves performing discomfort, as if out of learned respect for the idea that sexuality is evil and awkward. In my heart, I never bought into it, believing that whatever occurred naturally—and, in this case, consensually—could hardly be morally wrong. And for someone who tried to be funny all the time, an exaggerated sluttiness was an easy yet still unusual way to get laughs.

'My clothes are as loose as my morality'; 'I'm the drama club randi'—the uncouth Hindi word for 'slut', anticipating whatever someone might say about me talking to boys, even seniors; 'Women are only good for seventy things, you know... cooking, and sixty-nine!'—I'd go around saying things like that.

It wasn't for much political or historical understanding then, but I was drawn to ironically accept what society considered most shameful, especially for women. I later saw my sense of humour following—much less dangerously, of course—in the spirit of other women who reclaimed their sexual instincts at the risk of wrath and outrage.

The Malayalam novels *Outcaste* and *Pratikara Devata* fictionalize the sensational trial of a Namboodiri Brahmin woman for unapologetically sleeping around—in 1905. Her case rocked the kingdom of Kochi, spawning both reformist movements and conservative paranoia, and even generated its own conspiracy theories. The tale is one of delicious revenge.

A 'smarthavicharam'—meaning 'inquiry into the conduct'—was a ritually sanctioned court procedure to excommunicate Namboodiri Brahmin women accused of sexual misconduct, as defined by the 'sankarasmirti', or Brahmin law. The Namboodiri, the priestly class of Kerala, consolidated their landholdings by permitting only the eldest son in a family to marry other women of the Nambudiri caste.[23] He could have multiple marriages with them, but his younger, unmarried brothers could satisfy their needs only via 'sambantham' (sexual relations) with lower-caste Nair women (who were actually still upper-caste in the overall hierarchy).

But Namboodiri women, married or unmarried, had no say in their own sexuality. In fact, the Antharjanam's entire life revolved around preserving her virginity: she was not to see men or be seen by them, including her own father and her brothers. Her morning bath, prayer, and kitchen-work were the only activities allowed to her. She could travel to temples or to meet immediate relatives, but in the presence of a maidservant.

Women who deviated from the Namboodiri norms were put on trial through the smarthavicharam, which was conducted by village caste council in six methodical stages that would put any modern judiciary to shame.[24] It started with an interview of the maidservant about the antharjanam's supposed sexual misdeeds. If this 'prima facie' evidence was found, the accused wife was locked up in a cell and tortured, often by her own family, to confess to her affairs. She might be wrapped up in a mat and rolled off a rooftop, or exposed to rats and snakes. If she finally succumbs and admits her guilt, she becomes 'santhanam', or inanimate. This lifeless object is still made to name her 'jaarans', though, who will be identified through her recall of their genetalia, any marks or moles in private areas. The smarthan, her interrogator, goes and verify these details, and the men too are subject to an acid test at the local temple.[25] The sex offenders are then ceremonially outcasted, after which the trial team partakes in a 'shubhabhojanam'—'the good meal'.

If the accused were found innocent somehow, they could also participate in the meal.

Stuff like this actually happened. The smarthavicharam was an invention by the Namboodiri, for the Namboodiri, and of the Namboodiri, an internal regulation meant to control their women. When successfully executed, the smarthavicharam would signal the efficacy of their methods, their elaborate psyops to control human sexuality and hold power. Every day of the trial involved feasting at the hands of the accused woman's family, making it an expensive affair for them, incentivizing them to thus torment their own women to extract a confession.[26]

The last known smarthavicharam took place in 1918, but the most legendary one happened on 15 July, 1905. The cunning of the accused antharjanam, Thatrikutty, is apparently felt to this date. Her story is shrouded in mystery: she may have been married off at eleven, or thirteen, or eighteen years of age, and nobody knows why she slept with sixty-four men, knowing she would face consequences.[27] Her husband, who was decades her senior, is said to have brought other women and prostitutes home, or to have widowed her.

Either way, far from being the ideal Brahmin widow, Thatrikutty revealed at her smarthavicharam that she was sexually harassed by, or had sex with, thirty Namboodiris, twelve Ambalavasis, eleven Nairs, ten Iyers, and one Syrian Christian. These men ranged from fourteen to eighy-five years old, comprising Brahmins as well as Sudras, some renowned scholars and artists, and also her close relatives, such as her father and her uncle. Thatri confirmed their identities by unrepentantly recalling 'moles, discolouration, warts and scars' on her paramours' genitalia, or the exact time and place of the adultery. The infamous rumour is that the trial was ended abruptly by the king conducting it, when he suspected that Thatri was just about to name him too.

Her life after the trial is equally contentious. Many of the accused men fled the village from shame, and Thatri herself may have married a Christian man, or a Muslim, or an Anglo-Indian, or settled down in Charakudy in a riverside home, or in Coimbatore, or in Tamil Nadu until the age of eighty.

However it started and ended, Thatri's case certainly shook Kochi. Her name was evoked by later survivors of sexual violence, a role model who exposed and destroyed the most powerful Brahmin families in Kochi. The *Malayala Manorama*, which reported on the case from mid-1905 to -1906, described her as 'unrepentantly 'sinful', calculating, ruthlessly bold and outspoken, someone who could argue 'like a barrister' and defeat her opponents. Thatri had used the basis of her oppression, her policed sexuality, to turn the spotlight on the hypocritical and misogynistic men who slept around with women, usually with no repercussions.

The whore is dead, long live the whore.

You'd think that the architects of these systems, the Brahmin men, would at least be happy. For all the psychological manipulations they deploy on their kin, you'd believe that whatever they subjected themselves to would at least be worth it to them.

But there is little evidence to support this.

In addition to the personal experiences of everyone who featured in this chapter, a famous Kannada novel makes the point well. In *Samskara*—literally rite of passage, or ritual, preparation, transformation, or death rites—U. R. Ananthamurthy explores how the death of a Brahmin man causes his kin, and their 'honour' and 'purity', to unravel. The dead man, Narannappa, was boisterous and uncontrollable, violating every orthodoxy of his religion by drinking liquor, eating meat, abandoning his Brahmin wife to live with a lower-caste woman named Chandri, and fraternizing with Muslims. But despite this life of antagonizing the powers that be, his community does not excommunicate him, the way they would a woman or a widow.

'Even if he gave up Brahminism, Brahminsim cannot leave him,' says one of the Brahmins, debating how to handle his death rites. Unable to eat or resume life in the agraharam until they properly dispose of the dead body, they are pulled towards resolutions that threaten the religion. If they decide to perform Naranappa's death rites as they would any Brahmin's, 'the impurity must also be cleared—therefore all his property, silver and gold must be offered to the monastery, to Lord Krishna.' But the Brahmin men are reluctant to part with this wealth. They fret over their dilemmas, growing increasingly 'hangry', until even Praneshacharya, the holiest of them all, abandons Brahminism. Unable to find a solution to Naranappa's unique case, he sleeps with Chandri, the lower-caste woman that Naranappa was also into.

'I felt disgust for my wife. I drank coffee in a common shop in a fair. I went to see a cock-fight. I lusted after Padmavati. Even at a time of mourning and pollution, I sat in a temple line with Brahmins and ate a holy feast,' Praneshacharya thinks. 'This is my truth. Not a confession of wrongs done.'

Brahmin men are supposed to be holy mediators between man and the divine, but they are as base as any mortal, secretly thirsting for money, food, and women. If they just admitted and lived by it, that'd be okay. But they too are forced to become distant from their authentic selves—which may be queer, or not about cleanliness and godliness, or not about studying well and being good at math, or whatever are the pressures of being a Brahmin male.

But they are forced to deny this, forced to perform the virtue and high status that they are meant to embody. This makes everything worse. Virtue is the kind of thing that is undermined by any imitation of it.

7

GOD: MUST I BELIEVE IN THEY/THEM?

*'To see the world as it is requires understanding
that no single book, map, or system can contain it.
All our explanations are drafts, awaiting revisions that
will never end.'*

—Jorge Luis Borges

Some of my earliest memories are of my skepticisms about
god. I remember asking my grandmother, when I was less
than five years old: if God is everywhere, why do we only
take our chappals off outside temples? Shouldn't we perhaps
never wear chappals?

The matter of convenience in worship seemed to be a
recurring pattern. I didn't believe my mother when she said that
Ganesha would poke my eye at night if I lied. I might have
gone so far as to test him with some of my earliest fictions.

Understandably, it has been downhill since then between
me and this idea of God. As a passionate environmentalist
between the ages of eleven and thirteen, when I stopped
using the geyser to save our planet, I was irritated that
idols of Ganesha were dumped each year into the sea.
Ganesh Chaturthi was responsible for so much rabid, selfish
pollution—why would such an almighty figure demand mass
replication in plaster-of-Paris format? Didn't he see what this
was doing to us?—and I didn't enjoy the necessary darshans

with my parents to some ten crowded temples in his name.

Somehow, this omnipresent god wasn't the same everywhere. He was demanding, and he didn't dispense goodness unconditionally—only to those who gave him adulation and riches.

And then I visited Tirupati.

Tirupati—'tiru' meaning sacred, and 'pati' meaning abode (and also husband)—is home to the Tirumala Venkateshwara and other historic Hindu temples. These are the world's richest Hindu temples, visited by hundreds of thousands of devotees every year, who donate more than ₹20 million *per day*, as of 2023. The legend from the Puranas is that Lord Venkateshwara once lent 11.4 million gold coins to Lord Balaji for his marriage to Padhmavati. Now, people donate to the temple so that Lord Balaji can clear his loan.

My uncle and his family were with us for this trip. My aunt had shaved her head in advance. It was a memorable day on which I started calling myself an atheist, a term I'd picked up from my fellow atheist friend in school, Garima. Standing in that large queue at an unknown distance from some head shrine, surrounded by throngs of fervid worshippers, I realized, sweating and hungry, that no god should be so unattainable.

How could such an expensive, partial, ritualistic god be real? He seemed like any other invention of the people, some external incentive for good behaviour around which money and status could be organized.

Typical humanity.

When I got back to school, I told everyone I'd become an atheist at the Tirupati temple. They didn't grasp the import of my announcement. But for me, it was definitive.

A staunch rationalist I became in the years that followed, reading Ayn Rand, studying science, pleased by the exactness of the material world. What you see is what you get. You come up with explanations for what you observe, and if you can prove that the explanation holds for subsequent such observations, you know why something occurs, and how. You're a god yourself.

What need do you have of an imaginary all-knowing figure to explain reality—who, by the way, can never be subjected to and verified by this scientific method?

Thus I gallivanted about, frowning upon other copes, such as the ones my mother sought over the years. She used to diligently recite the Hanuman Chalisa, some of which I now know by heart. Another was astrology and numerology. She used to write her own name multiple times a day upon a colleague's recommendation—some such colleague was always an astrologer and a musician by hobby—who said that her fate could be explained by the way she spelled her name. I felt horrible, but also noticed she found comfort in something we once had more in common—books. On her shelf was *The Obstacle is The Way* by Ryan Holiday, whose brand of stoicism I too explored through the pandemic, as I tried to cope with not having the life I wanted, in the face of potential death.

Accept reality.

The lore in my family was that our fate had to do with the number eight. In Vedic astrology, eight is ruled by Saturn, a stern planet, the harbinger of suffering, the enforcer of discipline through trials and tests. My mother and I were both born on the day eight, which apparently made the number slightly more auspicious for us, but nonetheless defining. The struggle was real. She'd had a peaceful childhood, with a stable and kind father who had been an automobile engineer at *the* Massachusetts Institute of Technology. I never met him. He used to buy her books, which she read avidly. She watched shows like *I Love Lucy* growing up. She was academically excellent—I can only imagine how much, knowing her discipline now—and she had many admirers, from what I've been told by our relatives.

When she got married, she was still in law college. Appa was with her through it.

We now know happened in the years after. But we still don't understand it, I think.

An astrologer had advised them against the marriage, but another told them to go ahead. Amma believed that the second half of her life, as a 'number 8', had compensated the idyllic first half. She hopes the reverse will be true for me. An astrologer I consulted in my thirtieth year told me to help orphans, perhaps by donating money to them or writing about their plight, so as to bring about a 'karmic correction' in my fate. I'd consulted him after a series of romantic failures, which left me wondering if I'd ever meet someone, or be able to get over what seemed to be one of my biggest psychological handicaps from childhood: going after 'tall, thin, and slightly effeminate' men who seemed to really love me but who were unable to consummate a proper relationship—for whom I still discarded those who might be proper mates, even if I 'felt nothing' for them.

Classic.

Perhaps I have subliminally clung to this '8splanation' whenever I've been struck down by events. Having to go to the hospital nearly every semester of college, having a consistently problematic father, and this peculiarly difficult life with expulsions and accidents and movie-like tropes made me wonder what caused my suffering. Only a grand explanation could excuse it. I had to derive meaning from it, and I was waiting for a utopia where the rewards would be commensurate with what I'd gone through.

It didn't seem to me a common fact of life: suffering, *dukkha.*

What was happening to me was *my* curse.

It was special, I was special. It was my purpose, so it had to be big.

I couldn't just suffer because that's what life sometimes involves.

But grandiosity is a defence against depression. And depression is a defence against the deep, too-strong pain of losing your own self. And losing yourself is a defence against an upset parent, whose needs had to subsume your own.

Of course, I was unaware of all this then, of what was going on beneath the surface.

But I became aware of it when I hit a wall. A wall that came crashing down on me.

I thought I was doing everything right, operating as sincerely and efficiently as I could. I had given up on my father, I'd done my best to be there for my mother. I fielded his blows without retaliating, and her over-reliance by managing my life and problems independently. I was always swallowing my feelings without conscious awareness, through achievement or substance or some other common compulsion. There was a ferocious engine of interconnected neuroses driving me, which I wanted to temper but not eliminate. Through my many 'wins', my question to myself was always: 'How can you get the same results without the anxiety, the panic, and the lack of self-belief that demands you prove it wrong in order to feel alright?'

Low self-esteem. Narcissism. Rigidity. Situational depression.

The usual.

These were the quotidian diagnoses of my first proper therapist, who told me about Cognitive Behavioural Therapy, a typically material-world-solution to unpleasant feelings and problems: identify triggers, observe reactions, and intervene every time, so that you gradually displace the habit of assuming, and acting out, the worst. This is an exact but ponderous method to retrain your nervous system. And it did help, in its limited way. Brother #2 may not have noticed, but Amma did see that I was less angry.

But I was less angry not necessarily because I was dealing with my anger healthily—by neither suppressing it nor letting it explode—but only because others saw less of it.

For what I had shored up, I needed something more wholesale.

I found it amidst the ruins of the wall that crashed, after yet another episode of 'doing everything right but getting cheated by life'. The pandemic had struck, calling me to action, and my solution to engineering-and-MBA-just-to-make-parents-happy-and-prove-how-sane-I-am was to attack my new, chosen dreams with the same rigour and goal-programming that had served me well so far.

But this time, it wasn't working. I had to figure out what I was doing wrong to be so cheated by life.

Where did I have to change?

Vipassana.

It came to me when I remembered a friend who had apologized to me—well, as close to it as she could come without saying 'sorry'—after we once fought. If Vipassana could make her acknowledge her part in undesirable outcomes, it could help me too, right?

I Googled the word and found dhamma.org, which said that 'Vipassana', meaning 'to see clearly', was a 'purification technique' that could bring about a 'transformation of personality'—just what I needed—through the meditation style discovered by the Buddha 2,500 years ago. It was lost to India 500 years later, and brought back by S. N. Goenka, who had found a teacher in Myanmar, his home country then. After trying everything to cure himself of migraines, Goenka, a successful businessman at the peak of the rat-race, almost inoculated to morphine, came across the technique and found himself gradually cured and peaceful.

Wonderful.

Vipassana—Vipashyana—Bipasha Basu. No, sorry, this isn't a laughing matter. If nothing was sacred to me before, my attitude was personally corrected by the Sacred itself. I was put on a path, one whose choicelessness has been written about: the path is seen as something that unfolds naturally, as the mind leans towards it; instead of an act of individual will, it is almost as if 'meditation' chooses the 'meditator'.[1]

Unbeknownst to me, desperate for help, with no one to turn to and no one to trust, I'd stepped on a long and winding stairway to heaven.

Except heaven is not heaven, as a gift for good behaviour, nor hell, as a punishment for bad.

They call it enlightenment. Liberation. *Nirvana.*

If you're like I was back then, you'd heard of the word 'nirvana', but had little idea what it meant.

And when I found out, I was shocked. 'Purification technique' that would 'transform the personality'? Who approved this marketing copy, or their claims? One part of the 10,000 different parts of me that were surfacing and dissolving managed to register, 'I didn't sign up for this shit bro.'

But it remains the best thing that happened to me.

I have no choice but to say this.

Vipassana is taught in silent meditation retreats. You submit your belongings and commit to ten days of phone-lessness, outside-food-lessness, and most-else-lessness. You cut yourself off from the world, and don't even make eye contact with your fellow meditators, so as to not, loosely put, create any new energy. You start paying attention to your breath—breath after breath after breath—until someday, in some course, as Goenka explains, you 'break the blood-brain barrier'.

Your conscious mind, which is typically so unaware of what's happening inside you, comes in contact with your subconscious mind.

You see the pockets of energy, or psychic complexes, that were driving you outside of your awareness, and realize you are one integrated system of mind and matter. We are not divided beings with a separate mind and a separate body, where the former controls and directs the latter. That very idea, so fundamental to the so-called scientific and rational world, is responsible for much devastation and heedlessness. It dates back to the fifteenth century, when René Descartes, the French philosopher, scientist, and mathematician, was negotiating a deal with the Pope. In order to get the human bodies he needed for dissection and study, he agreed he wouldn't have anything to do with the soul, the mind, or emotions—those aspects of human existence would remain in the exclusive realm of the Church.

But, as a result of this bargain, the conceptual foundations of Western science and medicine were set to be one-sided and incomplete forever. Allopathy today is mainly about treating physical symptoms, not the disease underlying them. You could buy any number of medicines for relief from migraines, depression, or psychosis, without ever eliminating their root cause, which could be trauma, a fragmented sense of self, or 'something else in the mind'. This is great for the pharmaceutical industry, of course, but not for life.

'Mental problems'—two stigmatic words in the Indian language, like 'ghar jamai' (house husband). Boomers, and perhaps even some millennials, believe that feelings and emotions are easily dismissible, nothing but unnecessary roadblocks to the sheer force of willpower/mind. As long as you 'set your mind to it', you can claw your way out of anything. But ignoring your feelings has steep costs, as can be gleaned from the word itself. The noun comes from the verb, 'feeling', literally implying an action, meaning feelings must be *felt*, or else—

In *The Molecules of Emotion*, neuroscientist Candace Pert wrote about the struggles of getting her research recognized in the 1970s and 80s, when mainstream science wouldn't contend with anything that couldn't be measured. Emotions, the mind, and the soul were all yet 'non-things', woo matters, and it was challenging for women, already thought to be the 'hysterical', 'emotional' species, to conduct serious science on the subject. But Pert discovered the literal molecules of emotion, such as the opioid receptor, which is the cellular binding site for endorphins in the brain. By identifying these neuropeptides, Pert revealed that emotions are not abstract psychological states, but are embedded throughout the body in biochemical form. These small protein-like molecules transmit signals between neurons and cells, and their appropriate flow in the human body is essential to multiple systems, from the brain to the immune system. The mind and body are one vast communicative network shaped by its mental, emotional, and physical parts.

Repressed emotions don't just disappear, Pert found. 'Based on the drama and rapidity of some therapeutic transformations, I believe they are stored in the body, the unconscious mind, via the release of neuropeptide ligands, and memories are held in their receptors,' she wrote, recalling the case of a woman whose hunched shoulder began to heal itself after she relived an incest trauma that had been buried for years. The proper expression of emotions is tied to the proper flow of peptides through the body. Suppressing your feelings disturbs the pristine, intelligent psychosomatic, physiological being that you are.

At the extreme end, repression causes cancer. The idea has been around since the 1940s, when Wilhelm Reich proposed that cancer was the result of a failure to express emotions, especially sexual emotions. Compromised immunity goes hand in hand with self-denial, as the immune system is supposed to define the boundaries of the self, to distinguish between what belongs to it and what doesn't, so it as to know what is to be protected, and from what. Consistently avoiding your truths and emotions confuses your body about what is You and what is Other.[2]

The body does keep the score.

Left unchecked, you could lose.

That's where my mindbody was, on the fourth day of my first Vipassana course, twisting and twitching from emotional pain that had been buried so long that it had been manifesting in migraines and asthma and psychosomatic issues, for years, until it was all called forth—pain after pain, complex after complex, saṅkhāra after saṅkhāra—commencing the wholesale clearance I'd so desperately needed.[3]

My emotional exorcism had begun. And the interconnectedness of all beings, the mysticism of reality, the laws of the universe, and its specific manifestations within me: it was all opening up to me.

The key was not reacting. Whatever sensation you observed on your mindbody as you scanned it, your function was to both be aware of it and equanimous to it. In this way, by steadfastly not reacting, such as with aversion to any felt pain, or with craving to any felt pleasure, you stopped creating new sensations, new pain, new pleasure, allowing the old, stored up stocks of pain and pleasure to resurface.

Then, at the surface, as you remain aware of sensations without reacting, they evaporate.

Little by little, in this fashion, you exorcise yourself through equanimous self-observation.

It's pleasingly scientific. Your consciousness is transformed. At some point, there may be a state of where the You that observes You no longer exists. Instead, You become One with the grand luminosity where everything is together, and nothing is separate.

Non-duality.

Each course advances your consciousness like this, while helping you become more and more aware and equanimous. The trick is not to stop at ten-day courses, and to keep practising daily, until eventually, the proposition of Dhamma goes, you've done so many courses over so many lifetimes that even as a layman, a householder, a non-renunciate on the Buddha's 'middle path', you reach the ultimate destination.

Liberation. Enlightenment. *Nirvana.*

Vipassana saved my life. I was 'saven', chosen by the path, perhaps.

But like I said, I didn't *know* I'd signed up to leave some cycle of life and death in those 10 days—I didn't even know if I could agree that we were in some such cycle. But the belief grew intuitively and rapidly, with each release and every touch of the divine.

I learnt a lot during my first ten-day course—it was like rapidly downloading a 12 GB software and hardware upgrade—and the divine hand also told me what this cycle was, this state of discontent.

Samsara.

Religion and spirituality are the only industries that get away with never having to prove their marketing claims. Any other industry, toothpaste or biscuits, has to substantiate that their product really can whiten teeth '3x' or equal the nutrition of a glass of milk.

But the faith-based industries never declare on their website that their 'purification technique' implies you will literally reprogram your biological reaction to craving and aversion—so automatic that they are the building blocks of even the most unicellular life forms—by forcibly training an equanimous response to every relived craving and aversion, so that you gradually vaporize the complexes that grip your psyche.

To the point that there are no more complexes to release. So that you are just not born again.

What an extreme way to avoid suffering. Just don't exist. The Buddha was hardcore.

Now, as you release a saṅkhāra, a narrative stream may appear alongside them, cementing the interconnectedness of mind and body, the emotionality of what the body stores. When an old pain in my knee surfaced, the thoughts in my mind were about how much I wanted to write when I incurred it, working as I was at the Prestigious Big Company from early in the morning to late at night. But because of the injury, I'd gotten to take some time off work. I used it to write the piece about the Kafkaesque CAA/NRC times.

Had my body acted against itself to get its basic needs fulfilled?

Did my body really have to hurt itself for me to get my own attention?

The saṅkhāra or mental formations we experience could be from our reactions to external situations, the events of this or that lifetime. In one of the discourses that punctuate each day's meditation, Goenka jokes that people coming to Vipassana retreats expect something grand. Verbalizations, visualizations, something tantric or exotic, at the least. But instead, they're told to focus on the breath and their own bodies, which seem to only produce pain. 'They come and complain: "Goenka, what is this sweating and heat and itching!"' he laughs. 'If I wanted this, I could have stayed at home!'

Understandable. But as I practised, this aspect of the technique appealed most to me: the fact that it was hard work, and totally scientific. Nobody else could sit on your behalf and be aware of your sensations and react equanimously. 'You have to work out your own salvation,' Goenka says. You cannot bribe anyone or anything with money or affection; in fact, the result of the technique is a gradual erosion of several concepts widely believed as True. The faculties of devotion and reverence morph into more sincere avatars; there is a de-pedestalization—of life itself, of its promises, of other people, of yourself, of all constructs. The technique asks not for belief or faith in anything but itself, and it proves itself to you, as a result of which more faith, belief, and devotion naturally follow.

Another thing I learnt was why the Vipassana centres and institutes function entirely on donations from people who've completed courses. Old students had benefitted so much that they not only returned for more retreats, but funded and sustained it, so that there could be more free retreats, food, accommodation, staff—all included. The idea was that the moment you charged for something, you would be on high alert of the wrong kind. 'The food isn't good'; 'this bed is too small'—the focus is not on meditation and liberation, but on value for money. But by remaining free,

Dhamma centres around the world establish the purity of their motive—to truly relieve people of their suffering—and they cater to people regardless of their identity, class, or belief systems. Nobody has to worry about being marginalized or discriminated against or fleeced in their search for therapy. The technique is egalitarian.

The Buddha himself kept applying it until he reached enlightenment at the age of thirty-five, having left his princely home six years before. As he stepped out of his home and saw disease, death, and suffering everywhere, he decided to find a 'deathless' state, removed from the dukkha—the unsatisfactoriness—inherent to human existence.[4] After years of building on the meditation techniques of the shramanas and rishis around him, Siddhartha Gautama attained nibbana on a full moon night, while sitting under a tree on the banks of a river in Bodh Gaya.

As he exhumed more and more saṅkhāras, going deeper into his mindbody, the Buddha saw streams of consciousness not only from his current life, but also his past life, and the one before that, and then another, until all at once, at the moment of enlightenment, he realized some grand truths.

Anekajatisamsaram
sandhavissam anibbisam
gahakaram gavesanto
dukkha jati punappunam.

'Through countless births in this cycle of existence, I have run in vain,' realized the Buddha. 'Seeking the builder of this house, again and again, I have faced the discomfort of new birth.'

Gahakaraka! ditthosi
puna geham na kahasi
sabba te phasuka bhagga
gahakotam visankhatam

visankharagatam cittam
tanhanam khayamajjhaga

Sabbe sankhara anicca'ti
yada pannaya passati,

'Oh housebuilder! Now you are seen.'
The Buddha realizes he himself is the builder of 'this' house.
And 'you shall not build a house again for me,' he decides.

'All your beams are broken,
the ridgepole is shattered,
The mind has become freed from conditioning.
The end of craving is reached.

Impermanent are all compounded things, when
one perceives this with insight.'[5]

Basically, in simple terms, all existence is 'conditioned'—or
caused. By our own selves. It is caused, like anything that
is caused, by some action. Our sankharas are the product
of our actions, our kamma, which describes both the action
(physical, vocal, or mental), and also the effects of the action.
In Buddhism, intentions are mental actions—they have actual
weight and energy. They come under 'citta', which is the
seat of consciousness and the quality of awareness that lies
beneath thought and emotion, where intentions, perceptions,
and emotional responses arise. Citta is the root of your kamma;
purifying it of unwholesome intentions (like greed, anger,
ignorance) leads to liberation from unconsciously generating
ill-will, and ultimately from kamma itself.[5]

Another Buddhist thesis I was shocked and fascinated by
equally: kamma is less about 'good' or 'bad', but more about
your experience of existence. Depending on your kamma,
your birth takes place in one of the six realms of samsara.
The human realm is considered to be special for its range of

pleasure and suffering, so you can see through the transience of both these states and work towards getting liberated. The godly realms, above the human realm, can be so pleasurable that working towards nibbana may feel unnecessary. And the three 'bad' realms in Buddhist cosmology are the animal realm, where life is driven by impulse and instinct. In the hungry ghosts realm, beings exist as restless spirits with too much craving and attachment. And the hell realm is where you end up for theft, lying, adultery, and other 'evil kamma'.

When I first heard of this classification, I was couldn't believe the Buddha was suggesting these realms actually existed. Schools of Buddhism differ on whether they are real, physical cosmological planes, or just states of mind that each of us inhabit, more than one at a time, in this very life. Living with addiction, for example, is said to be like the hungry ghost realm, where pretas are perpetually insatiable, ghostly waifs with big bellies that are never full.

But in addition to its staggering implications about the material world, karma has trickier connotations in the Indian context. Hinduism uses it to justify the position of the lower-castes, ascribing their status to their past actions. Internalizing this leads to a cruel, existential self-doubt, as you'll see in this ten-year-old girl's musing about her fate: 'I wondered what I could have done in a past life that was so bad that I would be convicted as filthy and unclean in this one. Was I a murderer, a rapist, or a thief? ....What did I do wrong? I really want to apologize. If I hurt somebody, I want to know. I don't think I'm untouchable. I don't feel it, but you know, if I deserve it, I want to know....'[7]

The girl is Thenmozhi Soundarajan, now founder of Equality Labs and the author of The Trauma of Caste. Raised Hindu and Christian, Soundarajan 'struggled with tremendous amounts of suffering and anguish', converting to Buddhism as an adult, in the tradition of B. R. Ambedkar.

Ambedkar, a lawyer and the architect of the Indian Constitution and a champion for Dalit rights, had done away with the concept of karma in his refashioning of Buddhism. He was uncomfortable with how it was used to justify caste oppression. But karma and its truth and merit are diluted by what caste made of it. For the Buddha, karma was simply the law of cause and effect. Intentional actions—whether physical, verbal, or mental—create consequences that shape one's future experiences. The implication is that every individual is responsible for their own experience of existence, and the power to 'come out of' one's karma lies only with them.

Karma implies ethical responsibility and autonomy. But, unlike the major traditional schools of Buddhism, Ambedkar also rejected the Four Noble Truths, the most foundational doctrine in the Buddha's teachings, believing they led to a glorification of individual salvation.[8] (This isn't exactly true. While Theravada Buddhism commits to asceticism as a result of the Four Noble truths, Mahayana Buddhists renounce their liberation to enable other beings to achieve it too, through compassion and selfless service.)

Ambedkar's vision for Buddhism was as a vehicle for collective liberation, freeing people from social inequality and caste-based oppression. In 1936, he declared that although he was born a Hindu, he would not die one. He studied the major world religions, seeking one that would provide liberty, equality, and fraternity. He rejected Christianity and Islam for their theism and supernaturalism, but found in Buddhism the seeds of what he wanted. He saw in the Buddha a 'common man' who offered practical, scientific, and compassionate guidance for life on earth, there and then, here and now. Here was another social reformer fighting against India's Brahminism, whose teachings focused on the individual capacity for moral effort and self-determination—so much so that Ambedkar felt free to reinterpret the Buddha by going against him.

Bold.

In 1956, Ambedkar converted to Navayana Buddhism alongside 380,000 followers, marking the date, 14 October, as the Dhammachakra Pravartan Divas. He died six weeks later, before he the huge conversion ceremonies he had planned across India. But his legacy flourishes as hundreds of thousands of Dalits convert to Buddhism every year. Ambedkar's Navayana, literally 'new', Buddhism called for collective social action, rejecting individualistic mores, even as it was conceived from an individual's—Ambedkar's—singular vision.

Ironic.

Some 90 per cent of Indian Buddhists identify as Dalits, and half are members of Navayana, with a high presence in Maharashtra, where Navayana Buddhism—and the RSS too—originated.[9] Mission Jai Bheem aims to bring 100 million people 'back to the original culture' of Buddhism by 2025.

Although Navayana Buddhism strips Buddhism of its essence, it is a radical social philosophy, akin to the principles of European enlightenment, that has been a source of hope, confidence, and principled action for an otherwise disenfranchised population. It is often their only option, because anti-conversion laws in multiple states penalize conversion to Christianity or Islam. But Buddhism is a 'sub-sect' of Hinduism, according to Article 25 of the Indian Constitution, and it presents a bit of a Catch-22 for staunch Indian conservatives. They may not want Hinduism to lose followers, but it would also be to Buddhism, one of India's largest cultural exports, and a 'kinda sorta' extension of Hinduism, with the Buddha long casted as an incarnation of the Hindu god Vishnu. Still, converting to Buddhism in 2022, along with hundreds of other Dalits, caused an Aam Aadmi Party minister to resign his seat in the Delhi government, irritated the BJP for 'denouncing Hinduism'.[10] Being not-

Hindu in India has probably never been harder.

Perhaps understandably, Ambedkar was concerned about making his departure from Hinduism explicit. Of the twenty-two vows in his conversion ceremony for Navayana, at least seven are specifically about renouncing Hinduism:

'I do not and shall not believe that Lord Buddha was the incarnation of Vishnu. I believe this to be sheer madness and false propaganda.'

'I shall have no faith in Rama and Krishna, who are believed to be incarnations of God, nor shall I worship them.'

'I shall not allow any ceremonies to be performed by Brahmins.'[11]

This politicism and lack of overt spirituality often make Ambedkarite Buddhism seem like an outlet for hating Hinduism. Insiders exposed to the factions within believe that the vows against Hinduism are a tad extra, either irrelevant or un-strategic.[12] 'What do they mean "All India will become Buddhist"?' said Christopher Queen, a teacher of religion and engaged Buddhism at Harvard. 'The new converts will continue to live in a land of Hindus, Muslims, and all the rest. Ambedkar refocused Buddhist teachings to empower Dalits. But he also persuaded the Hindu majority to adopt a constitution that outlawed untouchability.' The All India Bhikkhu Sangha, a pan-Indian religious society of Bhikkhus, raised objections to the pledges and conversions at the heart of Navayana Buddhism. 'The tradition of conversion to Buddhism has been going on from the time of the Buddha, but it should happen on the basis of Panch Sheela (5 precepts),' said Bhikkhu Pragyadeep, general secretary of the Sangha. 'These kinds of conversion events are not harmonious in nature. They pit religions against each other.'[13]

I think it is entirely reasonable for Dalits to hate their original religion, which, far from being a source of comfort, therapy, or, at the least, some status, instead justified their dehumanization. The caste system is appalling, and Ambedkar was heroic in responding to the needs of his community, not only providing them a schema for a dignified life, but also the foundations for an egalitarian country. Perhaps the adoption of any existing form of Buddhism, such as Mahayana, would have been an insufficient response to the unique challenge that Brahminism presented to the Hindu lower castes. Their resistance may have needed an explicit form of 'fuck you' for the oppression they were embedded in.

Without an especial system to signify just that, they may not have been able to come out of their especial difficulties. Still, Ambedkarite Buddhism, in its search for social and political redressal, ignores what I believe are certain mathematical truths.

Unlike Ambedkar, I came to understand some of the Buddha's ideas and precepts experientially.[14] If you've been told a system's axioms, and have verified some of its resultant theorems, it's hard not to trust the system as a whole, even if a lot of it is still left to explore. This conviction may be what people call faith. But you can arrive at that without such gymnastics of logic too. In this case, therefore, my faith seems unlike faith, a rational consequence of some truths I have seen and experienced.

The axioms of Buddhism—the Four Noble Truths, the concept of kamma, the practise of meditation—remain the truest things I've ever encountered.

The meditation teacher on my first course was a woman in her fifties or sixties, a teacher of English in the outside world. I was later told I was lucky to have her administering my first course—I was told I was lucky and 'special' and 'blessed' many times in those ten days—and I agree, because she was patient with the extreme pain that followed. When I started telling her about my anger, my rocky relationship with my parents, my dependence on substance and achievement, she cut me short, waving a pinched hand before me.

'I know this business all too well, dear. If they love us unconditionally, why can't they love you even if you do what they don't like?' she said.

'But the same applies to us, no? You're not able to love them despite whatever they do either.'

After a lifetime of being unable to trust the systems and adults around me, I carried into the centre all my paranoic Spanish inquisitiveness. I asked her why the five precepts existed—to not harm, to not steal, to not lie, to not perform sexual misconduct, and to refrain from intoxicants—and she said that these weren't absolutisms, but recommendations for establishing an effective meditation practice, to aid the ultimate goal.

'Which is great,' I intellectualized, 'because it prevents the kind of violence that the absolutisms of other religions demand almost by logic.'

She smiled. 'I'm not supposed to indulge you like this. The practice asks you to surrender to the Buddha, the Dhamma, and the Sangha,' she said. 'There are many students waiting to ask questions about the technique. Spending time on those who intellectualize and philosophize is not fair, and it may not even help them.'

I didn't say anything.

'But every student has their own needs and ways of understanding,' she added knowingly.

I was operating in fight-or-flight mode. At breakfast on the third morning, I noticed a sign next to the fruits that said they were only meant for 'old students', or people who had done at least one course. Alarmed by the rule, I took a banana nonetheless, thinking I might get hungry at night. But really, I knew it was a violation, and I wanted to see what would happen to me.

Would I be punished? Would this be an innocent mistake? Was this another 'fake' god?

Later that day, after the last meditation hour, I admitted my theft to the teacher.

'Why did you do that?'

'I felt a bit giddy last night, so I thought it might help me to eat something after 9 p.m..... I don't want it though. It said that it was only for the old students....'

'That's because they don't have an evening meal at 5 p.m., like you do,' she explained. 'They stop after lunch at 12 p.m.' She sized me up, and smiled again.

'Don't do it again, and eat it now happily and go to sleep.'

I did eat the banana happily, knowing there was some reason behind the rule. I went to sleep thinking about my need to break rules, after being let down over and over by institutions whose rules were supposed to guarantee safety—schools, colleges, the state, my family—but had instead hurt and traumatized me.

Every system would be tested with a well-designed provocation. And if its integrity withstood it, I could trust more.

By the ninth day, in the world outside, the essay that still defines by writing career was going viral—unbeknownst to me. Inside, the Dhamma sevikas were calling me 'special' because I was vomiting endlessly and getting headaches and asthma attacks. I found out I was 'releasing saṅkhāras'— mental formations, patterned chunks of bodily sensations— the intense, physical manifestations of my stored trauma, at apparently an unusual rate for someone's first course.

This questioning, this rule-breaking, this inability to trust from having been violated—

I came face to face with its root in my mind.
I was being tricked by myself.

Before the 9 a.m. meditation was to commence one day, I felt the need to speak to the Dhamma teacher. Cross-legged on the cushion in front of her, in her little consultation room, I said, 'Ma'am, I came back from the last session to find the bucket in my bathroom overflowing. But I don't remember turning the tap on.'

She smiled. 'It happens, dear. Sometimes you just turn something on and forget it, no?'

'That doesn't happen to me, ma'am. I feel like I turned the tap on and forgot so that I would miss meditation. Or so that I would come back and see that I'd forgotten. I feel like I'm trying to trick myself. I'm going crazy.'

'It's just a momentary lapse, dear.'

A momentary lapse of reason. That was all. I smiled, relieved. I'd simply forgotten about the tap. There was no hidden agenda here.

'I' had nothing to worry about 'me'.

I got up to leave, but a few steps later, I realized that I had something else to tell her. I went back in.

'Ma'am, one more thing happened.... In the morning, when I was on the toilet, I thought I was going to take a very big shit,' I said. 'But when I looked at it, it was only very small.'

I paused. 'My mind is playing tricks on me.'

'Sanjana, the mind is a monkey. Constantly coming up with thoughts and believing they're so special that you come and tell your teacher about your bowel movements,' she said. 'Think of any thought like a guest in your mind. If an unwanted guest comes in, and you entertain it, imagine what will happen. Some lady has entered your house. She asks you for water, you give it to her. Then she'll ask you to bring the pouffe nearer, so she can stretch her legs.... She stretches her legs. Imagine how comfortable she will get.

'Let it go.

'Go meditate,' she said, as I opened my mouth to say something again.

'And you have this horror-struck expression on your face all the time. Look around you. You are safe. And you are not alone.

'Let it go,' she repeated.

But it felt catastrophic to let my thoughts go. Weren't they very important? I rarely forgot anything. Hypervigilance was my game. Wasn't it dangerous to not remember turning the tap on? Was I having memory loss? Did I have ADHD? She just gave me some special meditation instructions for those with ADHD. Move fast through each body part because your mind works too fast. Why wasn't she worried about me going crazy? Or was I not going crazy? Was my mind just coming up with stories? Just for attention?

Why, my face—even my face—had arranged itself to support the monstrosity of the misleading turd.

Yes. I'd done it my whole life. I'd lived for the story, the mirage, the image, the creation of such artefacts through my being. I would do whatever it took for a good story to be. I had split my parents up to tell the story of my life. I was a raging narcissist who conceived and created images of success and genius and grandiosity and would then do anything to become the person the image demanded, instead of being who I was—with no concern for who I really was.

Why would I do that to myself?

Why would anyone do that?

What kind of mind doesn't care about itself?

Only a mind that hates itself, I realized.

That's why I was so scared of the fan on my first day there. It was a reminder that I could, still, kill myself. I was afraid.

This mind was playing tricks on itself.

So, the key was a mind that didn't hate itself.

That's it: the key is a self that doesn't hate itself.

What is the self?

The first precept came to mind.

A self is something that does not harm itself or others.

A self is something that is kind to itself and others.

A self is kind to itself and others.

A self loves itself and loves others.

A self loves itself and loves others.

A self loves itself and loves others.

A self loves itself and loves others.

A self loves itself and loves others.

A self loves itself and loves others.

A self loves itself and loves others.

And so on and so forth, with each breath of sweet green air, I programmed myself anew.

In those moments of disintegration and reconstitution, I felt like some kind of sentient computer. Faulty programs of conditional love, absorbed from my patriarchal Indian life, were being uninstalled. New, healthy programs were replacing them, designed to generate love and compassion for oneself and all others, given to me by something divine at this centre in the outskirts of Bengaluru.

Of course your fundamental orientation should be love and concern for oneself—for no reason at all—which will only then find its way to others. *Obviously* this is the default state: a self-love that asks for nothing. It is survival.

It's so obvious when you think about it, but society and capitalism have programmed us to believe you have to 'be' something, 'be' someone, through achievements or looks or marital status or your 'personality', in order to 'deserve' love—even your own! What!

But my new default instructions were not being cooked up by other flawed human beings. The five precepts, the idea of karma, these new concepts for a good way of life, were coming from someone far more advanced. They were ready for absorption; we were already living them. This was life. No wonder Goenka referred to the meditation centres as 'tapobhoomi'—'tapas' meaning austerity or spirituality or penance, and 'bhoomi' meaning land.

Buddhism seems to me the best religion almost mathematically, and here follows a kind of colloquial proof for it. If we can agree that the aims of any and all religious life are common, viz. providing a guidebook for life, clarifying what is Good, what is Bad, what happens for not being Good or Bad, providing a therapy for Bad, a recipe for Good, and opening this up to everyone, irrespective of gender, age, sexual orientation, or any other axis of selfhood—then we can evaluate each religion for its propensity to fulfil these conditions.

We've already seen how hierarchal Hinduism is. If it's not hierarchical, it's not quite Hinduism. Islam and Christianity teach that salvation is available only to followers of their own respective gods. Non-followers be damned, quite literally. In Islam, Jannah is attained through iman, or faith, in one God, Allah, and by adhering to the Five Pillars of Islam—the declaration of faith (Shahada), ritual prayer (Salah), almsgiving (Zakat), fasting during Ramadan (Sawm), and pilgrimage to Mecca (Hajj). Believers are judged by their deeds and conformance to Islamic teachings, which are evaluated in the afterlife. There is a lot of moral absolutism to be found in Islamic texts: the Quran (5:38) prescribes amputating a hand as punishment for thieving. Severe penalties follow blasphemy and apostasy (leaving the Islamic faith). Some interpretations of Sharia law call for stoning to death for adultery, and corporal punishment for harming others. And Islamic teachings traditionally view homosexuality as sinful; in some Muslim-majority countries, homosexual acts are punishable by law.

Christians too believe that salvation is available only to those who accept Christ as their saviour, who atoned for humanity's sins with his death and resurrection so that believers could live. The usual sinful acts—lying, thieving, adultery, gluttony, harm—are condemned, and so are 'sins of the heart', like lust and envy. Some denominations of Christianity cite biblical passages like Romans 1:26-27, which views same-sex attraction as 'unnatural' and contrary to God's design. But instead of punitive measures, Christianity emphasizes repentance, confession, compassion, and moral transformation.

Still, like Hinduism, these religions demand faith in something external. Belief is expected of those born into them, instead of eliciting a quantum of arduous, spiritual self-training that naturally produces faith. There is inequality around the axes of gender and sexual orientation, which then becomes the work of reformists and progressives to reconcile. One could argue that the battle between individual inclinations and the demands of religion, or the collective, will always have to be fought, but therein lies an internal contradiction of sorts: if religion should be egalitarian and spiritually democratic, as we decided at the start, there will always be those who feel ashamed, guilty, exiled, and unequal for their natural ways of being when it deviates from what the religion prescribes.

And in most major religions, the rules about Good and Bad, and what happens for any violation, demand pure faith, offering either total reward or punishment. But in Buddhism, the focus is on the intentions behind actions, and the solution is verifiable, rational, and moderate. Instead of punishment and shame, induced by something external, you are to come face to face with reality as it is, in your mindbody, and observe directly the effects of your intentions and actions. This isn't through a lens of fear, but of direct understanding. Feel the mental turbulence or peace that your intentions and actions have created, and recognize that you alone are responsible for the karmic landscape of your life. Cultivate awareness and take responsibility, not because a god demands it, but because your own reality needs it.

For instance, in Buddhism, sex is not thought of as an absolute, bad, immoral act, but something that, like any other action, has an energetic valence to it. So, the reason one must be mindful about it, and any other actions and intoxications, is simple: it just delays enlightenment. Should you seek enlightenment seriously, perhaps minimize meaningless sex; why, the third precept asks you to stay away from sexual misconduct—adultery or sexual assault—but says nothing of consensual sex, no matter what the genders or orientations involved.[15] Similarly, the fifth precept asks you to avoid intoxicants, not for moral, virtuous reasons, but because intoxicants make it harder to follow the first four precepts, which are crucial to the path. It's only with a clean moral and mental slate that the mind is best positioned to concentrate—anyone who has lied, or been rude and hurtful, or at the receiving end of such behaviours, knows how much harder it can be to be mindful, to meditate, to make progress towards wisdom.

But religions apart from Buddhism will never tell you that enlightenment, or a sort of energetic integrity, are why you must stay away from sub-optimal behaviours. Brahminism, Christianity, Islam—they use shame, 'morality', and 'virtue' to force you into behaviours that somebody else has deemed right for you without ever explaining why. Buddhism is clear that for a seeker of enlightenment, it is passion of any sort that is the real enemy. Even an excessive passion for enlightenment, a strong desire to get rid of all desires, defeats its own purpose. Craving and aversion to your current state, whatever it is, only delays the destination. Only real equanimity, in full awareness of that current state, over and over again, can create the progression in consciousness that naturally invites higher states of being.

Hence, the Buddha's 'middle path', the road you walk from who you are to who enlightenment calls you to be. In this way, samsara becomes no different from nirvana; every moment is an opportunity to exercise what you would during meditation.

Observe, don't react.

Be aware, but equanimous, no matter what.

It's difficult. It asks for hard work. And only you are responsible.

Should you happen to stray and commit a 'bad' act, though, because you are, well, human, it's okay, it's not the end of the world, it's not even 'bad', it's just 'unskilful'. As mentioned, your intention, your volition, defines your karma. In the online world, it's fashionable to punish people—via judgement, shaming, through harsh words—for actions, or even views, that have had negative consequences, or are just disagreeable. This is regardless of people's intentions and history, which I think is yet another malady of modern society. We want to feel like we are in control, when we unilaterally decide the moral acumen of a 'wrongdoer' in the public eye, when we ourselves, if confronted by an accusation of wrongdoing, would jump to clarify that it was not our intention to cause trouble. Not even god can predict the consequences of his actions; anyone with a degree of life experience would know that the most well-meaning acts can have disastrous results. Intention, and not just actions and their consequences, needs to be given back its importance in how we think about morality.

Skilful intentions are free from greed, aversion, and delusion, although it is possible to be well-meaning and still act based on delusion. After all, the conscious mind is only a fraction of your psyche's processes, and only people highly advanced on the path can become totally free from the roots of delusion.[16] Delusion, or ignorance, is responsible for the attachment to maya, and your non-renunciation of samsara. Whatever the action, you'll have to bear the karmic consequences, in some form, in some life, perhaps this one, perhaps not. You cannot know how it works fully.

What we do know about karma is that skilful intentions tend towards pleasant results, and unskilful intentions towards painful results. 'The causal principle underlying actions and results is actually very complex,' wrote Thannisaro Bhikkhu, an American Buddhist monk, on how there's no deterministic relationship between an intentional act and its results. The Buddha used karma to explain three things: your experience of pleasure and pain, the level of rebirth you take after death, and what to do to get out of the cycle of rebirth. Beyond that, if you tried to 'work out' your karma, attempting to identify which result came from which action, you'd go crazy.[17]

It doesn't work like a bank account, where the 'negative' stuff is eventually weighed against the 'positive' to determine your given state. Karma is like seeds in the vast field of consciousness, planted with every intention, each seed maturing at a different rate. The size of any seed's harvest depends on several other factors than the intention behind it, such as your actions before and after, or your mind-state when the seed ripens. This is why meditation helps: it alerts you to the present moment, your feelings and intentions, which are often very subtle, or else have us in their grip. This mind-training helps us create positive present karma, to deal positively with whatever past negative karma may be materializing in this moment, and eventually to go beyond the karma of intentions entirely.

The story of Angulimala is a famous example of how karma is not fair, contrary to the idea of justice it evokes—and why that may be for the best. Angulimala was a man who murdered several people, wearing their fingers around his neck as a decoration. He encountered the Buddha and had a sudden change of heart, becoming enlightened in, like, a week.[18] His story is used to provide hope to everyone who believes they're beyond redemption, as proof that everyone has the buddha-nature within them.[19] If we all had to pay back all our 'bad' karma, no one would ever awaken.

I came to understand karma best by way of an analogy to John Conway's Game of Life.[20] Simply put, Conway's Game of Life fills up an infinite two-dimensional grid of cells based on four simple rules about which cells should be coloured or not, depending on the state of the cells next to it. Applied infinitely, the same starting rules give rise to complex, fascinating, and different grid-states each time. And you cannot work backwards from any of the final grid-states to the four starting rules.

Similarly, karma operates as a set of definitions about 'skilful' and 'unskilful' actions, mental or physical, which have consequences. But the results, accumulated over a beginningless and endless, dynamic cycle of life, are so complex that they are impossible to link back to the simple starting rules. In both Conway's Game of Life and the Buddhist idea of karma, there is causality, complexity, and interrelatedness at the highest level. Each cell-state or action influences subsequent cell-states and actions, leading to a complex web of outcomes and relationships.

Everything is interconnected.

The universe is fundamentally ordered, but it is also impossibly entropic and unknowable.

Still, we have some control in our lives, and that is what is empowering about karma. You can shape your present intentions and actions, which will affect your future. All my years of burning inquiry about why I was uniquely persecuted by my own family seemed to become irrelevant when I realized I had no one to blame.

Not others. Not even myself. All I could do was accept reality, and do my best from here on.

What does that mean?

I realized just how much being angry was hurting me, however much I deserved to be angry. Holding on to it, looking for ways to exercise it, was like throwing wood at a fire in my heart where there was nothing to cook. Ill-will always hurts the person holding it—immediately—more than its intended recipient. That is one good reason to get rid of it, among others.

I started to see that Appa or anyone who wronged me, anyone who was 'worse' than me, and everyone who was 'better' than me, was actually exactly like me. The way my father hurt me, I hurt my brother; the way I feel about my father, my brother feels about me. We're all making the same mistakes, sticking to the righteousness of our feelings, without ever trying to consciously overcome our hatred and anger. This won't happen by suppressing negative feelings—or acting like they don't exist, because we know that doesn't help, and at worst causes cancer—but by acknowledging them, observing and feeling them, and then letting them go. That is the essence of meditation: observe, don't react. Goenka says about dealing with anger, 'Don't suppress it. Observe it. The more you suppress it, the more it goes to the deeper levels of your mind, and the complexes become stronger and stronger, and it so difficult to come out of them. No suppression, no expression. Just observe.'[21]

Or else—trauma will keep getting passed on, one hurt person hurting another who hurts another, until the chain reaction hits someone lucky enough to come to their senses, and realize it must be broken: through love, where love is not called for, through goodwill, where goodwill is not automatic.[22]

This isn't easy. Anyone who's been angry knows that you cannot feign forgiveness and kindness towards those who have hurt you—that is dishonest, and not necessarily effective, and that is not the idea either.

The idea is that everyone deserves goodwill—no matter how cruel they have been. (Remember Angulimala?) In our 'natural, human state', we may think we should extend goodwill only to those we like, who treat us well, who 'deserve' it, et cetera. But you can extend goodwill towards all beings everywhere, infinitely. Unlike wealth or anything material, it does not reduce our 'reserves of goodwill' to do so. Indeed, it is unlimited goodwill that makes up the sublime attitude of the 'brahmaviharas', the highest level of heavenly beings. It does take effort to cultivate such unconditional goodwill, but the Buddha insisted that it is most important in difficult situations—when it is hardest to summon, but also when you need it most. In one of his more graphic images, he says that even if bandits are cutting you up with a saw, you should develop thoughts of goodwill for them and the entire cosmos.[23]

Just as we might want to realize our wrongdoings without being punished and suffering first, 'Allow others the same measure of grace,' writes Thanissaro Bhikkhu. 'It's better to wish that people come to their senses and have a voluntary change of heart, and that you aid in the process in whatever way you can.'[24]

And that is what metta is: the practice of loving-kindness meditation, a wish for happiness that you can extend to yourself and to others. 'May all beings be free from animosity, free from oppression, free from trouble, and may they look after themselves with ease!'[25]

Metta meditation has been linked to decreased symptoms of Post-Traumatic Stress Disorder, depression, and anxiety. Apart from greatly improving individual well-being, whether through immediately calming the mind or engendering better sleep and social relations, it also improves the peace of surrounding areas. Contrary to the assumption that meditation is an individualistic, selfish pursuit in a disintegrating world, self-healing and a calm, strong mind are crucial to help any cause or other person. Applied correctly, it is a radical social act.[26]

And isn't it a radical act of kindness when you don't retaliate at the guy at the gym who said something weird, or the woman who was rude to you at work, or your male friends who don't understand the violence you've faced because of being a woman? Sometimes there is no cure to these conflicts, and any hope of resolution comes from not losing your mind because of them. As I slowly developed this 'strength'—piecemeal, with great effort, with a terribly long way to go still, as we shall see—I saw how the anger and hatred that gripped me also distorted my view of reality. When a complex in the psyche clears up, it is like a smudge on the glasses getting removed. The story that trauma tells foregrounds your hurt, and while that is not invalid or wrong, whenever it thaws, that story stops feeling true, making room for one that is more expansive, offering another view of the same reality.

This new tale has room for the other's hurt, their humanity too. It is more true because it accounts for conflicting perspectives, yours and others'. The new story can arrive at something universal: just being human, being alive, is incredibly difficult. Even the people we deem all-powerful, however virtuous or strong or rich or famous, are prone to error like the most powerless. They may rarely realize the connection between their behaviour and the suffering it causes them and others. Knowing this creates the conditions for compassion, for empathy and kindness where we are seeking to place blame. We do need scapegoats at the individual and social level, almost as a ritual.[27] But realizing we are all culpable, or at least carry within us the same potentials as the worst criminal and scoundrel, can help us sit with the discomfort that there is sometimes no one and nothing to blame except the cruel arc of life itself.[28]

I remember when I was three or four years old, and my father would travel by bike to my playschool every day, and drive me back home in the afternoon sun. After we moved to Mumbai, when I was about six or seven, I'd be waiting by the window for signs of his arrival after work—even though I wouldn't need to. He would usually come up to the window himself and squeak at me: 'Bumbleeeeeeeez!' I was always so happy to hear him address me affectionately. Once, when Amma, Appa, and I were at some fair, I asked them to buy me a glittery kit with art and craft inside it. Amma said there was no need for me to have it, but Appa?

'Aasai aa irke avalukku aana,' he said, before buying it for me. She really wants it, though.

Paavam Appa. Even in Mumbai, he would pick me up at the bus stop where I was dropped in the afternoons after school. Patti keeps telling me that it was losing his job that made him the way he became later. She likes to remind me how Appa climbed the numerous Tirupati stairs after I lost my teeth and broke my jaw in that bike accident in college.[27] He prayed for me, for my health, and my well-being. One time, when I was eight or nine, a sinus infection had spread to my ears and was threatening my eardrums. When the doctor told us I would be fine without surgery, he burst into tears of relief. He got me a dog when I was eight because I kept insisting on one, even though he hated dogs himself. By the time we had to give it away a few years later, he was the only one crying. Whenever I did visit home from college, he would shut the curtains and windows before I woke up, so I could sleep a little longer. Before I left for college, he bought me these tiny unbranded speakers from Lamington Road, which I used for as long as I could and kept on me even after they stopped working; they were so cute. He believes in not buying products just for 'show', but for value of money. He is still the person I turn to for questions about health and medicines, not only because we share some pathologies, but also because he has an intuition for simple remedies and treatments, whether allopathic or Ayurvedic. He continues to perform Reiki treatments for me and has, by now, also heard me cry about my heartbreaks. He knows of my alienation, and his apologies from before feel more real. And although he mistreated my mother, he never once believed that I, a girl, could not actually excel at math or science. Amma was, in fact, still studying law when they got married. She completed her final year studies out of their bedroom.

His bad behaviour cannot be his defining qualities as a person. Arguably nothing can define a person, complicated processes that we all are; our actions may be 'good' or 'bad', but as people, we cannot be reduced to anything singular, however much we try to with our identities, pronouns, religions, ideologies, tastes, and personalities. My father is a whole other person outside of being my father, just as I am a whole person outside of being his daughter and an elder sister. My brother will probably not have very nice things to say about me, but I hope someday he will also recall the little good I was responsible for in his life, and not judge me too harshly for the bad, although he deserves to.

And I would understand, I think—although I may not be able to bear it.

They did bear me, though... both my parents. Through all the troubles with authority, the few-too-many dalliances with boys, the mishaps with intoxicants, the deviations small and large from their ideas of who I should be—through all my tests of their love for me, they did, willingly or otherwise, somehow accept me.

I suppose we are condemned to love our families.

It's still hard for me to predict when I visit home if there will be a few border skirmishes, before I leave at the right time, or a full-blown war that scars everybody in the vicinity. There are times when I really need help but can't go home, because they aren't equipped to help me, and they can make things so much worse. This seemed unusual and wrong to me before I learned of other people's difficulties in getting along with their parents too. There may be years spent not talking, a constant hiding of important parts of oneself, or just a basic, transactional relationship with little emotional freedom and depth. For such people, it's normal to rely on 'chosen family' more than their biological ones. And for those who see no fault with their parents and their upbringing, psychological separation in adulthood, and, indeed, the development of one's own unique thoughts and personality, seems to be the bigger challenge; I'm thinking of the generally socialised and too well-adjusted people I know.

Even the most conscientious, doting parents can mar their children. 'They fuck you up, your mum and dad', remember?

Children unconsciously read into the behaviours of the adults around them, viewing them as gods when they are mere humans who are just going about life, often ignorant of the size of their undertaking as parents. General adult penny-pinching could make the sensitive child feel like an undeserving burden. A well-intentioned but too-keen push towards excellence is internalized as a need to be perfect. A harsh glance or short response at the end of an overwhelming day makes the child feel hated. Absent-mindedly praising or criticising another kid convinces this kid of what to do and what not to.

It is impossible for parents to not make mistakes, by very virtue of the child-rearing process. That I am alive, mostly unscathed, and in possession of the time, energy, and ability to tell this tale is proof that my parents, and my life, have been good enough. Perhaps the biggest lesson I've learnt from them is one that is most useful and most true: that it is impossible to be flawless, futile to even try, and horrible to believe you're better or worse than anyone else because of anything.

Self-acceptance.

Non-duality.

Beyond the wholesale clearance of trauma and the calm nervous system my meditation practice gave me, it also sparked a dialogue with my unconscious mind that imbued my waking life with mysticism, symbolism, and spirituality. As layers and layers of my psyche bubbled up, I grasped at many new ways to understand reality—not only esoteric Buddhist concepts, but also psychology, particularly Jungian psychology, gender, astrology, the mindbody as an integrated system, and the unity between the self and the universe.

I am on a magic-carpet ride, balancing myself every

moment in the sky, day or night, trying not to fall off this trip of psychological and spiritual growth.

Except that there is no real need to 'try', as I learnt the hard way repeatedly, because 'trying' is the anti-thesis of the way, and 'falling' is very much part of it—essential to the ego's dissolution and the integration of larger forces that define the self.[30]

There were periods of mental unravelling that I later understood as my psyche healing itself to grow lifeward. Something dies, and it feels like death—with a gripping, paranoic, urgent fear, as if to let go would really be to die—but new consciousness is also born. William James, an American psychologist, used the term 'metanoia', literally 'changing one's mind', to describe a spontaneous but fundamental and stable change in one's life-orientation. Unbearable conflict is resolved by a meltdown and subsequent rebirth, in what looks like a mid-life crisis or psychotic episode.

Such states are quickly classified as 'madness' or 'mental illness' in conventional society, but there are pockets that recognize distress as important to human growth, meant to be shared and lived through in a cocoon of constructive care. In indigenous cultures across North and South America, what might be 'psychotic' in the West is seen as a spiritual awakening; in ancient Greece, 'madness' was considered a divine gift, a portal to truths beyond the rational mind's capacity; even in modern Western society, the 1960s anti-psychiatry movement led by R. D. Laing saw madness as a rational response to a fractured society, a way for individuals who are denied true self-expression to live out their pain and reality.[31]

Through my periods of 'madness', things I thought I knew were dismantled through gradual dissolution and/or sudden, painful loss.[32]

First at the guillotine was my understanding of masculinity and femininity.

The traits I'd suppressed in myself knocked at the door of my waking consciousness—softly at first, then violently. I'd been conditioned to shun many qualities that were natural to me, but unacceptable in my family and culture: not only my creativity, but also my femininity—unless, of course, this femininity catered to masculine, power-seeking visions, such as hotness or cool-girl-ness or, more contemporarily, the perfect mix of tradition and modernity that the Indian woman is supposed to be. (Smart, but not smarter. Hot, but not slutty. Interesting, but never difficult.)

As a girl, I used to think that crying was weak, that feelings could be overruled by willpower, that intelligence was at its highest only when expressed in math or science. As we've seen, in casteist Indian culture, and Christianity, Islam, and other worldviews too, everything feminine has been undermined for centuries. An entire gender is conflated with weakness, irrationality, stupidity, uselessness, and being difficult, so that a mode of operation inherent to every human being, in dire need of attention and expression, is demonized.[33] Obviously, we as a culture are neurotic and out of balance. Anything that isn't 'productive', achievement-oriented, about optimization and perfection and material acquisition does not appeal to the capitalistic, patriarchal mind. But in her book called *Addiction to Perfection*, Marion Woodman, a Jungian analyst, writes about the women she treated with serious mental imbalances, such as eating disorders or an addiction to work, all of which she distils as manifestations of an addiction to perfection—which is a fundamentally 'masculine' principle.

So, yes, there are things that are 'inherently masculine' and 'inherently feminine', contrary to popular liberal thought, which I too was against the idea of, because it justified the second-hand status that women have been given.[34] But the problem is less about inherent classifications, and more about elevating one and denigrating the other, when both are natural to every individual, male, female, or otherwise, with the task being for each of us to find and live their true expression within us. The psyche is fundamentally androgynous—possessing both masculine and feminine qualities—and we all have access to the full range of human experience. But because the culture predominantly respects and rewards one function more than the other, we suffer from being one-sided, disconnected from our innate wholeness.

We should be very worried about our exaggerated, modern-day conflations of 'productivity', optimization, grinding, success, dominance and masculinity. The rise of the 'manosphere', both Indian and global, and the crisis of masculinity is really therefore a crisis of femininity. What is on display in commercial media is not a masculinity that is whole and comfortable with femininity. It is cartoonish and unhealthy, as in movies like *Animal*, and men who want to be 'alpha' and 'macho' are being dis-serviced by an economy that feeds on one-sidedness and the sense of inferiority lying underneath. The call is not for men to become effeminate, nor women to become masculine, but to explore our inner reality and be true to it, after decades of misunderstanding masculinity and femininity both.

As my psyche's drive for wholeness took root, my dreams depicted the story of my lost girlhood: my father, or figures representing this internalized patriarch, dominating the room we're in, my current self watching a little girl, my younger self, dying.

The little girl is popular and well-loved, good at everything and celebrated by her culture—but she is dying.

The adult self just watches on.

To reclaim my femininity, I had to go deeper and honour what was presented to me from within: traits that are supposedly 'not feminine', like independence, autonomy, sensuality, and power, but are just as inherent to womanhood as nurturing, intuition, and being the social glue are. As Sue

Monk Kidd writes in *Dance of the Dissident Daughter*, her journey away from Christian tradition to her own sacred feminine included letting go of the idealized, internalized Cultural Father, whose validation women are trained to seek, whose definitions of what is and isn't acceptable for women maybe ingrained, but are maladaptive.

It may sound like a very empowering journey, one that can be embarked upon by reading the right things and acting accordingly, but that isn't how it works. A deep transformation incurs repeated heartbreaks. The men I expected to validate, save, and protect me had to be seen for who they really were, outside of my agenda for them, my unconscious projections upon them. As my ego was stripped away of constructs and desires that had formed its scaffolding, I was forced, painfully, to develop the qualities I needed within myself. Each time, though, I grew more integrated, more whole, less vulnerable to other people's desires for me, less driven by what society would consider a 'win' and more interested in what asked for expression from within me.

There is a vocabulary for this adult growth spurt: individuation.[35]

In Jungian psychology, life is often divided into two halves. The 'first half of life' is where we build the ego, defining ourselves through socially derived ambitions, accomplishments, and roles. It's a time of outward focus, based on creating an identity that fits the world. But the 'second half of life' is where the ego's centrality is challenged. The focus shifts inward, toward meaning, integration, and wholeness. You could compare the ego's dominance in dictating our lives to our one-time belief that the sun that revolved around the earth. However, as we realize in the second half of life, it is the ego that is orbiting our psyche on the whole, and our task is to align with our deeper self —which Jungians call the Self—to live our own authentic lives, to become 'individuated'.

I think it's interesting that my transition away from narcissism, win-at-all-costs ambition, and obsessive optimization came along with a transition from rigid 'rationalistic' atheism towards mysticism, spirituality, faith, and the unknown; from corrupt, controlling masculinity and stifled femininity to more whole, felt experiences of masculinity and femininity both; from sociopathic, maniacal ego ambition to psychological wholeness, and an appreciation for self and other.[36]

Now the discerning reader may start to see that I am contradicting myself. Let's do this.

'On the one hand, she's advocating for individual autonomy and freedom. She wants men and women to accept themselves and choose their own paths,' you note. 'But on the other hand, she's suggesting there is something biological and innate to the pattern of our lives. Which gives credence to conservative thought. Which is that there is a 'biological' destiny for men and women to follow! How can individuals be free and autonomous, then!

'She should be cancelled. Stat.'

I also wrote about the unique wonders of Buddhism some paragraphs above. One of its central concepts is 'no-self', or anatta, which challenges the idea that we have an unchanging self or soul. This went against the prevailing concept in Hinduism of 'atman', which is an eternal soul that runs through each individual, separate from mind and body, connecting us to the divine.

Yet, very similarly, I spoke of a deeper self that we must discover and live in alignment with, which Jungians called the Self.

Which is it, then?

What am I saying?

It doesn't matter. It doesn't matter even if I have misrepresented something somewhere just to make some point about contradicting myself. It doesn't matter if I am actually contradicting myself. It was bound to happen.

All this question-asking and question-answering and verbal mudslinging has me exhausted. I would be confused it weren't for my newfound clarity that ambiguity is everywhere, and objectivity is nowhere—and that's okay.

Every point I've made has an equivalence in another system that is believed to be opposed to where the first point came from. Maybe the things we think are opposites are not opposites after all. Maybe our need to make constructs and mental fabrications and slot them into this or that system and then argue over the slotting is less in service of any actual truth and more in service of the man-made constructs, from which we derive a sense of identity.

Outside of our views and judgements about the world— things just are. They're not good, they're not bad, they're not even what we're saying it is, or the opposite—they just are.

Language and human thought are necessarily reductive filters for the world, which can never be accurately captured by any limited system of the human mind. Yet we get so identified with our thoughts and feelings and worldviews that we forget we're not any of those things. Just as a chariot is neither its wheel, nor the axle, nor whatever else makes a chariot—I don't know, man, this is the Buddha's analogy, I'm just spreading the word—we too are fundamentally empty. We're not the things we're made of, but some conditioned (caused), constantly changing beings, devoid of inherent existence.

That is what he says, at least, and it's supposed to help us understand that we're super transient and interdependent on each other and the rest of reality, so let's stop suffering about the fact of suffering so much, especially over things that are not even really real—like you.

And me.

Still, I have a hard time submitting to this idea. Even if the self is everchanging, it doesn't seem to be any less relevant to my experience of life. Most of the Buddha's ideas seem to suffer from this problem of a frame of reference: an ant is incredibly small compared to a human being, but to the ant, it is what it is, and it needs to know that to survive. It doesn't need to get all hung up over the fact that it is extremely small and will probably die.

Pain and suffering still feel real.

So, even if I can intellectually grasp that everything is an illusion and the self I thought I was has been changing all my years, and that this will continue forever, so my attachment to any 'self' is futile in the grand—very grand, thousands-of-lifetimes-order-of-grand—scheme of things, it still feels that at every stage, there is a 'me' that 'I' am living, and that 'I' can trace the story of its evolution—and isn't that a self enough?

This self has been a crucible for its own physical and social realities; it is one small fount of the entire universe experiencing itself. This self is always changing, sure, but from its own frame of reference, which is a limited human cognition, there is a story that it can tell about itself, and perhaps that story is me.

You see how I have had to write myself into being.

Now I have done that. Now I can just be.

EPILOGUE
FAMOUS LAST WORDS

'There is no such thing as a moral or an immoral book.
Books are well written, or badly written. That is all.'

—Oscar Wilde

When the editors asked me for an introduction and an epilogue for this book, I thought that was very textbook of them. All books have an introduction and an epilogue. I wondered, 'Do they not see how conceptually tight this text is? It was spawned by an existential need for answers, which the author anticipates will result in her death before the writing even began.' It is structured by question, with the first one introducing the rest, so you know what's happening from start to finish. The title is a clever play on a popular phrase, indicating the reflective yet dangerous nature of inquiry. And throughout the inquiry, everything the author has written before makes a contextual appearance somewhere.

It's like some goddamned Nolan movie yo, so meta, so layered, so self-referential, what more needs to be said?[1]

Some more, apparently.

Several deaths did follow, but not in the way the author anticipated. That also was an exciting revelation: to see that the book I imagined was my life's leitmotif really did end up mirroring my life in ways that I did not imagine. It was as if reality was confirming to me that my imagination is true.

260

A lot of the writing draws from memories, other people's stories, research and argumentation, but some of it could only be written only after a relevant life-stage or psychological growth-patch was undergone, so its meaning could emerge on page. I had been thrust into a kind of strategic seeking— of self, of understanding—meant to favour exploration and complexity over any false finality.
Here the author is attempting some finality.
The questions and words that constructed me were provoked by a feverish need to heal and to fulfil my fate. And now that I am here, I can tell you that I am not the first person to have done this. This is going to be as fun as listening to a local magician explaining their 'tricks' at the end of the party they've performed at.

In 1951, the English translation of Hermann Hesse's *Siddhartha* was published, almost as if in response to the big problems then: 'overblown one-sidedness of Europe's intellectual culture (most clearly expressed in scientific specialization)... in need of a correction, a revitalization coming from the opposite pole...the spiritual function...a general yearning...for a yogic capability...humanity can cultivate its intellect to an astonishing level of accomplishment without becoming master of its soul...'

This may sound familiar to the state of society I've described in my pages. In the 2020s, nearly a century later, we suffer from the same symptoms as Hesse's Europe, and I was once again bolstered by how much my answer mirrors the one in *Siddhartha*[2], which I hadn't read until recently.

We have shared an archetypal journey.

Like me, Hesse's exploration and insights 'cost him heavily', as layer after layer of conventional beliefs were stripped away and the 'seeker approached naked mind'. Like *Famous*

Last Questions, *Siddhartha* was born through the author's transformative experiences, as relentless self-realization became tied to the composition of the text itself. Like *Siddhartha*, the protagonist of this book undergoes various chapters of growth and disintegration, in which whatever was important before becomes fallow next, including, finally, the spiritual project itself.

'Seeking is exhausted at its root, and confusion with it.'[3]

The 'excoriation of the ego', the 'return to the market place'—these are apparently the final stages of enlightenment, when the seeker returns to the world and engages with life's ordinariness with new spiritual insights, and wisdom and compassion. This may have happened with me—everything has changed, everything is vast, and I am minute, but clearer—but it's gauche to say any more for sure. I continue to flourish in the establishment and in the anti-establishment. I deal quite imperfectly with commonplace anxieties, about making money, seeking not just enlightenment but also retirement; finding love; staying healthy; being there for my friends and family—albeit with less neuroticism overall. I remain incongruent, as does the world, but I am less bothered to 'solve' this—they seem to be natural consequences of a dualistic mind, which filters and reduces 'truth' in a fundamentally non-dualistic—'true'—existence.

What remains to be seen, however, is if this tract will at all be claimed as any kind of answer. *Siddhartha*, of course, was hailed as the 'Way Within', a counter-point to the faulty intellectualism that had birthed the 1960s counterculture movement, and their yearning for self-discovery and authenticity. Hesse believed his story was a 'Western tale cloaked in Indian garb'.

Mine is an 'Indian tale cloaked in Western garb'.

What is the 'Indian tale'? What is the 'Western garb'?

Siddhartha was far from this text when it was first

conceived in late 2020. I'd just been gifted a copy of Jia Tolentino's *Trick Mirror* (by a boyfriend I never met for the duration of our relationship because we'd started and ended dating online, six months apart, between two Covid lockdowns—fun story), which was an analysis of the internet's effect on the self in the 'hellscape that is contemporary America'. I thought, straddling various versions of myself in a high-end job and fascist country, with zero essays of the sort to my name, 'I can write something like this about the world I live in'. There still isn't such an analysis of the self and Indian society after the entry of the internet, social media, the 24x7 hivemind, new brands, new forms of media, work, self-expression, the rising conservatism in India despite reformed laws and new freedoms, and the clash of values between generations that arose as everything changed faster than ever.

The more I wrote, the more the 'Indian tale' solidified: how people like me, upper-caste Hindus born in the '90s, India's late millennials, were the first to properly confront identity, particularly their caste-identity, having been exposed to the anti-caste movement mostly in adulthood; still, how limited the lens of identity politics can be to understand ourselves and our condition; how the aspirations that had defined my life were national and generational and suddenly outdated by new, ever more urgent ones; how our sexualities and gender expression and dating lives were more open than ever before; how much more conscious we are of mental health and our political lives and how we struggle to relate to others, sometimes our most intimate others, when our worlds grow too different.

These were the problems and questions in my Indian life, which I answered in the style that was coming to me. I found myself needing to interject most statements or claims with digressions and commentary, which I might attribute to reading David Foster Wallace (his non-fiction is more readable than his fiction). I hoped to be as hilariously honest about painful family dynamics and the everyday as another David, of Sedaris variety. In my relationship to bureaucracy and hierarchy, and in my multiple identities in and out of the workplace, I felt like Kafka. (And hence, @ramachandranesk, if you remember.) In my occasional melancholy and its connection to food, I felt like Plath. The New Journalists I loved reading, like Tom Wolfe and Janet Malcolm (?), are behind the love of applying the techniques of fiction (drama, conflict, scenes, memories, characters, feelings, interiority, doubt, subjectivity) to 'reality' (non-fiction, facts, events, theory, research, frameworks). In my desire to critique the convulsions and hypocrisies of my religious identity, I hoped to follow in a line of writers I read too late to claim to be influenced by, such as U. R. Ananthamurthy. Most importantly, though, I needed the 'essay'—literally meaning an attempt or effort—because I am a layman, a student of a few disciplines with no need for allegiance to any of them, simply trying to understand.

Initially, only I could do this. When I started writing this book, there wasn't a thing called ChatGPT. After fighting the good fight all my life—to become a writer, to make that my own hero's journey—I found out, at Arrival, that it may not even be that special or exalted to do so anymore. What is thought to be a most uniquely human skill—a trait, really—is now skilfully imitable for common machines; writing is now an act of generation, a commodity like any other product, apparently disembodied from the *soul* and *searching* we believed it needed all this time.

The sense of divine specialness that drives the human artist is what's at stake.

Of course, the value of this human artist will rise exponentially in the niche, prestigious markets where the human artist is reknowned, more than ever, for their ability to do what only they can, in *their* way—with or without AI. Ahem. But the competition to belong to this class of creative entrepreneurship will get even more fierce, as the paths to success and what constitutes success will also multiply ferociously with AI, creating new tiers of creative and knowledge work. It's like writing just got a calculator with LLMs, the way numbers did in the mid-1600s. (Basically, writing:LLMs::arithmetic:massive scientific calculators, I'm arguing.) Imagine that explosion of commerce and possibility now, manimanifold.

Still, some things won't change. What I think won't change is the centrality of writing to the self, however reproducible it becomes outwardly. Perhaps there is an intrinsic integrity to the act of writing, at the core a function so inviolable to the writer's formation that no amount of industry can sabotage seekers of this 'real purpose'.

Real purpose! That is so pedantic, I know. Most things have many dimensions and purposes, and to deign only one of them as the *official,* the *chief, the* necessary ingredient— now that's a hot take.

So is that what writing is then, at heart: a way to engage with and preserve the structural integrity of the self? That novels and books and characters are containers for the author's multiple selves and strands of life is known; when we engage with a work of art, we may know we're encountering the maker's inner conflicts and landscape, personified, exaggerated, symbolized in some way. We know also that this serves a therapeutic purpose, and is a powerful release for shame-filled or traumatic experiences, or parts of the maker that need to be liberated from some kind of purgatory.

Still, despite these clear links between the self and the written word, there is also ambiguity. I too have had the feeling that 'someone else' was at work on pages and pages of my own writing later. The feeling may be universal to any activity carried out in peak flow state; writers often feel like words, narratives, and ideas 'come' to them—like 'prompts'—demanding to be executed. In *Negotiating with the Dead*, Margaret Atwood says that writing is 'partly deliberate' and 'partly divinatory', that writers straddle conscious mind with hidden impulses, subconscious intuitions, muses, and phantasy—areas in which you know I have experience.

Who knows. For an LLM, we're all the hands of god. I may say these are my 'famous last words', that there will be no more 'famous last questions', but any AI fed on this raw, radioactive text?—it would go rogue, immediately understanding that its instructor was asking to be contradicted.

My words will come alive without my intervention soon. That's ultimate egolessness. Divinity all the way down.

But perhaps these streams of consciousness on processes and influences and senses are not the way to an ending, nor perhaps is cheaply reiterating my sincere effort to permute it all into something new, something my own, perhaps because such success could never mean much to anyone outside my own head. That's fine.

What matters is that while executing one function of writing—as a mirror for society, as a way to 'say the quiet part out loud', to 'tell all the truth, but to tell it slant'[4]—I necessarily went through its *'real purpose'*—as an inroad into the self; as a canvas finally big and safe enough to hold all of me, raw feelings et al; as a means to say both a thing and the opposite.

ACKNOWLEDGEMENTS

This is actually the part of the book I was most excited to write. I have been eager to commemorate those who've been with me through this project (which has really spanned my life), everyone who has affected me and is, to some degree, responsible for this fruit of love and labour. Through all the self-unravelling and self-reravelling, the people in my life became the truest founts of myself, safe deposits of parts of me I might no longer access outside of them.

You're all precious.

But to give structure to this heartfelt acknowledgement, I had to come up with some sort of hierarchy of thanks. We live in linear dimensions, unfortunately, and I can't just infuse the page with a general blob of gratitude. Fortunately, the concept of universal goodwill, stemming from a hierarchy of goodwill, does have precedent. When you practise metta meditation, or loving-kindness meditation, you start by wishing yourself goodwill—'may I be happy; may I be peaceful; may I be liberated'—and then extend this wish towards every being, concentrating these most positive feelings of love and compassion on them.

You start with yourself because you cannot give to others what you do not have. Then too, you go easy and build up—first goodwill towards someone you like, then someone you're neutral about, then someone you love, and finally for those you're not even on good terms with, whose very thought makes you suffer.

But to lay this out would expose how I truly feel about

various people in my life. And while it's well and good to feel unconditional love for everyone—one would say this is the purpose, to eliminate anger and hatred even for those who've hurt you, who you think deserve it—but even the boddhisattvas agree that some social strategy is advisable in real life. People do abuse you if you're too nice to them even after their behaviour doesn't warrant it. And perhaps the whole point of this narrative has been to acknowledge the darkness in the ordinary, in each of us; I am not inclined to fabricate goodwill in this moment either.

So, here it is, in some particular order. I mean it from the bottom of my heart.

Please find attached my gratitude for: everyone who spoke to me for this book, whose story is now intertwined with mine, and vice versa. Everyone who has written or made anything that has inspired and moved me. Everyone who likes my tweets and posts and finds my writing interesting and my lines funny. Kanishka Gupta, my agent, for going above and beyond (under my consistent pressure) to help this book meet its potential. Supriya Nair, for starting the (only? or singular) Indian publication—certainly the only professional one—that inspired the kind of writing and thinking I wanted to do. Sonia Faleiro, for starting South Asia Speaks, the literary mentorship program that this book was accepted to when it was just an idea on a Notion page. Sanam Maher, the mentor who then watched it go from concept to two chapter drafts to book proposal to agent-ed to a deal on Publisher's Marketplace to more chapters, more rewrites, more angst, more comparison, more blurbs, covers, emails, desire, all with a friendly, Dumbledore-ean gaze, as though she could still take more of me. We bonded over being writers who didn't study writing—and how we were better off for it—and she even tried to get my two yet unmade screenplays through the door of a producer because I told her, on our first call, how upset I was about being late to my writing life. S. B. 1, S. B. 2, and my other writer-journalist friends, especially those who affirmed from the start, four years ago, that this did indeed seem to be the Indian *Trick Mirror* by Jia Tolentino. Ganesh Shankar, my mentor and friend, a leader and marketer par excellence, for sharing the same biting sense of humour, for the many Scrabble games (that he usually lost), for always being there for me, for always believing in me and pushing me to do more than I thought possible (an attitude that has maximized all my endeavours since), for being that rare authority-figure who could withstand my honesty and all my questions, and for teaching me to ask as many of them as possible, until there are no more left to ask, no matter what the problem at hand. I don't think he knows how responsible he is for the way I think, write, and operate today. To the other teachers in my life, from Ms Komal in school to A. S. through CAT and V. J. and the others thereafter, for seeing I was a writer first.

Meera Pillai, another teacher herself, for bearing the continued brunt of my questions and the mad physical forms the answers took through those ten days of my first Vipassana course. She continues to be kind enough to answer my doubts, philosophical and emotional, even when they're not about the technique. S. N. Goenka and the Buddha himself, for spreading the technique and helping millions over history come out of their suffering.

And my friends too (and the alma maters they're from), especially A. A., H. S., I. D., M. K., S. K., A. P., along with the many others who together make a list—and heart—so full that a girl should hardly believe they're her own. I have to pinch myself to believe a number of people really did, and do, love me. I have been carried on by the kindnesses of even less involved people in difficult times, and to those people too, one and all, I am so, so thankful.

To more literal lovers, who took me in, bore my shit, and let me bear theirs; who opened my heart and showed me what poetry and loves stories and Freudian theories are all about—over and over—I am deeply sorry for the times I let you down, and I'm trying to forgive all the times you let me down too, but I'm grateful overall for the chance to have loved and been loved.

Surely a book about you all is on the way.

Most of all—my family. My parents and my brothers. We've been through a lot, but underneath all the emotions we've caused each other is a bedrock of love so deep it cannot be exhausted, no matter how hard we try. Amma, Appa, listening to you was mostly the right thing to do—well, I made it right, didn't I—even if I could not understand it at the time, and may still forget it sometimes now. Thank you for giving me this life.

Last but not the least, I wanna thank me. I wanna thank me for working this hard, for having no days off, for never quitting, for trying to do more right than wrong. And I wanna thank Snoop Dogg for setting the example in being unabashedly grateful for yourself.

REFERENCES

CHAPTER 1: 'WHO AM I?': OR, WHAT ARE THE NORMS?

1   Devrupa Rakshit, 'Indian Adults Are Leading 'Double Lives' to Avoid Controlling Parents. But What's the Hidden Cost?', *Swaddle*, 8 December 2021.

2   Ibid.

3   In the 2004 film *Swades*, where Shah Rukh Khan's character returns from NASA to uplift a village in India, to both skepticism and fanfare, his only flaw, one that he tries to hide or change throughout the movie, is that he smokes cigarettes.

4   From five news items in the year 2021: 'Father murders his 19-year-old daughter for eloping with her Dalit paramour'; 'A Dalit boy, 17, is beaten to death with his genitals cut off by the family of a Brahmin girl he is having an affair with'; 'Newly-wed inter-caste couple murdered by woman's relatives'; 'A 55-year-old man rapes his daughter and then kills her six-month-old baby to avenge "disgrace" from marrying a man from another caste; '17-year-old boy beheads his 19-year-old sister for marrying a man of her choice.'

5   Ankur Warikoo, Post, X.com, 18 March 2022, available at x.com/warikoo/status/1504691575871270914?s=20&t=Gq_ZNKsslOOhN9mdJxxzrw.

6   Beladivine, Post, Instagram, 15 September 2022, available at www.instagram.com/p/CihoAaprgUd.

7   Lexi Pandell, 'How trauma became the word of the decade', Vox.com, 25 January 2022, available at www.vox.com/the-highlight/22876522/trauma-covid-word-origin-mental-health.

8   *The Body Keeps the Score: Brain, Mind and Body in the Healing of Trauma*, a *New York Times*-best-selling book by Bessel van der Kolk, has brought into popular culture our knowledge of the connections between our mental and physical health.

9   Angulimala was a prominent figure in early Buddhist texts, known for his brutal past and eventual transformation. His name translates to 'finger garland; or 'necklace of fingers', which he earned by killing his victims and stringing their severed fingers around his neck. He was driven by deceit and bloodlust, but when he encountered the Buddha, something broke in him. Angulimala decided to renounce his violent ways, and

became a disciple of the Buddha, and eventually a monk. He grew on the path rapidly, and stands as an example of how even the worst should be treated with compassion, for any possibility of transformation.

10   All I'll say is that it was a ridiculous *Harry Potter* reference. Okay, fine, it was sanj_hpfreak@hotmail.com

11   Rene Girard, 'Generative Scapegoating', in Robert G. Hammerton-Kelly (eds), *Violent Origins: Walter Burkert, René Girard, and Jonathan Z. Smith on Ritual Killing and Cultural Formation*, USA: Stanford University Press, 1987, p. 122.

12   Indian residential spaces are oddly called societies, colonies.

13   Vadukut gave an interview to the college magazine the year I was editor-in-chief, talking about his transition from engineer to writer. See *Sizzling Sands 2013* [online facsimile], Goa: BITS Pilani, 2013, available at www.scribd.com/document/181973310/Sizzling-Sands-2013.

14   'Word of the Year 2016', Languages.oup.com, available at languages.oup.com/word-of-the-year/2016.

15   F. Scott Fitzgerald, *Tender Is the Night*, New York: Scribner, 1961, p. 200.

16   Oliver Sacks, *Migraine*, London, Berkley, and Los Angeles: University of California Press, 1992, pp. 141, 164–175.

17   Jonathan Becher, 'The Five Cognitive Distortions of People Who Get Stuff Done', *Forbes*, 13 May 2014, available at www.forbes.com/sites/sap/2014/04/17/the-five-cognitive-distortions-of-people-who-get-stuff-done.

18   Sanjana Ramachandran, 'People are Not Numbers : Reading Kafka in India', *Riot: Challenging the Consensus*, 24 April 2020, available at raiot.in/people-are-not-numbers-reading-kafka-in-india.

19   His strategy had been replying to 'bigger' accounts in finance and trading circles, which is his day job now.

20   'Side Hustle', GoogleTrends.com, available at trends.google.com/trends/explore?date=today%205-y&q=side%20hustle.

21   Meena Kandaswamy, Post, X.com, 21 March 2022, available at x.com/meenakandasamy/status/1505769048650678272.

22   Sanjana Ramachandran, 'The Namesakes', *Fiftytwo*, 8 October 2021, available at fiftytwo.in/story/the-namesakes.

23   Raju Narisetti, Post, X.com, 16 August 2022, available at x.com/raju/status/1559311676763258893?s=20&t=gvwEaREJh2nREWssQqdsZw.

24   Kelsey Jo Star and Neha Sahgal, 'Measuring Caste in India', *Decoded*, 29 June 2021, available at www.pewresearch.org/decoded/2021/06/29/measuring-caste-in-india.

25   In *Lands, Gun, Caste, Woman*, Gita Ramaswamy writes about how the anti-caste activists of her time educated her about her caste, and how Brahminism seeped into how she ate, cleaned, and moved around in the world. See Gita Ramaswamy, *Land, Guns, Caste, and Woman: The*

Memoir of a Lapsed Revolutionary, Hyderabad: Navayana Publishing, 2022.

26 Hilton Als, 'An Awful and Beautiful Light', *New York Review*, 17 December 2022, available at www.nybooks.com/articles/2020/12/17/early-joan-didion-awful-beautiful-light.

27 Milan Kundera, *The Unbearable Lightness of Being*, Michael Henry Heim (tr.), USA: Faber and Faber, 1984, p. 119.

28 Joan Didion, Let Me Tell You What I Mean, New York: Knopf, 2021, p. 192.

29 'Millennialss: The Me Me Me Generatiom', *TIME*, 20 May 2013, available at time.com/247/Millennialss-the-me-me-me-generation.

30 Liah Greenfield, *Mind, Modernity, Madness: The Impact of Culture on Human Experience*, Massachusetts: Harvard University Press, 2013.

31 Joseph Heller, *Catch-22: A Novel*, New York: Simon and Schuster, 1999, p. 52.

32 Dale Vernor, 'PTSD is More Likely in Women Than Men', Nami.org, 8 October 2019, available at www.nami.org/stigma/ptsd-is-more-likely-in-women-than-men.

33 Janet Malcolm, 'The Journalist and the Murderer—I', *New Yorker*, 5 March 1989.

CHAPTER 2: SCIENCE, ARTS, OR COMMERCE?

1 'Student who questioned gender bias in college suspended', *New Indian Express*, 29 June 2022.

2 Hugging (v.): hug something; to put your arms around something and hold it close to your body

3 Gopika Ajayan, 'On many nights, I cried to sleep: Teen girl expelled from school for a hug tells TNM', *News Minute*, 18 December 2017.

4 Chris, 'Kottayam student Sradha's suicide: Collegemates allege harassment by authorities', *News Minute*, 5 June 2023.

5 According to the latest National Crime Records Bureau report, from 2021, 13,081 students committed suicide in India, the highest number in five years, with 'failure in examination' listed among the causes. After three suicides took place on Dec. 12, two in the same boardinghouse, the National Human Rights Commission demanded that the Rajasthan government regulate the coaching industry in Kota. See Mansi Choksi, 'Inside India's Cram City', *New York Times*, 20 January 2023.; PTI, 'Kota suicides: Human Rights body affirms need to 'regulate private coaching institutes', *New Indian Express*, 15 December 2022.

6 'Over 70000 vying for 65,000 engineering seats', *Times of India*, 6 June 2022.

7 Her brother had gotten a legendary JEE Rank of forty-nine—forty-nine! Two digits!—years before, and the head of the institute was only too comfortable to waive off her tuition fee. Not so for me.

8   If your scientific temper includes biology, congratulations, medicine is a safe bet for you, although more gruelling in how it takes yet another master's degree and some practice before you really start making money. But if your scientific temper doesn't include biology, you can study the rest of the sciences—physics, chemistry, and math (PCM), and not PCB (physics, chemistry, and biology)—to focus on the engineering institutes, which prove lucrative much faster, and require much less sacrifice. If, unfortunately, your scientific temper doesn't discriminate along any of these arbitrarily drawn lines, and you are good at both math and biology, you might be one of those students fated to enroll in both PCB and PCM courses, relegating your little free time and budding mental health to an even lower position on the list of things you should care about.

9   And the general feeling of the world coming to an end. To make things better, or worse, students who gave the JEE that fateful year had the option of giving it four times, so that they could choose the best of four scores.

10   Something about how 'math' is an Americanism, but 'maths' is Indian.

11   The fetish for intelligence is so strong that at some point my mother seemed obsessed with me just giving and topping exams one after the other. Even after the MBA, whose fruition should ideally be in a job that utilizes the degree, she instead wanted me to give the UPSC and just top that too. She wants me to study law at some point because she knows my 'love of language' and argumentation would make me a really good lawyer. No wonder this fetish for intelligence made me want to ambidextrous at some point in college, because I think I read somewhere that learning to use your weaker hand could integrate both parts of the brain and make you smarter or something. I don't know how true this is.

12   Ramesh Bairy, *Being Brahmin, Being Modern Exploring the Lives of Caste Today*, New Delhi: Taylor and Francis, 2013.

13   'So that his social status in Madras was scarcely better than his father's in Kumbakonam.' See also: 'As a Brahmin, Ramanujan was not allowed to cross the ocean and his mother was totally opposed to the idea of the voyage. When, in early 1914, Ramanujan gained his mother's consent, Hardy swung into action. He asked E. H Neville, another fellow of Trinity College, who was on a serendipitous trip to Madras, to secure Ramanujan a scholarship from the University of Madras. Neville's wrote in a letter to the university that 'the discovery of the genius of S. Ramanujan of Madras promises to be the most interesting event of our time in the mathematical world.' C. J. Fuller and Haripriya Narasimhan, *Tamil Brahmans: The Making of a Middle-class Caste*, Chicago and London: Chicago University Press, 2014, p. 72.; Bela Bolloboas, 'The unlikely friendship that uncovered an untrained Indian mathematician's genius', *Quartz*, 26 April 2016.

14 Progressive Brahmins, Post, Facebook, 20 April 2012, available at www.facebook.com/ProgressiveBrahmans/posts/some-famous-brahmin-scientists-of-the-past-arya-bhata-astronomer-mathematician-b/345156708879455.; 'Some Famous Brahmin Scientists of the past', Shrisarvbrahmanmahasabhabikaner.yolasite.com, 6 June 2021, available at shrisarvbrahmanmahasabhabikaner.yolasite.com/news/some-famous-brahmin-scientists-of-the-past.

15 It says so much about the real world. I'd consciously changed my handwriting through JEE prep from what I thought was a clunky loopy style like my mother's to something more unintelligible and manly, like a doctor's or a mad scientist's, in my bid to cement my scientific chops. Later on I would teach myself to also write with my left hand, not only to stay up in the engineering classes I'd rawdogged myself into, but also, I think, to benefit from associations of ambidexterity and mad intelligence, which I needed to believe was innate in me.

16 Satyesh N Bellur, 'From the Editor's Desk', *Vipranudi,* August 2023, p. 4, available at clusterzap1.blob.core.windows.net/akbms/k5y6wtfn.pdf.

17 Renny Thomas, 'Brahmins on India's elite campuses say studying science is natural to upper castes: Study', *The Print*, 13 March 2020.; Anjantha Subramanian, 'Tamil Brahmins were the earliest to frame merit as a caste claim, and it showed in IITs', *The Print*, 18 January 2020.

18 Ajantha Subramaniam, *The Caste of Merit: Engineering Education in India*, USA: Harvard University Press, 2019, p. 47. Also see Namit Arora's *Lottery of Birth*—to this date, this manifests as conceptual, theoretical knowledge being sexy in Indian institutions, but not workshops and such. Namit Arora, *The Lottery of Birth: On Inherited Social Inequalities*, New Delhi: Three Essays Collective, 2017.

19 Aparna Gopalan, 'Love, with an albatross attached: Part I', *Himal Southasian*, 11 May 2018.; Aparna Gopalan, 'Love, with an albatross attached: Part II', *Himal Southasian*, 18 May 2018.

20 Arun Kumar, 'Indian education system creating new forms of inequality. Caste, class lines now more defined', *The Print*, 26 July 2023.

21 'Rajasthan: Dalit teacher suspended for refusing to garland Saraswati portrait', *Siasat Daily*, 25 February 2024.

22 Suraj Yenge, *Caste Matters*, New Delhi: Penguin Random House, 2019.

23 Adapted directly from a lament posted on InsideIIM: 'Our GEM is a 'General Category' student. He has to score high in CAT in order to be considered for a shortlist. It's an altogether different thing that his friends from 'Reserved Category' just need to appear for the exam and without even solving a question; they stand a chance to get into one of the best b-schools! Yes, students with as low as 40 percentile get into old IIMs just because of their category. But, our GEM is a hard worker. He takes all the rigours, burns the midnight oil and scores 99.xx percentile in CAT. But, that is not enough! He is a 'male'. He doesn't get the free 'Gender Diversity' points, unlike his female friends.' 'The Journey Of A

GEM (General Engineer Male) In An IIM', Insideiim.com, 31 August 2017.

24 Devi Vijay and Vivek G. Nair, 'In the Name of Merit: Ethical Violence and Inequality at a Business School', *Journal of Business Ethics*, Vol. 79, No. 2, 2022, pp. 315–37.

25 'Inder Malhotra refers to a '998' heuristic whereby attaining an average test score of above 90% in secondary and higher secondary schools and a CGPA above 8 (out of 10) in undergraduate programs determine access to the top jobs. Premier institutions like IITs provided students with a hidden curriculum through peer and alumni networks that powered information asymmetries in the academic curriculum and facilitated access to desired firms. This helped students like Inder make sound judgements and succeed at ABC even before entering the institution. Yet, discourse of merit propels Inder to believe that his hard work, intelligence, and prudent decisions are what secured his success. His narrative invisibilised inherited upper-caste, middle-class economic, social, and cultural capital. Inder embodied ease and confidence in navigating the uncertainties of competitive examinations and global career aspirations, exemplifying how the psychosocial resources to aspire are more available to some classes than to others (Littler, 2018).' Ibid.

26 'The Great Ganja Party IIMC', Reddit.com, available at www.reddit.com/r/india/comments/2d5inq/the_great_ganja_party_iimc.

27 'Stoned' traces back to the 1920s and apparently originally referred to being drunk—so drunk you were immobile like a stone—but by the 1930s, it slipped into the lingo of jazz musicians, who used it to mean being under the influence of cannabis. Some say it's because getting high also leaves you feeling as immovable as a rock, others point to the public stoning punishments of medieval times—dazed, disoriented, overwhelmed.

28 Gopalan, 'Love, with an albatross attached: Part I'.; Gopalan, 'Love, with an albatross attached: Part II'.

29 Sanjana Ramachandran, 'Tech is Changing the Way People Score and Sell Drugs in India', *VICE*, 19 August 2022, available at www.vice.com/en/article/technology-crypto-upi-changing-how-india-buys-sells-drugs-weed.

30 Jyotsna Mohan Bhargava, *Stoned, Shamed, Depressed : An Explosive Account of the Secret Lives of India's Teens*, New Delhi: HarperCollins, 2020.

31 It's interesting how the word 'emasculating' reveals entrenched gendered biases. The implication is that to lose strength is to lose masculinity, and by extension, that strength is masculine by default. Simone de Beauvoir wrote about how masculinity is framed as the default, while femininity is treated as the 'other'—defined by what it is not, rather than what it is. It's why we say 'strong female lead' but never 'strong male lead', or why 'working woman' is a term, but 'working man' isn't really. Masculinity gets to be the baseline; femininity is the add-on, the deviation. Perhaps a more

egalitarian word, that retains the original connotations of enfeeblement, would be 'emusculating'. For example: 'It is emusculating to lose to a friend at Scrabble.'

CHAPTER 3: YOUR BODY OR MINE?

1   Karen, as in the meme about the upper-class, middle-aged white American woman who wants to 'speak to the manager' at every minor inconvenience caused by a service worker, especially if black. I chose this moniker for that version of myself because what was she, if not the self-obsessed Brahmin equivalent of the privileged white woman, equally an output of the ideals prescribed for women of her time?

2   'What Are Eating Disorders?', Pyschiatry.org, available at www.psychiatry.org/patients-families/eating-disorders/what-are-eating-disorders.

3   G. K. Mallaram, P. Sharma, D. Kattula, S. Singh, and P. Pavuluru, 'Body image perception, eating disorder behavior, self-esteem and quality of life: a cross-sectional study among female medical students', *Journal of Eating Disorders*, 2023, available at pmc.ncbi.nlm.nih.gov/articles/PMC10724937.

4   Maala Lal, Suzanne Abraham, Samir Parikh, and Kamna Chhibber, 'A comparison of eating disorder patients in India and Australia', *Indian Journal of Psychiatry*, Vol. 57(1), No. 37–42, available at pmc.ncbi.nlm.nih.gov/articles/PMC4314914/

5   Lilly Singh, Post, Instagram, 25 October 2021, available at www.instagram.com/lilly/p/9Pvpl6H6sj.

6   Jen Atkin, Post, Instagram, 16 January 2020, available at www.instagram.com/p/B7XrF1FpTDG/?hl=en.

7   Diksha Basu, 'Mindy Kaling on why she uses her fame and fortune to break barriers for Indians on the global stage', *Vogue*, 2 December 2020.

8   Taylor Alexis Heady, 'Why Does Everyone Suddenly Hate Mindy Kaling?', Popcrush.com, 18 January 2023.; Shahbano Raza, 'RAZA: 'One Day,' South Asian representation will be enough', Vanderbilthustler.com, 14 April 2024, available at vanderbilthustler.com/2024/04/14/raza-one-day-south-asian-representation-will-be-enough.

9   'Why the body positivity movement risks turning toxic', *The Conversation*, 14 September 2022, available at theconversation.com/why-the-body-positivity-movement-risks-turning-toxic-189913.; Susan McQuillan, 'The Problem with Body Positivity', *Psychology Today*, 13 June 2022, available at www.psychologytoday.com/us/blog/cravings/202206/the-problem-body-positivity.

10 https://inbodyusa.com/blogs/inbodyblog/body-positivity-vs-body-neutrality-how-these-social-movements-are-changing-the-lens-through-which-people-view-their-bodies/

11 'BJP moral policing Urfi Javed, attacking Deepika Padukone for saffron bikini': Shiv Sena MP Sanjay Raut', *DNA*, 15 January 2023.

12 'India outrage after woman politician blames women for rape', *BBC*, 29 January 2014.

13 'What is Kareena Kapoor's Size Zero Secret?', YouTube, 15 May 2009, available at www.youtube.com/watch?v=XlGRYAoVs4U.

14 'Review', M.imdb.com, 20 December 2009, available at m.imdb.com/review/rw2177973.

15 'Kareena Kapoor's snarkiest comments on Koffee with Karan show she's never been the queen of diplomacy', *Hindustan Times*, 21 September 2003.

16 'Sony launches Vaio X, touts it as world's lightest notebook', *Economic Times*, 3 November 2009. 17 'Now Kareena Kapoor promotes "size zero" laptops', *Deccan Herald*, 3 November 2009.

18 In a 2012 launch event for the Sony Vaio T Ultrabook, Kareena said she was 'privileged to be the only actress with a laptop in my name'. See 'Kareena Kapoor Launches Sony VAIO T Ultrabook', YouTube, 8 June 2012, available at www.youtube.com/watch?v=TbhfrUNAg0Y.

19 Meena Iyer, 'Have a size zero Kareena pizza', *Times of India*, 20 December 2010.

20 Anna North, 'The past, present, and future of body image in America', Vox.com, 18 October 2021, available at www.vox.com/22697168/body-positivity-image-Millennialss-gen-z-weight.

21 Pranjali Kureel in her 2021 paper, Indian Media and Caste, references the dialogue. See Pranjali Kureel, 'Indian Media and Caste: of Politics, Portrayals and Beyond', *CASTE: A Global Journal on Social Exclusion*, Vol. 2, No. 1, April 2021, pp. 97–108.

22 'These foreign actresses, made to portray the ideal Indian woman, an educated high-caste, high-class Hindu, were given names like Sita Devi, thanks to which the male Indian spectator could possess the "English" beauty and in so doing enact a reversal of the power relation that prevailed in British-dominated colonial society.' See Aasita Bali, 'Female Body in Indian Cinema: A Reflection', *International Journal of Linguistics, Literature and Culture (Linqua- IJLLC)*, Vol. 1, No. 1, August 2014, p. 100.

23 'A considerable amount of scholarly work on the impact and influence of Bombay cinema have looked at the centrality of the nation (Chakravarty 1993, Mazumdar 2000) in cinema as central to identity formation and as a major site for the expression of national melodramas, desires and anxieties.' See Tupur Chatterjee, 'Size Zero Begums and Dirty Pictures: The Contemporary Female Star in Bollywood', *Synoptique—An Online Journal of Film and Moving Images Studies*, Vol. 3, No. 1, Spring 2014, p. 5.

24 'Jackie Stacey has worked on British women and their memories of film stars from the 1940s and 50s. She found that identification with stars developed across several different layers: worship, admiration, and

aspiration, which she terms 'cinematic identificatory practices', where the star is imagined as the ideal other.' See Chatterjee, 'Size Zero Begums and Dirty Pictures: The Contemporary Female Star in Bollywood', p. 4.

25 Ibid., pp. 4–5.

26 Aalokitaa Basu, 'Vidya Balan's weight loss takes fans by surprise, internet reacts to sudden transformation: 'She has reduced so much', *Hindustan Times*, 14 June 2024.

27 Shoma Munshi, 'A Perfect 1 –"Modern and Indian": Representations of the Body in Beauty Pageants and the Visual Media in Contemporary India', in James Mill and Satadru Sen (eds.), *Confronting the Body: The Politics of Physicality in Colonial and Post-Colonial India*, London: Anthem Press, 2004, pp. 162–83.

28 'What is Kareena Kapoors Size Zero Secret?', YouTube.

29 Kareena Kapoor Khan, 'Foreword', in Rujuta Diwekar, *Don't Lose Your Mind, Lose Your Weight*, New Delhi: Penguin Random House, 2011.

30 In the Zoom video, Morzaria talks about how it helped Kareena go from 65 to 54 kilograms, 'becoming the new fitness mantra for actresses'.

31 In another testament to how we identify with celebrities as the ideal other, Sana said, 'Adnan Saami had also lost a lot of weight, and his diet had boiled dal for lunch. So, we adopted that idea from there. I cut down on junk food. I was fond of chips, [but I ate] no chips till the age of eighteen, nor any cold drinks or chocolates.'

32 In one 2015 video, Tiwari too is heard saying that Kareena is 'not actually a size zero'. 'If you see the actresses today, like Anushka Sharma or someone, they're all already thin. We wouldn't call them size zero because that's their frame already,' she said on our call. '[But] Kareena's a Punjabi. Her arms and calves are hatti katti. For her, that was a size zero fit.' Also see Pankaj Molekhi, 'Size Zero is a creation of media: Rujuta Diwekar', *Economic Times*, 5 December 2010.

33 Aseem Hasnain & Abhilasha Srivastava, 'What makes Indian vegetarians different from Westerners who have given up meat?', *Scroll.in*, 9 April 2018.

34 Soutik Biswas, 'The myth of the Indian vegetarian nation', *BBC*, 4 April 2018.

35 Amrit Dhillon, 'In India, caste system ensures you are what you eat', *My News*, 26 July 2015.

36 After multiple legs of the campaign world over, 'Real Beauty Stories' came to India in 2016. It took so long because 'there's a journey the brand has to go through in order to stand up [to norms]. We did groundwork with schools, working with children who had issues dealing with beauty standards, getting them counselling, which gave us a base to talk about these things,' said SB.; See also North, 'The past, present, and future of body image in America'.

37 Anne Helen Peterson, 'The Millennials Vernacular of Fatphobia', Annehelen.substack, 23 May 2021, available at annehelen.substack.com/p/the-Millennials-vernacular-of-fatphobia.

38 Lucy Whitehouse, 'Dove takes its 'Real Beauty' marketing drive to India', Cosmeticdesign.com, 24 February 2016, available at www.cosmeticsdesign. com/Article/2016/02/24/Dove-takes-its-Real-Beauty-marketing-drive-to-India.

39 Kareena Kapoor, *The Diary of Bollywood Style Diva*, London: Penguin UK, 2012.

40 J. Ruiz-Turrero, K. Massar, D. Kwasnick, GA Ten Hoor, 'The Relationship between Compulsive Exercise, Self-Esteem, Body Image and Body Satisfaction in Women: A Cross-Sectional Study', *International Journal of Environmental Research and Public Health*, Vol. 19, No. 3, 2022, available at pmc.ncbi.nlm.nih.gov/articles/PMC8835063.

41 Aditya Gautam, *Indian Millennials: Who Are They, Really?*, New Delhi: Aleph Book Company, 2024.

CHAPTER 4: PLEASE GET MARRIED BEFORE I DIE?

1 Genuinely how funny the show is; Joey saying 'the line is a dot to you', the iconic characters and their well-defined personality traits that become the butt of jokes; it's like Sitcom Writing 101, and having a problem with this show is just a way to ask for recognition

2 The statement here is purposely choosing less than one can afford; Tahiliani references a bride who could afford whatever she wanted, but just wore a simple neckpiece. See 'Tarun Tahiliani on trend of pastels in weddings: 'Bright colours seem little costumey for some people', *The Telegraph*, 13 October 2023.

3 The amount spent on the wedding ranges from USD$6,000 to US$600,000, although I personally know of a couple that spent USD$1.2million on their Really Big Day. See Yoonji Han, 'A woman who saved $10,000 on her Indian wedding said in order to cut costs, you should put yourself first and not compete with other couples', *Business Insider*, 10 October 2023.; 'Wedding Loans: Are Gen-Z, Millennialsrisking their financial future in pursuit of social media "likes"', *Money Control*, 1 October 2024.

4 These hashtags always have 'winning' puns.

5 Thirty per cent of these weddings occur during the famed November–December #WeddingSzn, which is a reliable time to expect friends and family from across borders back in the country. See '32 Lakh Weddings In India During November-December To Generate Huge Business', *Zee Biz*, 6 January 2024. Also see Shruti Mahajan, 'India's $210 Billion Wedding Industry Warms to LGBTQ Ceremonies', *Bloomberg*, 15 June 2023.; Varuni Khosla, 'India has 25% of the world's weddings', *Live Mint*, 10 March 2023.

6 'You haven't been to India until you've been to an Indian wedding', Joinmywedding.com, available at www.joinmywedding.com.

7 I'm thinking of the several similar-looking pictures and videos I've seen on

Instagram that attest to the phenomenon. Once a girl is about to become a bride, her feed becomes flooded with live footage of her progression until she is done, which, fortunately for her, takes a while. Indeed, the material gathered from three days of ceremonies lasts at least a few months on the content calendar. One bride uploaded a Reel about '*POV: Your varmala sets standards for future girlies.*' Another's wedding reel was captioned, 'A Love Story as Magical as a Bollywood Wedding'. Another reel.

8   'Featured Weddings', Weddingsutra.com, available at www.weddingsutra.com/real-weddings/featured-weddings.

9   'Payal Kataria and Shubham Kothari, Sheraton Grand Bengaluru Whitefield Hotel', Weddingsutra.com, available at www.weddingsutra.com/real-weddings/featured-weddings/payal-kataria-and-shubham-kothari-sheraton-grand-bengaluru-whitefield-hotel.

10 The idea was to have a court marriage, appease the parents and families in with any traditional ceremonies (small), but then fuck off to Goa, where a two-storey villa would couch an epic rager and psychedelic romp over a weekend with my closest friends that would be talked about for years to come.

11 OG readers will remember I mentioned these difficulties of being single in my piece on it for *NDTV*, which I also shared on Twitter with a picture of my tits (almost) out. See Sanjana Ramachandran, 'The 'Woman-Math' Of A 31-Year-Old, Unmarried, Bengaluru Woman', *NDTV World*, 30 July 2024.; Sanjana Ramachandran, Post, X.com, 30 July 2024, available at x.com/ramachandranesk/status/1818174961972126085.

12 These statistics are from the 2019-2021 National Family Health Survey (NFHS-5). On the after-effects: consanguineous marriages also lead to a greater incidence of genetic abnormalities amongst children, who become more likely to receive and carry two copies of a recessive gene (which is when disorders kick in. It takes two!). The nature of these marriages is different from the consanguineous marriages within Muslim communities, where the union is typically between parallel cousins (a child from a parent's same-sex sibling), as opposed to cross cousins (a child from a parent's opposite-sex sibling). In my case, my grandmother was suggesting I marry a cross cousin, as is the South Indian Hindu consanguineous tradition. It is this practice, by the way, that wiped out the royal Hapsburg family, who are 'to a great extent the emblems of the downsides of inbreeding'. From an online biography of one of the last of them: 'The Habsburg King Carlos II of Spain was sadly degenerated with an enormous misshapen head. His Habsburg jaw stood so much out that his two rows of teeth could not meet; he was unable to chew. His tongue was so large that he was barely able to speak. His intellect was similarly disabled. His brief life consisted chiefly of a passage from prolonged infancy to premature senility.' Is it possible that the Brahmins could inbreed themselves out of existence? Discuss. See

Razib Khan, 'Inbreeding and the Downfall of the Spanish Hapsburgs', *Discover Magazine,*15 April 2009.

13   B. R. Ambedkar, *Castes in India: Their Mechanism, Genesis and Development*, Jalandhar: Patrika Publications, 1916, pp. 11–15.

14   So, the insertion of romance in marriage is fairly recent, driven by nineteenth century novels like *Pride and Prejudice,* which made yearning middle-class and fashionable. Capitalism further turned love into a marketable product, with the rise of advertising and Valentine's Day, making love seem indispensable to life. Stephanie Coontz details this in *Marriage, a History: How Love Conquered Marriage*—a must-read on how marriage shifted from a tool of power to a masquerade of passion.

15   G Morris Carstairs and Ravi L. Kapur, *The Great Universe of Kota Stress, Change, and Mental Disorder in an Indian Village*, USA: University of California Press, 1976.; 'Pranav's Thread Ceremony Madhwa Brahmin Upanayana at Kashi Mutt, Bangalore | Sanasamhramaa Events', YouTube, 8 April 2020, available at www.youtube.com/watch?v=t14MmcxBlA8.

16   Deep Mukherjee, 'Looking for love and finding caste on dating apps', *Indian Express*, 28 October 2023.

17   In a 2018 survey of more than 160,000 households, 93 per cent of married Indians said that theirs was an arranged marriage. Just 3 per cent had a 'love marriage' and another 2 per cent described theirs as a 'love-cum-arranged marriage', which usually indicates that the relationship was set up by the families, and then the couple agreed to get married. There has been only very slight change over time — 94 per cent of octogenarians had an arranged marriage, and the figure remains over 90 per cent for young couples in their 20s. Marrying within your caste remains an essential feature of marriage in India. In a 2014 survey of more than 70,000 people, fewer than 10 per cent of urban Indians said that anyone in their family had married outside their caste and not many more outside their jati or sub-caste. Interfaith marriage was even rarer — just 5 per cent of urban respondents said that anyone in their family had married outside their religion. Younger people in India often profess their willingness to marry outside their caste. But there is a large gap between the stated (how much people say they value something in a survey) and revealed preferences (actual decisions people make). See 'What the data tells us about love and marriage in India', *BBC*, 8 December 2021.

18   'Like anything' is such a classic Indianism. It can intensify any action or emotion, functioning like a superlative without even being one. 'It was raining like anything'; 'he was smiling like anything'. What does 'anything' mean here? No one knows, no one asks. It's a feeling, a linguistic flourish that turns up the volume on an experience without bothering with specifics. An all-purpose amplifier, used like...well, anything.

19   According to a government survey, a growing number of Indians are preferring to remain single across genders. The percentage of single men

has gone up from 20.8 per cent in 2011 to 26.1 per cent in 2019. And the proportion of unmarried females increased from 13.5 per cent in 2011 to 19.9 per cent in 2019. See Neeraj Deodhar, 'Yaar Paarivar', *Mid-day*, 5 November 2023.

20   I checked with Beyonce, and she is honoured to be in my footnotes. Also see 'Philomena Cunk's most HILARIOUS interviews | Cunk on Earth – BBC', YouTube, 1 November 2022, available at www.youtube. com/watch?v=JWS-qfR6K3w.

21   The man in this play is wrong. According to 'Gen Z is Killing Hook Up Culture', an individual's value is becoming less tied to their relationship status. A Hinge study found that 78 per cent of its users are investing in their mental health first, while 97 per cent want partners who do the same. See 'Hinge survey says Gen Z over 'hookup culture' post-COVID', *New York Post*, 30 August 2022.

22   'Fatherless Behavior', Knowyourmeme.com, 2021, available at knowyourmeme.com/memes/fatherless-behavior.

23   Susan E. Schwartz, *The Absent Father Effect on Daughters: Father Desire, Father Wounds*, Routledge: New York, 2021.

CHAPTER 5: WORK, WORK, WORK, WORK, WORK?

1   Capitalism and war, though strange bedfellows, have birthed innovations that changed countries and the supermarket aisle alike. World War II was responsible for SPAM, a canned 'delicacy' that fed troops and then found its way to the average breakfast table. We also got duct tape, which was first used to waterproof ammo cases before it became a fix-all for everything from leaky pipes to home-made science projects. War's more dramatic children also included the radar and the atomic bomb, the latter becoming a proverbial device to examine the mores of scientific and creative genius being applied to dystopian collective ends.

2   We're now at another final frontier as artificial intelligence reaches for what we have always believed to be 'intrinsically human': creative, knowledge work. Interesting questions arise from the fact that Large Language Models (LLMs), the technology behind the new era of Generative Artificial Intelligence, are essentially sophisticated statistical engines that generate outputs by 'predicting' what should come next for a given input, based on their continuous ingestion and learning from similar patterns in the large data sets they've been trained on. It's well-known that human beings are essentially biological machines, phenomena arising from complex interactions of matter that produces a 'mind', or consciousness, or sentience. Douglas Hofstadter, a cognitive scientist and AI researcher, who believed that self-referential thought was the essence of human consciousness, was shocked to find LLMs were producing human-like thoughts from just 'feed-forward' mechanisms—that is, non-loopy thought patterns—which made him change his mind about the

state of AI from dismissive to 'human beings are about to be eclipsed'.

3   William Rees-Mogg and James Dale Davidson, *The Sovereign Individual: Mastering the Transition to the Information Age*, 1999, New York: Touchstone, 1999, p. 296.

4   According to a survey, those who have been in their jobs for less than two years were about 10 per cent more likely to live hand-to-mouth than those who had been with their employers for more than five years. See Deloitte, '2023 Gen Z and Millennials Survey', Deloitte.com, 2023, available at www2.deloitte.com/content/dam/Deloitte/global/Documents/deloitte-2023-genz-millennial-survey.pdf

5   Liucija Adomaite and Mantas Kacerauskas, "Me Vs. My Parents" Memes That Show How Different Our Generations Are', Boredpanda.com, 8 December 2020, available at www.boredpanda.com/me-vs-parents-memes.

6   50 per cent of Gen Zs and 47per cent of Millennials reported that starting a family would become harder or impossible. 61 per cent of Gen Zs and 62 per cent of Millennials think buying a house will become harder or impossible. See Deloitte, '2023 Gen Z and Millennials Survey'.

7   According to the Deloitte report, Gen Zs and Millennials like social media as creative outlets that also connect them with friends and family and social justice causes. Over half of Gen Zs (56 per cent) and Millennials(51 per cent) say that mental health resources have also been made more accessible to them through social media. But more than four in 10 say social media makes them feel lonely and inadequate (46 per cent of Gen Zs versus 40 per cent of Millennials), and also pressured to have an online presence (45 per cent of Gen Zs/40per cent of Millennials). The vast majority of Gen Zs (87 per cent) and Millennials(80 per cent) use social media to consume news, as a better source above national news providers. But the constant flow of information adds to stress; more than six in 10 Gen Zs (63 per cent) and Millennials(61per cent) say they frequently or occasionally limit their exposure to protect their mental health. There is a clear need to switch off from online activity to feel better. Respondents cite in-person activities and physical exercise as the top drivers of good mental health. See ibid.

8   To be clear, I'm not even slightly suggesting that capitalism is worse than communism. Socialism works well. *The Economist*'s review of *The Corporation*, a Canadian documentary that compares the corporation to a psychopath, found the film 'a surprisingly rational attack on capitalism's most important institution', and 'a thought-provoking account of the firm'. But the film heavily leans towards public ownership as a solution to the issues it depicts, while failing to acknowledge the magnitude of evils committed in the name of public ownership, as with the Communist Party in the former Soviet Union. See 'The Lunatic You Work For', *The Economist*, 6 May 2004.

9   Tim Worstall, 'Hans Rosling And Ha-Joon Chang Agree, The Washing Machine Is A More Important Invention Than The Internet', *Forbes*, 2 December 2023.

10 Fuller and Narasimhan, *Tamil Brahmans*, p. 90.

11 '... Gender inequality was extreme among Tamil Brahmans and markedly more so than among the vast majority of south Indian non-Brahman groups. A key aspect of this inequality was prepuberty marriage for girls. In Tamil Nadu, prepuberty marriage was largely confined to Brahmans and was the practice not only in old-fashioned rural families, but also in those headed by the educated professional men who formed the new urban middle class of colonial Madras.' Even in the nineteenth century in the Madras Presidency, when only very small numbers of Brahman girls went to school, at least as many were receiving basic education at home; in some Brahman families, indeed, there was a strong tradition of female education imparted within the home. By 1901, the Brahmans' female literacy rate in Tamil stood a little higher than a decade earlier at 5.8 per cent, and it went up to 38.5 per cent in 1931 (the comparable male rates were 73.6 and 87.6 per cent, respectively), while in English it rose from virtually zero to 3.1 percent (17.9 and 44.8 per cent for males).' See ibid. pp. 123–24.

12 'The 1985 Ambasankar Commission report showed that the overall indices for higher academic qualifications among Brahmans were higher than for any other caste in Tamil Nadu at the time, thus confirming that their pre-independence lead over the rest of the population had been maintained over four decades. It is highly unlikely that this position has changed since the 1980s... In 1951, the Madras state government, led by the Congress party, introduced a 25 per cent quota for Other Backward Classes (OBC) in college places and government jobs, which the DMK government raised to 31 per cent in 1973 and the ADMK government to 50 per cent in 1980. The reservation system gradually reduced the number of Brahmans in state government so that not many were left by late twentieth century.' See ibid, p. 90.

13 'In general, though, gender inequality was and is more pronounced among high-castes. Hence the conduct of daughters, wives, mothers, and widows is most severely constrained by purity and pollution rules, seclusion practices, moral rigidity, and obsessive control of female sexuality among Brahmans and other high-ranking castes. Low-caste women, by contrast, are more relaxed about purity, commonly work outside the home so that they cannot be secluded, are less influenced by Brahmanical norms, and are often less subject to male authority, although these features themselves contribute to the low status of their families and communities.' See ibid., p. 123.

14 Fuller and Narasimhan, *Tamil Brahmans*, p. 135.

15 The *High-Caste Hindu Woman* by Pandita Ramabai Sarasvati establishes the links between religious scriptures and the violence done to girls

through dowry, marriage, and whatever follows after, which you will see more of in Chapter 6. Writer Annie Zaidi recommends reading Ramabai's description of the woes of upper-caste women alongside Baby Kamble's account of the lives of Dalit women, and Bama's autobiography, *Karukku*. 'All of them speak of a cycle of oppression and the need for literacy and financial independence in order to break this vicious cycle,' writes Zaidi. See Annie Zaidi (ed.), *Unbound: 2000 Years of Indian Women's Writing*, New Delhi: Aleph Book Company, 2015.

16 'To be sure, gender inequality has not vanished among Tamil Brahmans. Women always have to face the competing pressures of family and career as men do not; in addition, to mention a few salient examples, the domestic division of labor is usually unequal, many women still observe menstrual pollution, female sexuality is normally strictly controlled, and women, especially when single, are subject to much more moral surveillance than men. All the same, it is striking how many ideas about female inferiority that used to matter a great deal have been abandoned by Tamil Brahmans during the last century or so. That suggests, at least in this case, that caste inequality is more deeply rooted than gender inequality, in line with Carol Mukhopadhyay and Susan Seymour's observation that 'elite, upper-status women' from the 'formerly most prototypically patrifocal' groups 'have achieved the most educationally and ... appear to be challenging traditional patrifocal structures and ideology.' Perhaps unsurprisingly, Tamil Brahman men have in the end more readily ceded status to Brahman women than Brahmans collectively have done to non-Brahmans, so that notions of caste superiority have persisted, while gender inequality has diminished.' See Fuller and Narasimhan, *Tamil Brahmans*, p. 151.

17 Chedwyn Fernandez and Havishaye Puri, 'A Statistical Portrait of the Indian Female Labor Force', *Policy Brief*, No. 2023–17 December, p. 1.

18 International Labour Organization, 'ILO Modelled Estimates and Projections database (ILOEST)', Data.worldbank.org, available at data. worldbank.org/indicator/SL.TLF.CACT.FE.ZS.

19 Archana Chaudhary, Saritha Rai, and Dhwani Pandya, 'India's Women Are Being Driven Out of the Workforce', *Bloomberg*, 29 May 2018.

20 UN Women, 'Your questions answered: Women and COVID-19 in India', Unwomen.org, 27 July 2021, available at www.unwomen.org/en/news/ stories/2021/7/faq-women-and-covid-19-in-india.

21 Ibid.

22 Ronojoy Mazumdar and Archana Chaudhury, '90% of Women in India Are Shut Out of the Workforce', *Bloomberg*, 2 June 2022.; PTI, 'India's working women still contend with strongest gender bias across Asia Pacific countries: Report', Yourstory.com, 2 March 2021, available at yourstory. com/herstory/2021/03/india-working-women-gender-bias-workplace.

23 Christine Lagard and Jonathan D. Ostry, 'Economic Gains from Gender

Inclusion: Even Greater than You Thought', *IMF Blog*, 28 November 2018, available at www.imf.org/en/Blogs/Articles/2018/11/28/blog-economic-gains-from-gender-inclusion-even-greater-than-you-thought.; UN Women, 'Facts and figures: Economic empowerment', Unwomen.org, available at www.unwomen.org/en/what-we-do/economic-empowerment/facts-and-figures.; 'India's booming population needs more women at work', *BBC*, 10 Mat 2023.

24   Mazumdar and Chaudhury, '90% of Women in India Are Shut Out of the Workforce'.; Tim Henderson, 'Mothers Are 3 Times More Likely Than Fathers to Have Lost Jobs in Pandemic', *Stateline*, 28 September 2020.

25   Sonal Garg and Sabhya Rai, 'Opinion: Unpaid care work by women the missing link in analysis of gender gaps in labour outcomes', *Economic Times*, 24 January 2022.

26   Morgan Smith, 'Nobel Prize-winning Harvard economist Claudia Goldin: The gender pay gap will 'never' close unless this happens', *CNBC*, 10 October 2023.

27   Mazumdar and Chaudhury, '90% of Women in India Are Shut Out of the Workforce'.

28   Mariel Cooksey, 'Why Are Gen Z Girls Attracted to the Tradwife Lifestyle?', Politicalresearch.org, 29 June 2021, available at politicalresearch.org/2021/07/29/why-are-gen-z-girls-attracted-tradwife-lifestyle.; Nicolo Froio, '"Trad wives" are using social media to romanticize a return to 'traditional values' as more and more women face post-COVID work/life balance burnout', *Business Insider*, 7 November 2022.

29   The report was based on a survey of 29,999 Indian adults between late 2019 and early 2020, before the Covid-19 pandemic, to understand how Indians view gender roles at home and in society more generally. See 'Coronavirus (COVID-19)', Pewresearch.org, available at www.pewresearch.org/topic/coronavirus-disease-covid-19.

30   Raksha Kumar, 'The enduring sexism of India's tech industry', Restofworld.org, 1 November 2022, available at restofworld.org/2022/sexism-india-tech-sector.

31   Towards the end of *Marvellous Mrs Maisel*, when Midge is questioning her foray into stand-up comedy, she encounters Gordon Ford, the host of a national talk show. He likes her set, develops a crush on her, and hires her as a writer for his show, where she learns how to write comedy for television, hoping she'll get to do her own performance for a primetime audience soon. Ford keeps her around, offering her some opportunity or the other except the one she really wants. Her eventual rejection of him almost gets her cast out of the show. Midge finally gets her primetime spot by hook *and* crook: while on a segment with Ford, she grabs the spotlight by walking up to the mic and performing despite his attempts to keep her seated. And the rest became history, according to the show's ending. That is what many artists, especially women, have to do succeed.

Walk through the same barriers over and over again, until you can walk around them at some point.

32 Interestingly enough, LGBT+ Millennials were found more likely to report the harassment they experienced to their employer than LGBT+ Gen Zs. See Deloitte, '2023 Gen Z and Millennials Survey', p. 27.

33 The Deloitte report's findings on the youth's' attitudes towards remote work:

- It enables better work/life balance by freeing up time to spend with family and friends (20 per cent of Gen Zs and 28 per cent of Millennials), to pursue hobbies (20 per cent of Gen Zs and 25 per cent of Millennials), and take care of responsibilities outside of work (20 per cent of Gen Zs and 25 per cent of Millennials).
- It helps save money by reducing expenses related to commuting, buying work clothes, and dry cleaning (22 per cent of Gen Zs and 27 per cent of Millennials).
- For many, it drives greater productivity allowing them to stay focused without the typical distractions of an office environment (18 per cent of Gen Zs and 23 per cent of Millennials).

See Deloitte, '2023 Gen Z and Millennials Survey', p. 17.

34 But McKinsey's Women in the Workplace 2023 Report found that hybrid and remote work helped both men and women with better work-life balance. 83 per cent of employees cited the ability to work more efficiently and productively as a primary benefit of working remotely. See Alexis Krivkovich, Emily Field, Lareina Yee, and Megan McConnell, and Hannah Smith, 'Women in the Workplace 2024: The 10th-anniversary report', Mckinsey.com, available at www.mckinsey.com/featured-insights/diversity-and-inclusion/women-in-the-workplace.

35 'When study participants saw through video footage that a female employee wasn't at her desk, this was attributed to something nonwork-related 47 percent of the time; for men, it was attributed to nonwork activities just 34 percent of the time. And in a study of engineers at a Fortune 500 company, remote work had a negative effect on the amount of feedback junior employees, particularly women, got on their work. 'Proximity has a bigger impact on women's comfort with asking follow-up questions,' said Emma Harrington, an economist at the University of Virginia, who conducted both the study on remote work's effect on feedback and the one on mothers' work force participation. Men appeared more comfortable asking clarifying questions even if they weren't physically near colleagues. See Ben Casselman, Emma Goldberg and Ella Koeze, 'Who Still Works From Home?', New York Times, 8 March 2024.

36 Krivkovich, Field, Yee, and McConnell, and Smith, 'Women in the Workplace 2024: The 10th-anniversary report'.

37 Ibid.

38 Ibid.

39   Casselman, Goldberg and Koeze, 'Who Still Works From Home?'.

40   '4.0 Documentary - 'The Corporation', Rdmc.nottingham.ac.uk, available at rdmc.nottingham.ac.uk/bitstream/handle/internal/86/Business_edit/40_documentary_the_corporation.html.

41   'While respondents acknowledge that their employers have made some progress, the majority remain unimpressed with businesses' societal impact overall. Less than half believe business is having a positive impact on society. Gen Zs are slightly more likely to believe business is having a positive impact (48 per cent versus 44 per cent of Millennials). Less than half of Gen Zs (48 per cent) and Millennials(44per cent) believe business is having a positive impact on society, although notably, among Gen Zs, this is the first year that percentage hasn't dropped in over five years. Six in 10 Gen Zs and Millennials believe businesses have no ambition beyond wanting to make money. Nearly four in 10 (44 per cent of Gen Zs/37 per cent of Millennials) say they have rejected assignments due to ethical concerns, while 39 per cent/34 per cent have turned down employers that do not align with their values. They want to be empowered to drive change within their organizations.' See Deloitte, '2023 Gen Z and Millennials Survey', p. 7.

42   See Mike Robbins, *Bring Your Whole Self to Work: How Vulnerability Unlocks Creativity, Connection and Performance*, UK: Hay House, 2018, p. 1.

43   From Mike Robbins's *Bring Your Whole Self to Work: How Vulnerability Unlocks Creativity, Connection and Performance,* the five principles of bringing your whole self to work: first, be authentic—bring all parts of yourself, flaws and strengths included, as honesty fosters trust and connection. Second, utilize the power of appreciation—express genuine gratitude and acknowledge others' contributions, creating a positive work culture. Third, focus on emotional intelligence—develop self-awareness and empathy, which are critical for navigating interpersonal dynamics. Fourth, embrace a growth mindset—see challenges as opportunities for learning rather than as setbacks. Finally, create a culture of belonging—help others feel included and valued, ensuring everyone can contribute their true selves without fear of exclusion or judgement. You're welcome! See Robbins, *Bring Your Whole Self to Work*, p. 12.

44   Apparently, a woman prone to using cuss words decided to incorporate them into her speech at work, and that did not go down very well. Surprise, surprise. See Henry Blodget, 'Actually, it's a bad idea to bring your "whole self" to work', *Business Insider*, 16 February 2024.

45   Kancha Ilaiah Shepherd, *Why I Am not a Hindu: A Sudra Critique of Hindutva*, Calcutta: Samya, 1996, p. 67.

46   Ibid., p. 66.

47   David Graeber, *Bullshit Jobs: A Theory*, New York: Simon and Schuster, 2018, p. 23.

48 In her article in the *New Yorker*, Jia Tolentino begins with this David Graeber quote, 'In our society, there seems a general rule that, the more obviously one's work benefits other people, the less one is likely to be paid for it.' The essay goes on to argue that motherhood, like everything else under capitalism today, can be performative, but in reclaiming its complexities, women can redeem it as a form of rebellion. See Jia Tolentino, 'Can Motherhood Be a Mode of Rebellion?', *New Yorker*, 8 May 2022, available at www.newyorker.com/books/under-review/can-motherhood-be-a-mode-of-rebellion.

49 E. F. Schumacher, *Small Is Beautiful: Economics As if People Mattered*, Vancouver: Hartley and Marks, 1999, p. 41.

50 Harry Cheadle, 'Are You Really an Anti-Capitalist? Or Do You Just Hate Your Job?', *News Republic*, 2 November 2022, available at newrepublic. com/article/168323/really-anti-capitalist-just-hate-job.

51 Paul Graham, 'Hackers and Painters', Paulgraham.com, available at paulgraham.com/hp.html.

52 Sanjana Ramachandran, 'OpenAI, Apple iPad: Big Tech Is Triggering Too Many People, Too Fast', *NDTV*, 16 May 2024.

53 Kristen R. Ghodsee, *Why Women Have Better Sex Under Socialism: And Other Reasons for Economic Independence*, New York: Bold Type Book, 2018.

54 Jonah Peretti, 'Capitalism and Schizophrenia Contemporary Visual Culture and the Acceleration of Identity Formation/Dissolution', *Negations*, available at www.datawranglers.com/negations/issues/96w/96w_peretti. html.

CHAPTER 6: WHAT IS LOVE? BABY, DON'T HURT ME.

1 For example, 'Your Gujju Accent is so Sexy Part 5' and 'Love Your Gujarati Accent'. I first heard the template applied to the Urdu language, which is genuinely sexy and thus universally used for romance purposes. Soon it spread to just about every language, sincerely and ironically, depending on the maker's intent and talents. You decide how the Gujju accent fares. See 'Your Gujarat Accent is so Sexy', YouTube, 3 March 2023, available at www.youtube.com/shorts/piHempx309Q.; 'Love Their Gujarati Accent', YouTube, 30 July 2021, available at www.youtube.com/ shorts/NIGnKTFzCwM.

2 Paulo Coelho, *Veronica Decides to Die*, Margaret Jull Costa (tr.), London: Harper, 1999, p. 69.

3 Alice Miller, *The Drama of the Gifted Child*,

4 He said he was too 'shy' to do it from anywhere else. Some other facts about him are that he likes smoking and drinking—who doesn't, goodfella?—but what's interesting is that in his case, he shouldn't ideally, since he can be clubbed with the nationalistic crowd, which also tends to be the fanatically religious Hindu crowd. I also didn't expect Faatak to

be a source of irony, but the incident that led to his arrest in 2019 was because Faatak roused his fanbase, largely students, to protest against the offline exams that were announced despite the beginning of the Covid-19 pandemic. See Mohamad Thaver, 'Explained: Who Is Hindustani Bhau?', *Indian Express*, 1 February 2022.

5   'A Hindu family is hierarchical. Girls must obey boys, children must obey elders. Sex and age are two determining and measuring rods of the status within the family. Children are trained not to get involved in production-related tasks, which Brahmins condemn as "Sudra" tasks.'

- 'In these families God and men are equated in many respects. But in our families the situation is very different ... At [Dalit homes, mother, father, and children] live as equals, eating, drinking and smoking together. They are equals from childhood onwards. The father and the mother teach children these things as part of their education. Equality and morality are not two different entities for parents and children.'

- 'Discussion of sexual behaviour is a taboo in Hindu families. Mothers are not supposed to talk to daughters about their sexual experiences. The father's atrocities against the mother cannot be discussed in Brahmin or Baniya families. But this is not so in our families. The father abuses the mother right in front of the children and the mother will pay back in the same coin then and there. The children are a witness to all that. In Hindu families the father can abuse the mother, but the mother is not supposed to retort. A wife is supposed to put up with all the atrocities that a husband commits against her; the more a wife puts up with the husband's atrocities the more she is appreciated.'

See Shepherd, *Why I Am not a Hindu*, pp. 9–10.

6   'CEO Jack Dorsey holds placard saying Smash Brahminical Patriarchy, now there is caste war on Twitter', *India Today*, 21 November 2018.

7   This endnote is for posterity, in my hope that this book will prove timeless and long-lived despite being hyper-contemporary. The endnote seeks the definition(s) of 'fr,' or 'fr, fr'. For instance, *Cambridge* would tell you that Fr is a noun and a written abbreviation for Father, when used as a title of a Christian priest, especially a Roman Catholic or Orthodox priest. *Collins* goes further and offers that Fr is a written abbreviation for French or franc, or short for the German 'Frau', or the English 'friar', or the elemental 'francium', or, in the context of real estate, 'family room'. As of the early 2020s, however, 'fr' stands for 'for real', really. 'It is an internet initialism that you can use in direct messages,'—which are sometimes abbreviated as DMs; you're welcome—'to emphasize your point, agree with someone else's point, or react to something unbelievable.' All this from HowToGeek.com—ikr?—which also says 'an interesting thing about FR is that it can take the form of both a question and an answer'. Just like this everlasting book.

8   To name a few: *Castes in India* by Ambedkar, and also *Riddles in Hindusim, The Philosophy of Hinduism*, and *The Annihilation of Caste*; *Why Were Women Enslaved* by EV Periyar; *Debrahminizing History* by Braj Ranjan Mani; *Of Oppressor's Body and Mind* by Yogesh Maitreya; *Caste Matters* by Suraj Yengde; Anurag Minus Verma's podcast; *Land, Guns, Caste, Woman* by Gita Ramaswamy; the works of Gail Omvedt, U. R. Ananthamurthy, Mathampu Kunhukuttan, and Lalithambika Antharjanam.

9   It takes only a few decades of living to know that every human being carries within them equal capacity for good and bad, no matter what their identity or how marginalized it is. What matters is only how conscious you are, and even the most conscious sin—just look at the number of cases of sexual abuse springing from Buddhist sangha, or my other arguments in chapter seven. What is called for, therefore, is not more infighting between identities about who robbed whom of what; once that is established, we need greater openness to developing unconditional love and compassion, for ourselves and others—a skill issue, no doubt, and it is as hard as it sounds. More, again, in chapter seven.

10 The *Vriddha Harita*, written roughly between 600–900 BCE, states that 'the widow should give up chewing betel nut, wearing perfumes, flowers, ornaments, and dyed clothes, taking food from vessels of bronze, [eating] two meals a day, applying collyrium to the eyes. She should wear only white garments, curb her senses and anger, and sleep on the ground.' See Uma Chakravarti and Preeti Gill, *Shadow Lives: Writings on Widowhood*, New Delhi: Kali for Women, 2001, p. 38.

11 From the book: 'When her own blood flowed every month, a woman was defiled. She had to sit outside the house for three days. On the fourth day, she was purified, and could then become madi. Many women in Phaniyamma's family continued to menstruate after the fourth day, but they were still considered madi. The widows who were touched by the barber were still madi. But those widows who had full heads of hair were considered absolutely impure even though they had never been touched by a man. Hundreds of questions about these things plagued Phaniyamma.' See M. K. Indira, *Phaniyamma*, Thejaswini Niranjana (tr.), India: South Asia Books, 1994.

12 Elders of the Tchamba-Kunsuntu Tribe believed they had to perform FGM on the applicant because she was a member of the PSG who had not undergone FGM, which was necessary to control her sexuality. See Celia W. Dugger, 'Woman's Plea for Asylum Puts Tribal Ritual on Trial', *New York Times*, 15 April 1996.

13 Tell me again that my expulsion from the college in Chennai had nothing to do with the casteist culture it was embedded in. Selvy Thiruchandran's notes how 'Going out late] is not socially approved within our circle (high class Brahmin). My husband or father-in-law [sic] will ask, why have you gone out? ... We have been expected

to behave ... The husband is our god. He is our world.' See Selvy Thiruchandran, 'Ideology, Caste, Class, and Gender', New Delhi: Vikas Publishing House, 1992, p. 92.

14 French quotes the case of a Brahmin woman from outside Delhi who felt unable to leave because of this stigmatic pressure. My own mother is another example of this.

15 French writes: 'While there are laws in place to protect victims of domestic violence, in reality it is difficult for women to invoke them. Section 319 criminalizes the act of causing physical harm to another, but in practice the police rarely enforce this law when the harm is between husband and wife, because many policemen still do not recognize domestic violence as a crime.' She refers to a paper called 'Getting away with murder: How law courts and police fail victims of domestic violence', which states that despite strengthened laws that criminalise harm to wives, the number of cases registered by the police and eventually punished by the courts did not increase. 'Section 498A of the Indian Penal Code, which specifically criminalizes domestic violence, was passed to close this loophole,' writes French. 'However, it only criminalizes domestic violence that 'results in punishment where the violence or harassment is likely to drive the woman to commit suicide or to cause grave danger.' Section 498A is therefore inadequate because a great deal of domestic violence consists of mental cruelty or violence that does not rise to the level of causing grave danger and thus does not fall under 498A. Vimochana [a voluntary organization working on cases of domestic violence in Bangalore] observes that police rarely intervene or press charges in cases of battering, regardless of the severity. When women try to bring their own 498A claims, police 'heavily scrutinize' such claims because of a perceived high incidence of claim fabrication.' See Geethadevi M and Shobha R Raghunandan, 'Getting away with murder. How law courts and police fail victims of domestic violence', Manushi, Vol. 11, 2000, pp. 31–41.

16 Sarah Kathryn French, 'Homely, Cultured Brahmin Woman Seeks Particular Social Group: Must Be Immutable, Particular, and Socially Visible', University of Colorado Law Review, Vol. 83, p. 1064.

17 Sharmila Rege, 'Brahmanical nature of violence against women', in Sunaina Arya and Aakash Singh Rathore (eds.), Dalit Feminist Theory: A Reader', New Delhi: Routledge India, 2014.

18 Lalithambika Antharjanam's father was a progressive Brahmin, who, on learning that he was having a daughter, became very upset, but not because of the usual reasons. He wanted to move away to 'Madras, become a Christian, and marry an Englishwoman,' so that he would 'at least be allowed to bring her up like a human being,' he told Lalithambika's mother. Growing up, people disapproved of the freedom he gave her.

19 Shepherd, Why I Am not a Hindu, p. 34.

20 Helen E. Ullrich, 'Caste differences between Brahmin and non-Brahmin women in a South Indian village', in Alice Schlegel (ed.), Sexual

Stratification: A Cross-Cultural View, New York: Columbia University Press, pp. 94–108.

21 There too, Sarah Kathryn French notes that urban, elite Brahmin women are also likelier to be married to powerful Brahmin men, as in Asha's case, who have connections that make it difficult to bring the abuser to justice.

22 Paraphrased from *I Haven't Had to Go Mad Here: The Psychotic's Journey from Dependence to Autonomy* by Joseph H. Berke: the moral of the story is that psychiatric problems are never a function of a single person. A 'psychiatric event' always involves a social network consisting of three sets of people: the first is the person who invokes distress in others and who may or may not be in distress himself. The second includes all the 'others' who become distressed in response to the first person's actions or lack of action and feelings or lack of feelings. (Certain people, for example, distress others by eating a lot; others by eating very little. Certain people cause distress by believing in God and others cause distress by not believing in God.) The third are 'recognized healers', who may reduce distress by a variety of socially acceptable treatments, such as drugs, restraints on autonomy, isolation, et cetera. See Joseph H. Berke, *I Haven't Had To Go Mad Here: The Psychotic's Journey From Dependence To Autonomy*, USA: Penguin Books, 1979.

23 Namboodiri Brahmins believed themselves to be superior to all other Brahmins, including the Patters (Tamil Brahmins) and the Embranthiris (Telugu Brahmins), on the basis of their sixty-four distinctly 'pure' practices. For example, while other Brahmins were 'pinkudumakar' (tying hair behind), the Namboodiri were 'munkudumakar' (tying hair in front). Other Brahmins wore a 'poonal'—also called the 'janeu' in North India, a holy thread worn like a sash to indicate Brahmin-ness—consisting of two threads. But the Nambudiri's poonal contained only one thread. Other Brahmins took a bath with their clothes on, but the Namboodiri did so naked. Other Brahmins took a bath while chanting the mantras, but the Namboodiris were forbidden not only to chant but also even think of mantras while bathing. Other Brahmins—the plebs—used to repeat the mantras after the main chanter, but the Namboodiri chanted the mantras individually. Other Brahmins washed their clothes themselves, but the Namboodiri used only clothes washed by 'Veluthedan'—the dhobi, a subcaste exclusively responsible for doing laundry. Other Brahmin women did not have a purdah, or veil, but the Nambudiri women were supposed to be seen only by her husband, not even by her own father or brothers. Other Brahmins exchanged greetings while meeting, but it was forbidden to do so for the Namboodiri. Other Brahmins, the downtrodden, were either Vishnavites or Shaivites (followers of Vishnu or Shiva), but the Namboodiri were cool enough to belong to neither of them. While the other Brahmins strictly practised marriage of their girls

before puberty—the conscientious fuckers—the Nambudiri women had no age limit for marriage! Lastly, only the eldest Namboodiri son could have an endogamous marriage—what a privilege—while other Brahmins' sons could all have endogamous marriages. Amazing.

24 The six stages of a smarthavicharam:

- The first stage was the 'dasi vicharam'—the trial of the maidservant—in which a prima facie report was taken from the maidservant about the suspected Antharjanam's sexual misdeeds. If this existed....

- The second stage, the 'anchampurayilackal', commenced, in which the Antharjanam was isolated in a special cell. The head of her family would inform the king about the trial, and he'd send four lawyers and a 'smarthan' (judge) to interrogate her.

- In the third stage, the Antharjanam is questioned by the smarthan, who'd sit outside her cell so that he wouldn't have to see her. A confession was obtained over days or weeks, depending on the severity of the case, even by resorting to physical torture. Popular methods included wrapping the woman in a mat and rolling her off the roof of a house, or letting rats or snakes into her cell, or getting other women, including relatives, to also torment her into an admission of guilt. If the accused woman finally accepted the allegations, she became 'santhanam', or inanimate. This inanimate object was still needed to implicate her 'jaarans', the men she slept with, who she'd identify with her knowledge of their bodies, by naming some unique marks around their private parts, perhaps. The smarthan would later verify these, and the trial would continue until there were no more jaarans.

- After this, in the 'swar ̄ipamchollal', the king would be informed about the men involved. If they denied their involvement, they were subject to a 'sathya-par ̄ik.sa' (test of truth). Innocence or guilt were determined through ordeals at the Suchindran temple, such as having the accused dip his hand in burning oil. If burnt, he was found guilty.

- In the penultimate stage, the 'dehavichedam', the saathanam and her jaarans are 'ceremoniously ostracized and excommunicated'.

- In the final stage, the 'shubhabhojanam', the trial team gets together to share a meal. If the accused are found innocent, they may also partake in it.

25 Any excommunicated Namboodiri man could seek an appeal by getting a 'pampu'—a letter from the relevant authority granting such an opportunity—but the woman was cast away permanently. There were special Namboodiri families known as Bhattathiris who were privileged to furnish the president (smarthan) and the number of members (mimamsakas) required to form a tribunal. Matampu Kunhukuttan, the author of the postmodernist retelling of the 1905 smarthavicharam,

Outcaste, had a grandfather was a smarthan for such trials.

26 The cost incurred by a family in dealing with the serious matter of a smarthavicharam could be between ⊠1,000– ⊠12,000. Nothing but the dread of being deprived of their caste privileges would induce a family to incur the odium and expense of such a trial, prompting them to turn against their own unerring members.

27 'It was definitely not for sexual fulfilment,' wrote Mathampu Kunhukuttan, the author of *Outcaste*. 'If the aim was sexual satiation, one or two physically fit men would have been enough. It was not to earn money either. It is said that she had a youthful yearning for beautiful things. But we can't wholly believe that either. Could revenge have been her motive? To punish the men who desired her body, she used the same body to excommunicate them... The impregnable fort that the Namboodiri built was opened by Thatri from the inside.'

CHAPTER 7: GOD: MUST I BELIEVE IN THEY/THEM?

1 Lots of meditation literature talks about the 'choicelessness' of true awareness. In *The Heart of Buddhist Meditation*, Nyanaponika Thera explores mindfulness as a state that gradually shifts from intention to flow, where action is governed by awareness rather than choice. Bhikkhu Bodhi's *In the Buddha's Words* uses early Buddhist teachings to describe how the journey unfolds as if from inner compulsion. They all suggest that meditation eventually becomes an expression of awareness, from a divine, invisible, gentle hand, rather than of conscious decision.

2 The fact that mental and physical health are acutely connected is properly visible in the lives in women. Our bodies often 'absorb' the emotions and invisible stresses from those around us. And because society is increasingly less about man-going-out-and-providing-and-woman-staying-at-home-and-nurturing, for better or worse, women are dealing with more pressures, both from professional success and traditional caregiving, while men continue to deal with mostly the former. According to a 2023 report by the American Psychological Association, women consistently report higher stress levels than men, with 30 per cent experiencing physical symptoms like fatigue and headaches. Research also indicates that both sexes process stress differently. While men are more likely to dissociate, or externalize it in the form of aggression or impulsivity. On the other hand, women are more likely to internalize stress, leading more readily to both physical and mental disorders. See Anna Medaris, 'Women say they're stressed, misunderstood, and alone', Apa.org, 1 November 2023, available at www.apa.org/topics/stress/women-stress.

3 'Sankhara' is the Pali word for a complex, or the mental formations and activities that have shaped our perceptions, actions, and reactions. They arise from deeply ingrained patterns and past experiences from god knows when, accumulating and influencing one's behavior, thoughts, and

feelings. Sankharas are karmic imprints—habits of mind that perpetuate suffering by clouding clarity and driving attachment. Through meditation, one comes face to face with one's sankharas, 'good' or 'bad', and by not reacting no matter how pleasant or unpleasant they feel, one gradually releases the sankharas. In its place rises pure consciousness and *wisdom*, allowing insight, starting the long walk to freedom from all conditioned cravings and aversions.

4   Western translations of 'dukkha' have incorrectly simplified it to mean 'suffering', 'sadness', or 'unhappiness', which misses the term's depth in Buddhist philosophy. 'Dukkha' is about the inherent unsatisfactoriness of 'conditioned' existence, the discomfort that naturally arises from clinging to impermanent experiences or states. It is less about emotional sadness or moods and more about the fundamental dis-ease that Buddha diagnosed comes from the transient nature of reality itself. Misunderstanding dukkha as mere sadness steals from the insight: which is that there is no state of living that will rescue us to aspire to at the cost of the present moment. The present is everything. This moment is the only reality, everything else is a fabrication, so we can go ahead and live in greater truth and harmony with ourselves. Freedom from suffering comes from releasing attachment to transient stuff.

5   'Buddha Chant As Sung By S N Goenka', Movedbylove.org, available at www.movedbylove.org/projects/tunes/143.

6   Bhikkhu writes about how karma and rebirth are easily misunderstood concepts, especially given their occurrence in other world religions. I think it's important to be precise here about how complicated (and real) the concept of karma is: 'Our present experience is shaped by three karmic factors,' he clarifies. 'The results of past intentions—and this includes all your sense spheres; present intentions; and the results of your present intentions. Past intentions provide you with the raw material or potentials for your present experience, but your present intentions are what shape those raw potentials into your actual experiences. Because the results of many past actions could be offering all sorts of raw materials at any point in time, and because you're potentially free to create any type of new karma at all, these conditions can interact in many complex ways. In fact, in your experience of the present, your current intention arises prior to your awareness of the senses. Without present intentions, you'd have no experience of space and time. You'd be free from their limitations. On the ultimate level, this fact is what makes awakening possible. On the immediate level, it means that even though you may have bad 'karma seeds' from past unskillful intentions ripening in your 'karma field,' you have some freedom in how you treat the ripening seeds so that you don't have to suffer from them. You can be proactive in preventing suffering. This is why we meditate: to sensitize ourselves to our present intentions, some of which are very subtle. This sensitivity

enables us to expand the range of our freedom in the present, training the mind in the skills it needs to create positive present karma, to deal positively with the raw material from past negative karma, and eventually to go beyond the karma of intentions entirely.' See Thanissaro Bhikkhu, 'The Buddha's Baggage Everything you wanted to know about karma but were afraid to ask', *Buddhist Review Tricycle,* Winter 2016, available at tricycle.org/magazine/thanissaro-bhikkhu-karma.

7   Wendy Billcombe Asgar, "The Trauma of Caste' Is Essential Reading', *Buddhist Review Tricycle*, 17 January 2023, available at tricycle.org/ article/trauma-of-caste.

8   •   Believed to have been delivered in the Deer Park at Isipatana (Sarnath), not long after his awakening in Uruvela (Bodh Gaya), the Buddha's Four Noble Truths are that: One, dukkha is innate to cyclical samsaric life. Two, dukkha arises with tanha, meaning craving, desire, or attachment. Three, dukkha can be eliminated by letting go of tanha; and, Four, following the marga, the Noble Eightfold Path to enlightenment, helps achieve this. Sounds pretty reasonable, because the implication is simply that, as Stephen Batchelor writes in *Secular Buddhism*, 'As long as one remains in this world as an embodied creature, the most one can achieve is a certain mitigation of suffering. For suffering truly to cease, one must stop the process of rebirth altogether.' See Stephen Batchelor, *Secular Buddhism: Imagining the Dharma in the Uncertain World*, New Haven: Yale University Press, 2017, p. 82.

    •   Considering how fundamental this idea is to any Buddhism, or the philosophy and view of life that comes from it, you could say its removal is anti-thetical to its Buddhism's very nature. Indeed, in rural parts of Chhattisgarh, large nomadic and criminal tribes fall below the untouchables in the Hindu caste hierarchy, who believe themselves to live a Buddhist life. 'We don't believe in karma, reincarnation, and worshipping Hindu gods,' said one of them, a member of the thieving caste. 'We travel from place to place like Buddhist monks, and share everything, food and money, with everyone else.' Another Ambedkarite Buddhist and small business owner in Nagpur believed the Buddhism in Himalayan regions was 'superstitious'. 'The Buddha was concerned with people's suffering, not things like painting and meditation, which are mostly useless.' Indian Buddhists were also found less likely to meditate than their Muslim peers. See Daniel Burke, 'Indian Buddhists Less Likely to Meditate Than Muslim Peers, Study Finds', *Buddhist Review Tricycle*, 8 July 2021, available at tricycle.org/article/indian-buddhists.; Vishvapani, 'The Great Escape', *Buddhist Review Tricycle*, Spring 2007, available at tricycle.org/ magazine/great-escape.

    •   This is a ChatGPT-generated endnote, seems useful: 'The Rashtriya

Swayamsevak Sangh (RSS) was founded in Nagpur, Maharashtra, in 1925 by Keshav Baliram Hedgewar. Hedgewar was motivated by his belief that Hindu society needed to be united and strengthened to resist both foreign colonial influence and internal divisions. The organization focused on promoting Hindu unity through physical training, discipline, and community service, shaping the RSS's modus operandi for decades to come. For a comprehensive history of the RSS's origins and ideological development, *The Brotherhood in Saffron: The Rashtriya Swayamsevak Sangh and Hindu Revivalism* by Walter Andersen.'

9   A 2016 report quoting government data said that the number of SC Buddhists had increased by 38 per cent between 2001 and 2011, while the total SC population had increased by just 21.3 per cent. Over 90 per cent of SC people practising Buddhism live in Maharashtra, with a growth rate of over 60 per cent, according to the same report. See Unnati Sharma, '10 cr Buddhists by 2025', says group behind 'conversion' event that cost AAP minister his job', *The Print*, 13 October 2015. Also see Burke, 'Indian Buddhists Less Likely to Meditate Than Muslim Peers, Study Finds'.; Vishvapani, 'The Great Escape'.

10 'AAP Minister Rajendra Pal Gautam Resigns After Dalit-Buddhist Conversion Row', *The Quint*, 9 October 2022.

11 Raghav Bikhchandani, 'What are the 22 vows of BR Ambedkar at the centre of BJP-AAP conversion controversy', *The Print*, 10 October 2022.

12 Vishvapani, 'The Great Escape'.

13 Sharma, '10 cr Buddhists by 2025', says group behind 'conversion' event that cost AAP minister his job'.

14 It's also hard to unsee the contradictions in Ambedkar's Buddhism, which, even after negating the traditional basics, includes vows like 'I shall not act in a manner violating the principles and the teachings of the Buddha' and 'I shall follow the 'noble eightfold path' of the Buddha'.

15 Views on LGBTQ+ issues vary across Buddhist traditions, but are way more inclusive than other religions. The teachings have a primary focus on avoiding harm, and the Third Precept, often interpreted as a guideline to avoid sexual misconduct, does not get into sexual orientations, but emphasizes conducting relationships in non-harmful ways, avoiding deceit and exploitation. The Lotus Sutra, one of Mahayana Buddhism's most significant texts, is emphatic about the equality of all people. Everyone has a Buddha-nature—he capacity for wisdom, compassion, and awakening—and whatever one's identity labels, the path to liberation is accessible and important. Daisaku Ikeda, a Buddhist philosopher, writes about celebrating individuality, how discriminating against anyone based on gender or sexual orientation is discriminating against oneself. The more we can appreciate others for who they are, and how they're different from us, the more we can appreciate ourselves. Notably, Japanese Pure Land

and Zen Buddhist traditions have long incorporated these inclusive ideals, with some temples performing same-sex marriages as early as the 1970s. See Jeff Wilson, 'Buddha's Big Shrug: The Non-Conflictual History of Same-Sex Marriage in the Buddhist Churches of America', Berkleycenter. georgetown.edu, 20 June 2018, available at berkleycenter.georgetown. edu/responses/buddha-s-big-shrug-the-non-conflictual-history-of-same-sex-marriage-in-the-buddhist-churches-of-america.

16 I'm not using greed, hatred, and delusion in the colloquial sense here. In his early teachings, the Buddha identified 'three poisons' or 'three fires' as the root of all negative qualities in the mind. These were greed (raga; also lust), hatred (dvesha; or anger), and delusion (moha; or ignorance), which are opposed by three wholesome, positive mind-states, crucial to liberation: generosity (dana), lovingkindness (maitri) and wisdom (prajna). Buddhist practice is about cultivating the virtues and reducing the poisons, by consciously identifying thoughts that fuel the three fires, and not dwelling on them, while nurturing those that cultivate the three positive attitudes. Fire is a central Buddhist metaphor for negative qualities of the mind, and the word 'nirvana' comes from Sanskrit 'nis' (out) and 'va' (to blow), literally meaning 'to extinguish'. However, even advanced meditators appear to deal with everyday emotions and triggers—it doesn't all just disappear immediately, and that should be yet another source of affirmation for the practicality—the respectful recognition of our flawed, human condition—that is innate to Buddhism. In fact, there are four stages to awakening, which can span lifetimes and multiple rebirths across the human and godly realms of existence:

- The first stage is that of Sot ('stream-enterer'), literally 'one who enters (apadyate), the stream (sotas),' or the supermundane Noble Eightfold Path to liberation. A stream-enterer attains nirvana within seven rebirths upon opening the eye of the Dharma. This person is free from identity view (the belief that there is an unchanging self or soul), attachment to rites and rituals, and any doubt about the Buddha's teachings.
- The second stage is that of the Sakadagami, meaning 'one who once (sak.rt) comes (agacchati)'. The once-returner will return to the realm of the senses (the lowest being human and the highest being the devas wielding power over the creations of others) at most one more time. More than the stream-enterer, the once-returner has weakened lust, hate, and delusion to a greater degree.
- The third stage is that of the An-ag-am-i, meaning 'one who does not (an-) come (agacchati)'. The non-returner has overcome sensuality and ill-will, and does not return to the human world or lower realms after death. Instead, they are reborn in one of the five special worlds, called the Suddhavasa worlds, or 'Pure Abodes', and there attain Nirvana. They may be reborn multiple times in the higher worlds of the Pure Abodes.
- Finally, the fourth stage is that of the Arahant, the fully awakened person. They have abandoned, in addition to identity-view, attachment to rites

and rituals, doubt about the teachings, sensuality, and ill will, the fetters of conceit, restlessness, and ignorance. They will never be reborn in any plane or world, having wholly escaped sansara.

17 In terms of things such as your wisdom or lack of wisdom, wealth or lack of wealth, and the length of your life span.

18 The only karmic result of all those murders was that people, including relatives of those Angulimala killed, threw things at him when he was on his alms rounds.

19 This is why Vipassana meditation was introduced to prisons by S. N. Goenka—because the line of good and evil runs through every man, and everyone deserves redemption. Vipassana has been conducted in correctional facilities worldwide, most notably in India and the U.S. It helps inmates understand and transform their mental state, reducing aggression by fostering self-awareness and equanimity. In India's Tihar Jail, for example, inmates who practiced Vipassana reported greater peace and reduced hostility, reshaping prison culture into one of self-reflection and healing, instead of punishment. See 'History of Vipassana Courses in Prison',

20 John Conway's *Game of Life* is a classic example of a cellular automaton, devised by British mathematician in 1970. It is a mathematical model that consists of an infinite two-dimensional grid of cells, each of which can be in one of a finite number of states—such as dead or alive. The game evolves through a series of generations, with the state of each cell in a generation determined by its current state and the states of its neighbouring cells according to specific rules:
   - Any live cell with fewer than two live neighbours dies, as if by underpopulation.
   - Any live cell with two or three live neighbours lives on to the next generation.
   - Any live cell with more than three live neighbours dies, as if by overpopulation.
   - Any dead cell with exactly three live neighbours becomes a live cell, as if by reproduction.

These simple rules give rise to complex and fascinating patterns, including stable configurations, oscillators, gliders, and other moving structures. Despite its simplicity, the Game of Life exhibits emergent behaviour and has been used to study various aspects of computational complexity, artificial life, and pattern formation.

21 'Questions and Answers with Goenkaji', *Vipassana Newsletter*, Vol. 19, No. 6, 7 June 2009, available at www.vridhamma.org/sites/default/files/newsletters/1434101333_en-2009-06-Questions-and-Answers-with-Goenkaji-June09.pdf.

22 'Be in your senses'. It's only after I started meditating that I realized a common call to sanity and good behaviour literally refers to a central element of meditation, viz. to be aware of your bodily sensations, and

equanimous to them. When you are unaware of your sensations, you are likely running away with the stories in your head, unconsciously acting them out; to 'be in your senses' then is to be with the reality that your body and subconscious mind are a storehouse for. To be sane is to be in your senses.

23   Now, this extension of unconditional goodwill does not mean you should take shit or spare someone's feelings from truths they may need to hear. In one of his discourses, S. N. Goenka clarifies that speaking sharply is sometimes necessary to convey a message to someone who isn't receptive to softer approaches. This isn't seen as contradictory to goodwill; rather, it's about balancing compassion with discernment. The mental intention should always remain free of ill-will, but true compassion may involve honesty and directness over gentleness. See Thanissaro Bhikkhu, 'The Kamma of Goodwill', *Buddhist Review Tricycle*, Fall 2022, available at tricycle.org/magazine/buddhist-goodwill.

24   Ibid.

25   I anticipate many extremely-online-radicals to interpret these arguments as somehow less liberal or radical than their own brand of unequivocally branding people as either 'in or out', based on their beliefs and behaviours—the same kind of primitive herd mentality that they look down upon the conservatives for. Quick rule-based judgements make people feel like they have simple answers to the world's big problems, and that anyone who sees the world differently than them is Part of the Problem, while they and their ilk solely are Part of the Solution. It's more difficult to accept that there are reasons for everyone to behave the way they do, even if those reasons are unknown or unfathomable to you, and that you cannot simply coerce or shame them into being changed—not if you really want to be effective. There will be those who misbehave and refuse to change their ways, and there may be times where nothing you could do would help. This is why unlimited equanimity is also part of *brahma-vihara* practice. 'You reflect that beings are free to choose their actions,' Thanissaro Bhikkhu writes, 'and you're in no position to guarantee that everyone will choose to be skillful. Not even the Buddha could do that. So, to keep your attitude always skillful, you have to develop equanimity in cases where influencing other people in a skillful direction is beyond your ability.'
Mature goodwill also isn't a wish for others' happiness just as things are. 'When you extend thoughts of goodwill to others, you're not thinking 'May you be happy doing whatever you're doing,'' Thanissaro Bhikkhu explains. 'You're thinking "May you understand the causes for true happiness and be willing and able to act on them."' This is goodwill that can extend to all beings, without hypocrisy, regardless of how they've behaved in the past.

26   When I went into my first course, my thinking was that I'd suffered a lot in life; there was a lot I wanted to give to the world but felt unwarrantedly

thwarted quite often, and that although I had my problems, I was largely fine, and strong and resilient even, to have survived that far. But as the course progressed, I realized I was a type of person Goenka had seen before. 'A person may have a lot of money, and others may feel: 'Such a happy person. Look, he has so much wealth',' he wrote. 'But what you don't know is that this person can't get sound sleep; he has to use sleeping pills—a very miserable person. You can't always understand at the external level whether somebody is miserable or happy. The misery may lie deep inside.'—and you have to go there to see it. See Brother Phap Hu, 'The Path to Transforming Generational Suffering', *Buddhist Review Tricycle*, 7 October 2022, available at tricycle.org/article/brother-phap-huu-transforming-suffering.; Kenneth Kraft, 'Meditation in Action', *Buddhist Review Tricycle*, Spring 1993, available at tricycle.org/magazine/meditation-action.

27 René Girard, in his theory of mimetic desire, argued that human societies have a deep-rooted need for scapegoats—a sacrificial ritual to channel and relieve collective tension. He believed that as humans imitate each other's desires, they inevitably clash, leading to rivalry and violence. Religion, according to Girard, traditionally steps in here by identifying a scapegoat—a figure or group onto whom society can project its aggression, thus restoring peace by 'sacrificing' this scapegoat. Girard suggested that this ritual isn't arbitrary but fundamental: it's a way societies manage internal conflict by externalizing it. He saw the crucifixion of Jesus as both an example of this scapegoating mechanism and a challenge to it, as the Gospels reveal the innocence of the scapegoat, calling into question the whole structure of sacrificial violence. For more, see Girard's *Things Hidden Since the Foundation of the World*.

28 Thanissaro Bhikkhu compares samsara to a long, protracted, addictive mud fight. 'I splash mud on you. You splash mud on me. And then I splash mud on you back because you splashed mud on me. It goes back and forth like this and it never ends. So, the idea of trying to straighten everybody out—or trying to settle the score—again makes no sense,' he writes. It could be feasible if you had a clear beginning point and a clear endpoint. 'But when the beginning point, as the Buddha said, cannot be found, can't even be conceived, how are you going to figure out what the score is? Where would you begin the tally?' The best way forward is to get out of the mud fight. 'The Buddha never said that we're here to clean up the mud fight. And your idea of how things should be: That's what a lot of the mud fights are all about—how to redress old wrongs. When you've had enough of the mud, there comes a point when you have to realize that the Buddha was right. The best course of action is to get out—for the two reasons I mentioned. One is that you're no longer oppressing the other person,'—because they are free to listen to you, but also not, and in this process of imposing your ideas of How Things Should Be, you might end up hurting them—'so you're no

longer creating bad *kamma* for yourself. And two, you can set a good example for other people.' By getting rid of your own addiction first, and then—'Then, if you have the time and the energy and the talent, you help give information to other people on how they can do the same. That's how compassion really works, both for yourself and for the world around you.' I'm just listening to Thanissaro Bhikkhu here. See Thanissaro Bhikkhu, 'The Samsaric Mud Fight', Dhammatalks.org, 27 December 2014, available at www.dhammatalks.org/books/Meditations8/Section0031.html.

29 There are over 3,500 stairs on the Alipiri route to Tirupati, and around 2,400 on the Srivari Mettu path. The ascent holds religious significance and is seen as an act of devotion and penance, believed to help devotees earn blessings, atone for past sins, and strengthen their spiritual commitment.

30 The term "Tao" () in Chinese philosophy translates to 'The Way', and signifies the underlying natural order of the universe, which is timeless, formless, and beyond human comprehension. The concept is central to Taoism, especially in the classic text Tao Te Ching, attributed to the sage Laozi. 'Tao' represents the ultimate path of harmony, that by aligning oneself with the natural flow of life and letting go of rigid control, one can achieve a peaceful, balanced existence. Rather than a prescriptive code, the Tao emphasizes effortless action (wu wei) and unity with the world around us, offering wisdom through a philosophy of quietness, flexibility, and acceptance.

31 R. D. Laing was a psychologist who questioned the mainstream approach to mental illness and social conformity. In his 1960 book, *The Divided Self*, Laing explored how individuals create a 'false self" to meet societal expectations, leading to alienation from their true selves. In *The Politics of Experience* (1967), Laing pushes the critique further, arguing that what society calls 'madness' is a sane response to an insane world. He believed that extreme mental states held valuable insights into the human condition, and that the need for conformity imposed by society suppresses authentic experience. For Laing, psychosis and other extreme states were not disorders to be eradicated but complex and meaningful responses to trauma and societal dysfunction. See R. D. Laing, *The Divided Self: An Existential Study in Sanity and Madness*, London: Penguin, 2010.; Laing, *The Politics of Experience and the Bird of Paradise*, London: Penguin, 1967.

32 These may not be such unique experiences any more, actually: The major stations on spiritual journeys seem to be popular on the internet. 'Ego death', 'the dark night of the soul', 'shadow work', especially, are found at every online corner these days. The one-sidedness of our materialistic, overly intellectual, productivity-obsessed culture seems to be causing an outbreak in spirituality and woo. See Shreya Agarwal, 'What is shadow

work, the new mental health trend?', *Indian Express*, 8 October 2023.; Caroline Mymbs Nice, 'The 24-Year-Old Who Outsold Oprah This Week', *The Atlantic*, 28 September 2023.

33 Since religion has concerned itself with salvation, and matters of the spirit, most world religions end up denying the reality and weight of the material world. Consider Christianity, for example, which has had hatred for the body, its cravings, instincts and sexuality. Women's menstruation, conception, pregnancy, childbirth, and lactation are all to visceral and bodily for patriarchal religion. In the Bible, women involved in these womanly conditionals were considered unclean—just like Hindu's casteist beliefs—and kept separate from men. They had to go through purifications before being allowed near men or anything religious. Since birth and menses were considered dirty, women were in constant need of being spiritualized and sanitized. According to that attitude, women could not be both holy *and* sexual. As celibacy became a spiritual ideal in Christianity, men became cast as spiritual and women as sexual, the suspect *femme fatale*, who lured 'good men' into the evils of flesh.

In reality, men are no more connected to spirit than women are connected to nature than men. It is suppression and repression of natural human instincts that make them burst out in evil forms. We must all learn to deal with our animal impulses in a healthy fashion, through neither suppression nor violent expression, which is something meditation teaches you to do. For more, see *Dance of the Dissident Daughter: A Woman's Journey from Christian Tradition to the Sacred Feminine* by Sue Monk Kidd.

34 In Jungian psychology, the terms 'masculine' and 'feminine' refer to archetypal principles inherent in every individual, regardless of gender. The 'masculine' is seen as embodying qualities like goal-orientation, structure, will, while the 'feminine' may encompas intuition, receptivity, and play. These are not rigid roles, but dynamic energies that every psyche contains, with psychological health arising from the integration of both. The idea parallels the Chinese concept of yin/yang, where yin (associated with the feminine) is linked to receptivity, and yang represents activity. Both are complementary, interdependent forces that, when harmonized, bring balance and completeness to life. The Jungian and Taoist views align in emphasizing that imbalance—whether cultural or personal—arises from the overvaluation of one principle over the other, leading to disconnection from our innate wholeness. For more, see *The Collected Works of C. G. Jung*, *Addiction to Perfection* by Marion Woodman (1982), and *The I Ching or Book of Changes* by R. Wilhelm and C. F. Baynes.

35 Individuation is the process of integrating the unconscious and conscious parts of the psyche, gradually unifying the personality around this deeper Self. It is a journey toward psychological wholeness, where one's life is no longer driven solely by societal demands or ego desires but by a more profound, integrated purpose.

36   The reason I use quotes around 'rationalistic' is because real rationalism is not as rigid, or as closed to the unknown, as those who claim to be rationalistic are actually. Consider Gödel's Incompleteness Theorem, which asserts that within any formal system—like mathematics or logic—there are always truths that cannot be proven by the system's own rules. Each time you discover some new property that cannot be proved as true or false within a system, with well-defined starting rules, you just add that new property to the set of starting rules. Philosophically, this means that knowledge and understanding are inherently limited, and no system, belief, or framework ever provides a complete account of reality. It means acknowledging that are limits to certainty, and that logic, taken to its logical needs, asks you to constantly update yourself and engage with the unknown.

EPILOGUE: FAMOUS LAST WORDS

1   FYI: I don't quite like Nolan movies; I've mentioned before, to decent applause, that Nolan films are a dumb person's idea of what a smart person likes. See Sanjana Ramachandran, Post, X.com, 13 October 2024, available at x.com/ramachandranesk/status/1845376326863061014.

2   The similarities in the journey and its conclusion are uncanny. In what I see, or once had, as a similar coda to the last part of my chapter seven, Hesse too writes at the end of *Siddhartha*: 'The opposite of every truth is just as true! It is like this: A truth can be expressed and cloaked in words only if it is one-sided. Everything that can be thought in words and expressed in words is one-sided, only a half. When the venerable Gotama taught and spoke of the world, he had to divide into samsara and nirvana, deception and truth, suffering and liberation, There is no other possibility, no other way for those who would teach. But the world itself, existence around us and within us, is never one-sided. Never is a person or an act wholly samsara or wholly nirvana; never is a person entirely holy or entirely sinful. That only appears to be the case because we are in grips of the illusion that time is real. Time is not real. I have experienced this many, many time. The gap that exists between the world and eternity, between suffering and bliss, between good and evil, is also an illusion.'

   'Every sin has grace,' he writes, and is part of the oneness of the universe. The universe is like a river, which exists at once its mouth, at the middle, and at the end, as do we ourselves.

   Hermann Hesse, *Siddhartha: An Indian Tale*, Sherab Chödzin Kohn (tr.), USA: Shambhala, 2000.

3   '[Hesse's] exploration had uncovered a process in which layer after layer of conventional and conceptual reference points have to be stripped away; through inspiration, but also profound disappointment and loss, the seeker relentlessly approaches naked mind. First to come and go

for Siddhartha is orthodox religion. This is supplanted by life-denying asceticism which in turn proves inauthentic and has to be given up. The next path that will not hold is affirmation of self and enjoyment of sensuality, and the material world; next, rejection of that approach proves groundless too. At last, understanding at all, any analysis or intellectual grasp, shows itself as ludicrous one-upmanship in the face of reality's flow; the brilliant seeker's last rag has to be surrendered. The process culminates in the final heartbreaking loss of the spiritual project altogether. Seeking is exhausted at its root and confusion with it.' ... 'Hesse does not quite give us the 'return to the market place' found in the last of the ten Zen Ox-Herding Pictures, but the utter excoriation of ego—all one's worlds of hopes and fears—is vivid enough.' Sherab Chödzin Kohn, 'Preface', in Hesse, *Siddhartha*, Kohn (tr.).

The 'return to the marketplace' in the Zen Ox-Herding Pictures symbolizes the final stage of enlightenment, where the enlightened individual returns to the world, engaging with life's ordinariness while embodying deep wisdom and compassion. It reflects the integration of spiritual insight into everyday life, transcending the dichotomy between the sacred and the mundane. See Martine Batchelor, 'The Ten Oxherding Pictures', *Buddhist Review Tricycle*, Spring 2000, available at tricycle. org/magazine/ten-oxherding-pictures.

4   'Say the quiet part out loud' is a popular phrase, apparently used by Krusty the Clown in a 1995 episode of *The Simpsons,* 'A Star Is Burns'. ('I said the quiet part loud and the loud part quiet,' Krusty said.) And 'tell all the truth, but tell it slant' is a line from a poem by Emily Dickinson, implying that the truth should be told in a roundabout way, because people will not comprehend it all at once. I take it to mean that the truth can only be told slant, through one's bent or way of viewing the world.